By Whom Introduced	Date
J. H. Osborne	
do	
H. Wood	
H. McAfee	April 21
do	
do	
Edw. Righter	
Jno. E. Collins	
Do	
Do	

At the Center: 175 Years at Cincinnati's Mercantile Library

At the Center

175 *Years*
at Cincinnati's Mercantile
Library

Robert C. Vitz

The Mercantile Library
CINCINNATI, OHIO
2010

First edition 2010.
Published by The Mercantile Library,
414 Walnut Street, Cincinnati, OH 45205
www.mercantilelibrary.com

© 2010 Robert C. Vitz

ISBN: 978-0-9788915-1-0
ISBN: 0-9788915-1-1
Library of Congress Cataloging-in-Publication
data available from the publisher

Book design: TRIAD Communications
Type design: Keith Bollmer
Printed in the United States of America
by CJK, Cincinnati

Photo credits:
Unless noted, all photos are from the collection
of the Mercantile Library.

*Like most institutions, the Mercantile Library
required strangers to register. Only one such
register survives from the nineteenth century.
The endpapers are taken from that volume.*

For
Riley Catherine Taylor
Evan William Taylor
and
Boden Emerson Bakermans Vitz

Table of Contents

Preface: Dale Brown... i

Introduction.. v

CHAPTER 1 ❧ "Banded together for self-improvement":
Beginnings of the Mercantile Library............ 1

CHAPTER 2 ❧ Finding Its Place....................................33

CHAPTER 3 ❧ Through War and Fire 63

CHAPTER 4 ❧ More Than Books..................................93

CHAPTER 5 ❧ A Change in Focus............................. 121

CHAPTER 6 ❧ The Doldrums...................................... 155

CHAPTER 7 ❧ Finding Its Voice: The Springer Years.......... 185

CHAPTER 8 ❧ To the New Millennium and Beyond 213

APPENDIX A ❧ Board Presidents................................235

APPENDIX B ❧ Librarians 239

APPENDIX C ❧ Art and Collectibles
Currently or Previously in the Library 241

Bibliography..255

Index 261

Preface

IN THE COURSE of long existences, organizations do many things, but one of them is write histories. Inevitably, a particularly articulate or knowledgeable member volunteers or is drafted for the job, someone is hired, or the task falls to the president, the historian, or another official. Perhaps it is the occasion of a big anniversary, as it is for the writing of this history, or perhaps it's some other milestone. At any rate, it happens from time to time, whether the result is a pamphlet, a hardbound book, or an article for an internal publication.

The Mercantile Library of Cincinnati has a rich tradition of histories, as one might expect from an organization that is dedicated to the written word. For example, there is John W. Ellis's very early account of the first ten years, written for the 1879 annual report. Ellis was one of the founders of the Library as well as founder of First National Bank of Cincinnati, a forerunner of the mammoth U.S. Bank. He gave posterity an extremely valuable personal recollection. Along with several other histories in the Mercantile's collection, it is considered not only useful, but, for the Library, priceless.

What is different about this history is that it was written by a professional historian. Of course, Robert C. Vitz is a member of the Library, just as were the other writers, and he, like the others, has worked tirelessly without benefit of monetary reward. For those who haven't pored over the vanishing ink of flowery nineteenth century minute-takers, there is no way to describe the task. But Dr. Vitz is a professional. And that is significant.

It has been said that the difference between an amateur and a professional is that the amateur gets it right some of the time; the professional all of the time. When it comes to writing history, it is challenging to button up every detail, to correctly shade every nuance, to frame every footnote according to the latest edition of *The Chicago Manual of Style*. There are occasions when even the professionals can't do it. But Dr. Vitz has been teaching and writing history for a lifetime, and his work reflects both the attention to detail and the confidence of that experience.

Professionals like Dr. Vitz bring other strengths to their projects as well. For example, their work is comprehensive. They keep pulling the threads of their stories from the beginning through to the end. The task probably wasn't easy for John Ellis when he sat down to summarize the Library's first ten years, but Dr. Vitz has had to track a 175 years. It is a long sweep to consider, and the job has been done unfalteringly.

Historians also put things in context. The good ones aren't simply recounting the tale of the librarian who died at his desk or reporting who donated the sculpture *Silence*; they're helping the reader understand how the events of the organization fit into the history of the city, the region, and the country. For history to be useful, it must inform the present, and Dr. Vitz's history of the Library does that well. The story offers not only the account of a noble institution, but also the taming of the frontier, the ups and downs of war, the flash of Halley's Comet, the digitization of America, and much more.

Good historians bring objectivity to their projects, and here Dr. Vitz has also excelled. As neither staff member nor board member, he has relayed the Mercantile's story without bias, simply laying out both the institution's accomplishments and its failings. Admittedly, he has treaded gently on the foibles and only occasionally smiled at the faults, but he has laid them out plainly for the reader to see. This history is neither public relations nor puffery.

Finally, historians, and, truly, all good writers, anticipate the reader's questions and answer them before they're asked. What is the meaning of the library's seal? What is the truth behind the rumors surrounding the Mercantile's infamous shell collection? When did women gain full membership? Readers want to know these things, and the professional historian makes sure he provides them with the facts.

Dr. Vitz has spent two years sifting, reading, writing, and evaluating on the reader's behalf. It's an invaluable service, for which the library is extremely grateful. There will be other histories as this institution moves into the future, but readers can rest assured that the definitive document for the first 175 years is in hand.

Dale Patrick Brown
Mercantile Board President
January, 2010

Introduction

I T IS NOT OFTEN that one is asked to write a book, especially a book about an institution as unusual, important, and interesting as Cincinnati's Mercantile Library, but that happened when I went to work as a volunteer at the Library in August 2007. This history is intended to help celebrate the Association's 175th anniversary. It has been a remarkably pleasant task, made even more pleasant by the opportunity to get to know the Mercantile as an institution and the many people who make it such a special place. In writing this history, I have tried to show how the Library has undergone changes of direction, survived various crises, and overcome a host of problems. Above all I have tried to place it within the broader picture of the city's development.

Much of the information about the Mercantile's operations comes from the board minutes, which have survived intact except for a stretch of about ten years during the 1850s. Most organizations' board minutes are extraordinarily dull, and the Mercantile's often are no exception. At times, however, especially during the Library's first forty years, board secretaries recorded quarrels, individual social observations, personal embarrassments, and even humorous comments. The board secretaries' handwriting varied considerably; this variability, coupled with occasional ink fading, and ink blotting, sometimes made the minutes difficult to read. This was a particular concern in identifying personal names; no doubt I made errors of identification as a result of this.

Because I used the minutes and annual reports so much, I have chosen not to footnote each reference to them. Unless another source is cited, the reader may assume that information based on board decisions or discussions comes from the Association's board minutes or annual reports. In most cases the month and year are mentioned in the text, so that anyone wishing to look up the original information can locate the source with only a little effort. The minutes and the annual reports are housed in the Library's archives.

One incurs many debts in writing a history. First, I want to acknowledge my predecessors, those Mercantile Library members who wrote informal histories of the organization, particularly Murray Merrihew in 1905 and Robert L. Black Sr. in 1935. Then, for the Library's lectures, both in the nineteenth century and in more recent years, Dale Patrick Brown's *Brilliance and Balderdash* and Buck Niehoff's *Something Funny at the Library* were invaluable sources of information. Librarians at the Cincinnati Historical Society Library (Cincinnati Museum Center) never complained when I asked them to bring out volume after volume of nineteenth-century newspapers for me to read, and I am especially indebted to Ann Shepherd and Rick Kesterman for their valuable suggestions, and to Linda Bailey for her assistance in locating possible illustrations. The Historical Society Library's collection of Cincinnati-based material is unsurpassed.

At the Mercantile Library, both collector Cedric Rose and administrative assistant Chris Messick helped locate material, answered operational questions about the Library, and listened politely to my sometimes corny comments, bad puns, and atrocious jokes. Sandra Geiser, Nourse Collection administrator, provided timely information on the Nourse family's connection to the Mercantile. Librarian Albert Pyle and literary programs manager Mary Gruber not only answered innumerable questions about the Library but also served as my editors on this project. They provided many suggestions and corrections. Dale P. Brown, current president of the Mercantile Library board of directors, read all the chapters as well, and her numerous suggestions have greatly improved the final product. Karen Feinberg, a Mercantile volunteer, served as copy editor, and her many corrections and suggestions have done much to improve the manuscript. Any remaining errors are mine alone.

Jean Springer, Albert Pyle, Buck Niehoff, Tom Huenefeld, and Mary Gruber kindly consented to be interviewed about their individual roles in shaping the Mercantile Library. No doubt I should have interviewed others, but pressure of time made that impossible. I hope I have not offended anyone who feels they should have been interviewed.

My wife, Margaret, has put up with two years of household disruption created by my taking over the dining room table at various times. She never complained. Three other people also deserve mention because they served as important and necessary distractions from the research and writing, so I am dedicating this book to my three grandchildren: Riley Catherine Taylor, Evan William Taylor, and Boden Emerson Bakermans Vitz.

"*[Cincinnati is] the seat of commerce, the arts,
the fashion, and literature,–the place to which every
one resorts for information upon the* manners and
topics of the day."

CINCINNATI CHRONICLE
AND LITERARY GAZETTE, 1833

"*[Fiction] pampers and bloats the intellect with
unwholesome food, and enfeebles and demoralizes
all future exertions of the mind.*"

ALEXANDER KINMONT, 1836

CHAPTER I

'Banded together for self-improvement'

BEGINNINGS OF THE MERCANTILE LIBRARY

B Y THE MID-1830s Cincinnati was poised to become the dominant city in the Ohio Valley, as it rapidly changed from a village of republican values to a commercial and industrial city. In just fifty years it had grown from a forest clearing to a city of unlimited promise. Already known as "Queen of the West," Cincinnati had survived a bitter winter followed by a major flood in 1832, a serious cholera epidemic in 1832-33, and a series of disastrous fires, as well as various economic disruptions triggered by President Andrew Jackson's attack on the Bank of the United States.

Situated on the Ohio River, a mighty artery of commerce, Cincinnati served both as a gateway to the western frontier and as its chief commercial and manufacturing center. On most days the public landing teemed with bales, barrels, and boxes, newly manufactured furniture and household items, piles of lumber, agricultural tools, leather products of all kinds, newly wrought ironwork, and pork products. A steady stream of horse-drawn wagons and drays moved between the riverfront and the three- and four-story warehouses and factories that constituted the city's economic heart. Seemingly hundreds of young men arrived each week to harness their futures to that of the fast-growing city.[1]

From this group came the impetus for the Young Men's Mercantile Library Association. Ambitious and industrious but often undereducated, these men, reflecting the spirit of the age, sought self-improvement. At a time when public schooling was in its infancy and the constraints of a class system lingered, aspiring merchants and clerks sought to educate themselves, and they accepted the necessity of taxing themselves individually to gain the benefits of knowledge. With an energy derived from a new nation and a new kind of society, these men invested in a variety of self-help institutions, and they formed a number of associations aimed at cultivating the mind. While the Franklin Society, the Cincinnati Literary Society, and the Cincinnati Lyceum all sponsored lectures and debates, those short-lived organizations were more for the contemplative mind than for the more utilitarian interests of the mercantile community.

These merchants wanted access to practical knowledge, and for that they needed a library. The Ohio Mechanics Institute, founded in 1828, provided exposure to science and the "mechanic arts" for the group of residents known as mechanics, but although its reading room and library were open to the public, it offered little for the mercantile class.[2] Other attempts at establishing permanent libraries had met with only

---

1   A detailed description of Cincinnati's commercial and manufacturing development may be found in Daniel Aaron, *Cincinnati, Queen City of the West,* 1819-1838 (Columbus: Ohio State University Press, 1992), 19-47.
2   "Mechanics" were those involved with creating products, and, as Frances Trollope pointed out, merchants considered themselves somewhat superior to mechanics; see Frances Trollope, *Domestic Manners of the Americans* (New York: Oxford University Press, 1984), 126-27.

limited success. As early as 1802, General Arthur St. Clair, Jacob Burnet, and Martin Baum, among others, had founded a subscription library, located in Yeatman's Tavern, but it soon disappeared. Twelve years later Dr. Daniel Drake, the man of so much civic energy, helped establish the Cincinnati Circulating Library, located on Fourth Street between Main and Walnut. By 1826 it boasted more than 1,300 volumes. In 1821 the Apprentices' Library, located on Main Street near Third, sought to provide reading material of "an instructive nature to youth." Benjamin Drake and Edward D. Mansfield, in their 1826 promotional guide to the city, singled out the Cincinnati Reading Room, situated behind the post office, where residents and "strangers" could find many newspapers and literary journals "free of expense." In the 1830s one could also take advantage of books from Waldie's Select Circulating Library (Philadelphia), which promised "polite literature" in five to six weeks from its London publication date. Although well intentioned, all of these early libraries proved premature.[3] They also failed to reach those young merchants who sought to better both their professional and personal lives.

Frances Trollope's critical comments also had a lingering effect. Mrs. Trollope had spent two years in the city, hoping to improve her family's financial situation, before departing in

3 Ernest I. Miller, "Libraries in Cincinnati," *Bulletin of the Historical and Philosophical Society*, 16 (July, 1958), 240; *Greater Cincinnati and Its People: A History*, edited by Lewis Alexander Leonard, (New York: Lewis Historical Publishing Co., 1927), 707-08; Charles Cist, *Cincinnati in 1841* (Cincinnati: 1841), 109-10; Benjamin Drake and Edward D. Mansfield, *Cincinnati in 1826* (Cincinnati: Morgan, Lodge, and Fisher, 1826), 44; William H. Venable, *Beginnings of Literary Culture in the Ohio Valley* (Cincinnati: Robert Clarke & Co., 1891), 139-53. In 2002 Edward G. Marks, on behalf of the Mercantile Library, researched whether the Mercantile was the oldest continuously operating library west of Philadelphia. He concluded it was, after learning that the Transylvania College library had closed during the Civil War, with its collection dispersed for safekeeping, and did not reopen until 1914; see Mercantile Library archives, shelf box: "Library Histories, Letters & Awards," folder: "History."

1830. Her book, *Domestic Manners of the Americans*, published two years later, included a rather unflattering description of Cincinnati and its residents. Even the region's weather did not escape her censure, although most residents, then and now, might agree with her on that point. For a young community unsure of itself, Trollope's words struck a nerve. To be sure, she brought a conservative, middle-class Londoner's bias to her work, but her personal barbs were not without accuracy; many Cincinnatians were quite embarrassed, especially about the lack of refinement and culture she observed. With the exception of the Massachusetts-born Timothy Flint,[4] she met no one, in her opinion, who could converse on literature or the higher forms of art. Although we find no evidence that the founders of the Young Men's Mercantile Library Association reacted personally to Trollope's criticisms, her acerbic comments surely must have strengthened their motives.

Thus in 1835 Moses Ranney, a junior partner in the grocery firm of Worthington and Ranney, provided the spark that led to the Young Men's Mercantile Library Association. As the organization's first president, we assume that he was the driving force in the library's establishment, but little information is available about the conversations that preceded the first official meeting. Certainly Ranney and others were aware of recently established mercantile libraries in Boston, New York, and Philadelphia, and they hoped to continue the process of democratizing knowledge.

On the evening of April 18, 1835, some forty-five men

4 Timothy Flint (1780-1840), trained as a Congregational minister, spent much of his adult life traveling in the Ohio Valley region. He lived in Cincinnati from 1825 to about 1835, founded a literary journal, helped establish the Historical and Philosophical Society of Ohio, and wrote extensively about the western country, including several popular novels.

assembled on the second floor of the Independent Fire Engine and Hose Company building on Fourth Street, just east of the recently completed Christ Episcopal Church. There they adopted a constitution and elected officers. The original constitution clearly spelled out their vision: to "adopt the most efficient means to facilitate mutual intercourse; to extend our information upon the mercantile and other subjects of general utility; promote a spirit of useful inquiry and qualify ourselves to discharge with dignity the duties of our profession and the social offices of life; have associated ourselves for the purpose of establishing a Library and Reading Room...."[5] Despite these lofty sentiments – and later accounts continued to emphasize the Association's self-improvement role – these young men were practical merchants, largely self-made men, who also saw in the Association an opportunity to access current commercial information and to develop a local networking system.[6]

The local press paid little attention to the Mercantile Library's humble beginnings. Newspapers of the time failed to mention the new organization. They preferred to entertain their readers with vivid accounts of Richard Clayton's balloon ascension which had taken place on April 8, witnessed "by the beauty and fashion of the city." According to Clayton's

5 [Robert Black], *The Young Men's Mercantile Library Association of Cincinnati, Ohio,* 1835-1935, (Cincinnati: 1835), 3-5. Besides Ranney as president, they elected the following officers and directors: Elbridge Lawrence and William N. Greene, vice-presidents; Charles G. Springer, treasurer; William R. Smith, secretary; and Samuel S. Spencer, Robert Brown, Rowland G. Mitchell, and Isaac D. Wheeler, directors.

6 For a fuller discussion of this aspect of the Mercantile Library's early years, see Sallie H. Barringer and Bradford W. Scharlott, "The Cincinnati Mercantile Library As a Business-Communications Center, 1835-1846," *Libraries and Culture*, 26 (Spring, 1991), 388-401. As the authors point out, not only did the Association establish both the Chamber of Commerce and the Merchants Exchange, it also spent almost as much on newspapers and journals as on books.

own account, he reached an altitude of 2½ miles and traveled some 370 miles, landing near Charleston, Virginia (now West Virginia). Newspapers also mentioned violinist Joseph Tosso's concert at the Bazaar (Mrs. Trollope's former emporium), the heated boundary dispute between Ohio and Michigan, and the mounting presidential "fever" for local resident William Henry Harrison.[7]

Lack of attention, however, did not deter the new organization. Some years later one of those first members, James Lupton, recalled the enthusiasm of those early days in his president's report. In lofty rhetoric that did not particularly reflect most of the men in the audience, he addressed the members:

> We are young men. We are banded together for self-
> improvement. Very limited, for the most part, have been our
> educational advantages, yet we believe in an enlightened
> age—in a land of liberty—the sun of knowledge, in its merid-
> ian splendor, is beaming down upon us. The World, itself, is
> waking up, and shaking off the lethargy of ages. Shall we be
> sluggards? Nay; but let us grasp at every means of improve-
> ment within our reach; let us read, think, act, in the living
> present; let us strive earnestly and heartily for that dignified
> and ennobling self-culture, to which every end, and aim, and
> object of life shall converge as toward a common center—with-
> out which man is of little worth, and with which he can

7   See *Cincinnati Advertiser and Ohio Phoenix*, April 8, 1835, 3, and April 18, 1835, 3; also the *Cincinnati Whig and Commercial Intelligence*, April 20, 1835, 2, and April 21, 1835, 2. In the 1840s Clayton owned a jewelry and watch store at the corner of Sycamore and Third Streets, which was known as Clayton's Balloon Store. For a personal description of Clayton's balloon ascension, see "Glimpses Into Cincinnati's Past: The Gest Letters, 1834-1842," edited by Charles Schultz, *Ohio History*, 73 (Summer, 1964), 171-72.

accomplish all things.[8]

The members needed all of that enthusiasm. Lodged in temporary quarters, they faced a multitude of questions. Unaccustomed as they were to meetings, proper procedures, and issues that lay far outside their business experiences, the organization slowly felt its way toward permanence.

During the first three months, the board of directors, working largely in the evenings, wrote a set of bylaws, raised more than $1,800 in subscriptions, and began purchasing books and periodicals. The Association's first quarters were in the second story of a building belonging to a Mr. Daniel Ames, located on the west side of Main Street, below Pearl Street. Here a library and reading room were opened.

The directors devoted considerable attention to establishing proper rules for the two rooms. Bylaws informed members that they were expected to converse only in whispers; smoking, spitting on the floor, and damaging the furniture were prohibited. Any mutilation of a periodical would result in a fine of four times the cost of the damaged item. No one was to conduct himself "in any way inconsistent with decorum." Furthermore, no one was to lend a book "to any person out of the dwelling house or counting room[9] of the member." In other words, members were not to loan an item to someone who was neither staying with them nor connected to their place of business. Books were expensive, often irreplaceable, and invariably the library owned only one copy. Members, however, could bring out-of-town guests to the facilities for up

---

8   Quoted in [Black], *Young Men's Mercantile Library*, 6.
9   A counting room or counting house was a merchant's office, usually at his place of business.

to one month, as long as the librarian recorded their names.[10] Given Cincinnati's rapidly expanding commercial network, the Library provided many important benefits to the city's merchants.

In the beginning the Mercantile Library was open only in the evening: six to ten from November through February, seven to ten in March, April, September, and October, and eight to ten from May through August. The emphasis on non-daylight hours reflected the changing length of a workday in the days before gaslight. Circulation of books to members was limited to one volume "if it be a folio, quarto, or octavo, and one book or set (not exceeding three volumes) if a duo-decimo or volume of life size." Folio- and quarto-sized books could be borrowed for three weeks, smaller books for a shorter time. Fines were also based on book size, ranging from 1¢ per day for a duodecimo or smaller to 4¢ for a folio size volume. After one week, fines doubled. The librarian was instructed to report violations to the board of directors. The board made the librarian responsible for keeping track of books, organizing them on the shelves, reshelving, and collecting fines.

Unfortunately, until the board could secure sufficient capital, a librarian could not be hired. Thus the daily operations fell to the officers and directors. These duties included not only those of the librarian, but also opening and closing the rooms, keeping the facilities clean, and trimming the lamp wicks. These men soon found themselves stretched to maintain the facilities. Finally, with the onset of summer's heat,

---

10 See Young Men's Mercantile Library Association minutes for April and May 1835; these are housed in the Library's safe. Unless indicated otherwise, information cited throughout the book concerning the decisions and activities of the Mercantile Library board of directors has been taken from the appropriate monthly minutes and/or annual and quarterly reports.

they closed the rooms.

In the meantime, they continued to meet regularly. Much of their time was occupied with securing new members, ordering books as funds became available, approving the payment of bills, and ordering newspapers and journals: the first were the *New York Daily Courier and Enquirer*, the *New York Mirror*, the *Niles Weekly Register* (Baltimore), the *Philadelphia Daily Enquirer* [sic], the *Daily Baltimore Patriot*, the *Richmond Whig*, and the *National Intelligencer* (Washington, D.C.).[11] They kept a cautious eye on all expenditures.

As these duties became increasingly routine, two concerns began to demand more attention. First, who was to be eligible for membership? As is typical of organizations then and now, the president appointed a committee to explore the question. In May the committee recommended that membership be open to "those whose interests are connected with, or whose course of business directly facilitates the operations of the mercantile class, namely those engaged in Banks and Banking Establishments, Insurance Officers, Manufacturers, Counting Houses, and those engaged in Counting Houses generally." Artisans, mechanics, and professional men were excluded.

The second issue was a permanent location for the Association. The initial rooms proved unsatisfactory. By early summer the board of directors had started a search for something better suited to its needs; the only necessary requisites were "cheapness and convenience." A central location

---

11 Newspapers from Boston, Mobile, Charleston (South Carolina), Pittsburgh, Louisville, St. Louis, London, and Edinburgh were soon added, along with *Blackwood's Magazine* (Edinburgh), *Metropolitan Magazine* (London), *Silliman's Journal* (New Haven), and *Littell's Museum Monthly* (Philadelphia), also known as *Littell's Living Age* or simply as *Littell's Magazine*. Within a few years the Reading Room carried newspapers from France and Germany.

appeared essential in order to avoid "all jealousy & dissatisfaction" and to preserve "perfect good feelings and harmony...." Sometime that summer the board took out a five-year lease on rooms located near Fourth and Main Streets, rented from Messrs. Ross and Gwynne, with an opt-out provision after the first year. The directors expressed their hope to soon have "a considerable stock of books, both instructing and interesting." The only drawback to the new quarters was the annual rent of $200, a $50 increase over the previous space. The need for new members now became even more acute, but the closing of the facilities over the summer months had discouraged many young men from joining.

By December 1835 more hopeful signs prevailed, both inside and outside the organization. In the community, discussion centered on the possibility of a railroad connection to Charleston, South Carolina, a plan strongly promoted by Dr. Daniel Drake and dear to the hearts of most merchants. For those seeking a more celestial sign that the situation was improving, Halley's Comet made its scheduled appearance that month. Then, at a special meeting in early December, President Ranney appointed Rowland G. Mitchell to ascertain how much money could be raised by subscription to engage Joseph S. Benham, a well-respected local attorney, to deliver lectures on commercial and maritime law. Two days later Mitchell confidently reported back that $116 had already been promised toward Benham's $200 fee. The Mercantile Library's long and illustrious association with public lectures had been launched.

At the January 1836 annual meeting, in a vote of confidence and appreciation, the members reelected the entire board. In his annual report at that meeting, President Ranney announced that membership had almost doubled since October: it now stood at 169, including fifty-four life members. With justifiable pride, he also announced that the library now held 767 volumes, over half fully bound or in boards; the collection consisted of "works of almost every department of Science & Literature... with a few exceptions of theological works, mostly of anti-sectarian character." Circulation had also increased, although Ranney noted that half of the active members had not checked out any books.

Despite the rather limited interest in religious works, apparently some members expressed concerns about the moral tone of several novels. Ranney finessed the issue by reporting that they had purchased only works "of an historical character... with but few exceptions strictly ethical." However, he added, future boards would not be bound by this criterion. A year later the issue resurfaced. A new board solemnly resolved that "the work lately purchased, entitled 'Boccacio,' be rejected as totally unfit for the Young Men's Mercantile Library Association, being composed of stories obscene and vulgar, and that hereafter no works of like character be admitted into the Library, also that the Librarian be directed to dispose of the above work."[12] The reference to the Librarian also informs us that the board had hired its first full-time employee, Benjamin F. Doolittle, a person of "gentlemanly deportment," who was to receive an annual salary of $200.

Problems with Librarian Doolittle soon surfaced; perhaps

---

12 The third quarter report for 1836 reveals a curious note. In pencil, board secretary William R. Smith wrote that the "April Report should be here but was taken from my drawer by the President in my absence & has been mislaid." Later he made an additional notation: "The July report of the Directors has been misplaced by the President." Moses Ranney may have been the Association's "founder," but apparently he lacked some basic organizational skills.

his name was prophetic. In May 1836, the board established two permanent committees, one on finance and one on the library. The need for the first committee may have been triggered by concerns over Doolittle's handling of accounts. A week after its establishment, the committee on finance reported that it had "demanded of the librarian explanation in regard to some obscure and unsatisfactory items in his account and that he failed to give them full satisfaction." They also demanded "a schedule of a part of his Book account &... after assenting, he addressed a note to the Committee in which he refused to comply and questioning their right to demand the same."

This board was not to be trifled with, and it quickly set a tone for Doolittle and perhaps all future employees. On motion by President Ranney, the librarian's actions received "the unqualified disapprobation of the Board of Directors." The board then voted to require Doolittle to submit "the receipts and expenditures from November to this time." The following month, the librarian handed over his accounts, but because "no balance" was included, they were returned to him "to be consummated by the next meeting." Curiously, on the same day, Doolittle requested a one- to two-month leave of absence, which was approved pending the procurement of a satisfactory substitute. Although this particular accounting issue apparently was resolved, it severely strained Doolittle's relationship with the board. On February 4, 1837, he submitted his resignation. Shortly thereafter, Nathaniel Holley took up the position.

The board also dealt with less stressful issues. In July 1836 it approved a seal for the Association, "a figure representing Commerce with the name of the Association engraved around it." After the State of Ohio granted a charter in January of that year, bylaws had to be rewritten in order to comply with the Act of Incorporation. This included an age requirement that limited initial membership to men under the age of thirty; fortunately this provision was soon changed. The directors set the first week in January for the annual meeting and the election of officers, with a quorum of twenty members required for transacting any business. They also created a procedure for removing any officer or director.

While the board worked through these necessary housekeeping chores, finances remained the major problem. In fall 1836 the board appointed an ad hoc committee "to procure subscriptions and members." Fees soon increased: the initial cost doubled from $1 to $2 for all "active" members, and a life membership increased from $25 to $50. Annual dues remained at $3 for both active and honorary members.[13] In December, when the Cincinnati Literary Society needed a place for its Friday evening meetings, the board was only too happy to rent space to it. This arrangement lasted about a year until the Society disbanded.

At the April 1837 quarterly meeting, the president sadly announced that the financial situation had worsened and that the Association had no way to meet its current debt of $160.69. The problem was clear: with a total of 180 members, each paying $3, the organization's income of about $540 did not meet the annual operating cost of about $800. Library

---

13 An honorary member had full use of the facilities but could not hold office or take part in meetings. This type of membership was apparently established for non-merchants, particularly those from the professions. A notable example was Salmon P. Chase, a rising attorney who was denied membership in July 1837 on the grounds that he was not eligible (as a lawyer he was not of the mercantile class). The following month the "honorary" category was created, and in October Chase joined the Association. This classification was eliminated after the Civil War, and an "honorary" membership took on its present-day meaning.

accessions ceased, and members were asked to donate books.

To resolve the fiscal dilemma, the board divided the city into several districts, and board members then were assigned to solicit new members within a specific district. The idea was that they would be more successful if they canvassed their neighbors. The strategy worked: by October membership had climbed to approximately three hundred.[14] Plans moved forward to have a catalog of the books printed; cost was to be covered either by purchase or by private subscription. The first catalog was printed in 1838. Still, the president cautioned, there was a "feeling of supineness [sic] and indifference, of apathy and unconcern among many of [the members]."

By the end of 1837, when several prospective members stated they would join if the Association would "provide certain newspapers," the board felt secure enough to reject their proposal. The board appointed director Peter Outcalt, at that time a clerk in A. J. Wheeler's exchange office, to inform them that if they were elected to membership they would have the privilege "of bringing into the Reading Room such publications as they may desire at their own expense."

Another nagging issue was the increasingly high turnover among members of the board, no doubt reflecting both the amount of time involved in holding a position and the economic turbulence caused by the financial panic of 1837. Director William Gallagher proposed a 25¢ fine for board members who failed to attend a regular meeting (unless ill

14 Early membership numbers are unreliable. Given the social and economic fluidity of the times, the Association had no effective way to keep track of those members who moved out of the city. This was particularly true for the large number of single males who lived in the city's many boarding houses. For an analysis of economic mobility in the city, see Walter Stix Glazer, *Cincinnati in 1840: The Social and Functional Organization of an Urban Community During the Pre-Civil War Period* (Columbus: Ohio State University Press, 1999) 112-22.

or absent from the city); the motion failed, but the problem remained. A year later, at the annual election, the board cautioned those who aspired to positions in the organization that they must be prepared to serve at least one year. The fairly frequent special meetings called to fill various vacancies on the board had an "injurious effect... in the eyes of the public." The admonition apparently had little effect, however.

Vandalism also proved vexing. Apparently some users were taking periodicals from the Reading Room without the librarian's permission. Theft and mutilation of books and periodicals remained a constant problem for the next twenty-five years or so, despite appeals to the membership and the best efforts of several librarians.

The board also passed a resolution to have members pay dues "yearly, in advance, instead of quarterly as heretofore". This would help the Association's cash flow. Attention was also directed toward ordinary matters such as procuring a sign for the outside of the building, selecting a speaker for the anniversary address, approving all purchases, and discussing how the board might determine more clearly who had relinquished membership and who still owed money.

While the board continued to spend large amounts of time on administrative issues, it also began to expand the Association's role in the community. The success of Joseph Benham's two lectures in 1836 led to the establishment of a more ambitious lecture series in 1838. Tapping into local talent, the board contacted Dr. John Locke of the Medical College of Ohio, the Rev. Dr. Robinson, Mr. Samuel Ellis, Edward D. Mansfield, Professor Charles L. Telford of the Cincinnati College, Judge Timothy Walker, Rufus Hodges, and William Holmes McGuffey, president of the Cincinnati College. It is not known how many responded positively, but Judge Walker, one of the founders of the Cincinnati Law School, inaugurated the series in February with a lecture titled "Commercial Law," for which he declined any remuneration. The profits from the two lectures went toward the purchase of two chandeliers and five dozen chairs.

The following year the board approved a resolution calling for a Board of Trade or Chamber of Commerce to be established. A quickly formed committee looked into the possibility, and its report on October 1, 1839, touched off an animated discussion. Apparently feathers were ruffled, and something was said about an inadequate report. When the committee stated that they had done enough, the president disagreed sharply, whereupon two of the three members on the committee resigned. A newly formed committee called a public meeting for October 15, and one week later the Chamber of Commerce was born.

Intended as an organization to collect commercial and financial information, to provide a place for discussion of leading mercantile issues, and to promote the amicable settlement of differences among businessmen, the Chamber was a true product of the Mercantile Library, and for several years the two organizations shared space. As the annual report for 1839 stated, the "elder portion of the mercantile community" had taken the lead in this enterprise, but the two organizations would "become the mutual stay and support of each other...."

All of this activity attracted public notice. The *Cincinnati Daily Gazette* pointed out that the Young Men's Mercantile Library Association benefited more than merchants, and that, for a "trifling sum," its "advantages are open to any respectable member of the community."[15]

The abrupt resignation of the two committee members, however, indicates internal dissension that may have originated in the annual election held on January 1, 1839. Considerable discussion and open disagreement had occurred regarding the votes cast for the three director positions. After it was first announced that James Wiles, A. P. Iglehart, and Thomas Spooner had been elected, several members questioned whether the latter two could be elected if only Wiles had received a majority vote. This question eventually led to a second balloting, and John Pullan replaced Spooner. To avoid future problems, the board decided at its next meeting to use a nominating committee. The rancor within the board soon resurfaced, however, and over a surprisingly minor matter. This suggests that something more personal lay below the surface of the disagreement.

The minutes of the April 2 quarterly meeting of the Association record that a "warm discussion" erupted over the proper anniversary day of the organization. Should it be April 4, 1835, when a preliminary discussion was held, or April 18, when the Association was actually established? Board secretary Ebenezer B. Hinman, a druggist, resigned at this point, and the meeting was adjourned until the following Saturday. No doubt considerable activity took place during the intervening days: at the next meeting Henry Shaw's motion to accept April 18 as the correct date was approved, although it was made clear that this was only for the current year. The fact that the earlier date had already passed may have been a

15 *Cincinnati Daily Gazette*, April 17, 1839, 2. Several of the Chamber's early presidents had been or remained very active in the Association, including Rowland G. Mitchell, James C. Hall, R. M. W. Taylor, James F. Torrence, J. W. Sibley, Joseph C. Butler, Theodore Cook, and John W. Hartwell.

factor in making the decision.

No matter. The minutes reveal that President Isaac D. Wheeler, vice-president John Buchanan, and director Wiles all resigned, perhaps hoping to force a reconsideration of the issue. A newly established nominating committee "retired for a few minutes," then returned to recommend the election of three new officers and one director. One of the nominees, however, Rowland G. Mitchell,[16] declined to be elected president because he supported the resigned officers, and William Parry withdrew his name for vice-president because there was "not enough time." The situation began to resemble a comic opera.

The nominating committee then put up Charles C. Sackett for president and James Findlay Torrence for vice-president.[17] Both were elected, although support for the resigned officers remained strong. Aftershocks followed: a few days later, Iglehart and Pullan resigned as directors and George W. R. Bouldin as secretary, although their particular concerns are not clear. On April 12 they were replaced.

The conflict was made evident when Henry Shaw, now the board's corresponding secretary, wrote Wheeler, the former president, requesting papers dealing with the Association's founding. Wheeler replied tartly that the old board "has ceased to be" and he was not "their head." He concluded by suggesting that Shaw had "hastily penned" his request "without due reflection as to my capacity to comply with its and

---

16 Rowland G. Mitchell, a wholesale grocer, was one of the forty-five original members of the Mercantile Library and served as its president in 1837; he gave the anniversary address in 1839. Perhaps because of the turmoil of that year he may have left the Association. In 1842 he became president of the Chamber of Commerce.

17 Sackett, a clerk at N. W. Thomas & Co., wholesale grocers, later became a founder and president of the Young Men's Mercantile Library of Sacramento, California. At that time Torrence worked as a clerk in his family's corn business.

your demands...."

As the new president, Sackett wrote in his annual report at the end of the year that the former president had withdrawn "all that friendship and sympathy of feeling, which we had so anxiously looked for, and had reason to expect...." Whether a clash of personalities or strong disagreement over board management lay at the bottom of this conflict, the Association almost foundered on the seemingly insignificant question of the appropriate anniversary date.[18]

Personal rancor aside, the continuing affairs of the organization had to be addressed. The Association went ahead with its anniversary celebration, on April 18 at the College Building, highlighted by Rowland G. Mitchell's address. Also, problems with the librarian rose again. At a special meeting held in April 1840 the finance committee reported that the Association's accounts were "in a very confused state" due to the "negligent manner of collecting": many members' accounts had gone unpaid for two or three years. Since collection was one of the librarian's responsibilities, the board removed Holley "solely on the ground of inattention to his duties." By July, the new librarian, James Wildy, had brought "a decided change for the better."

The board then turned to other matters. When the Cincinnati Lyceum failed, they discussed the possible donation of the Lyceum's library to the Mercantile Library. Apparently nothing came of this, however. Ambitions for enlarging the book collection also led to a search for more spacious quarters. A committee contacted the Odd Fellows Association, as well as a Mr. S. G. Brown, about rooms.

---

18 The 1840 election of the highly respected Moses Ranney as president may have been an attempt to smooth out the situation.

In late 1840 the Mercantile Library began renting rooms in the Cincinnati College Building, located on Walnut Street between Fourth and Fifth (the present site of the Library), where it shared its Reading Room with the Chamber of Commerce. Just five years earlier the handsome two-story brick building had been deteriorating—in a "dilapidated state," according to the *Daily Evening Post*[19]—but it had been resuscitated by the revival of the Medical College and the Cincinnati Law College. When the Mercantile Library prepared to move into its new quarters, however, it found "the late Medical faculty still occupants, and unwilling to yield their right."[20]

After lengthy communications, the Library obtained a three-year lease but had to pay the medical faculty half "in consideration of the permanent fixtures in [the] Library Room." In return for the $300 annual rent, the Association controlled rooms on the second floor, and from the windows along the south wall members could look out on a beautiful garden extending down to Fourth Street. To the east, elegant residences and the 285-foot spire of the First Presbyterian Church filled the view. Perhaps more attractive to many Library members was Mrs. Gooch's Boarding and Day School for Young Ladies, located just across Walnut Street.[21]

Finally settled into adequate surroundings, the Young

19 [Cincinnati] *Daily Evening Post*, October 26, 1835, 2. The Cincinnati College was founded in 1819, largely through the efforts of General William Lytle, but by 1830 it had lost most of its students.

20 The Medical College or Medical Department of the Cincinnati College, not to be confused with the Medical College of Ohio that was also in the city, had closed in 1839, but the faculty retained offices in their former quarters.

21 Mrs. Gooch advertised that young ladies in her boarding school would learn "orthography with definitions, Reading, Natural History, Mental Arithmetic, Geography, and Plain Needlework," all for $50 for a twelve-week session; see David Henry Shaffer, *Shaffer's Advertising Directory for 1839-40* (Cincinnati, 1840), 19.

Men's Mercantile Library Association enjoyed several years of relative stability. It had become a fixture in the commercial development of the city and seemingly could now look forward to growth and prosperity. Although the financial strain from the Panic of 1837 remained, local merchants, stout Whigs for the most part, drew great confidence from the election of William Henry Harrison in 1840.[22] Board meetings now settled into a routine of accepting bills for payment, electing new members, making necessary changes in the bylaws, appointing committees to look into specific concerns, and arranging for lecturers.

In an era when there was little public entertainment, especially during the winter months, lectures provided both education and amusement. Eventually East Coast notables would dominate the "lecture circuit," so vividly described by Dale Patrick Brown in *Brilliance and Balderdash*, but until railroad travel improved, the Mercantile Library depended upon local men.[23]

In the Association's first attempt at a public lecture series, held in 1838, Judge Timothy Walker of the Cincinnati Law College gave a "course of lectures" on law. In 1840-41, a Rev. Dr. Robinson[24] presented a series of six talks on American history, the board guaranteeing him a fee of $200. To protect the organization's operating budget, the board initiated a subscription drive to raise the $300 necessary to support the

22 Although President Harrison became a member of the Association in December 1840 shortly after he was elected president, there was another, apparently unrelated William Henry Harrison, a druggist, who belonged to the organization for many years. This latter Harrison, a brother of Learner B. Harrison, was a native of Franklin, Tennessee, and later became a prominent member of Cincinnati's business community.

23 Dale Patrick Brown, *Brilliance and Balderdash: Early Lectures at Cincinnati's Mercantile Library* (Cincinnati: The Mercantile Library, 2007).

24 Charles Cist listed a Reverend Samuel Robinson as pastor of the Reform Presbyterian Church in 1841; see Charles Cist, *Cincinnati in 1841* (Cincinnati: 1841).

series. After some difficulty it reached this goal, and the lectures even turned a small profit.

The following year, with more profits in mind, the Association sponsored two series, a twelve-lecture "course" in geology, held on Saturday evenings in the fall by Professor John Locke, and a winter series of "more varied character." Two dollars paid for admission to all of Dr. Locke's presentations. The winter series included such local luminaries as Timothy Walker, Edward D. Mansfield, and Lyman Beecher; the topics ranged from Unitarian minister James Handasyd Perkins' "Saints and Miracles of the Middle Ages"[25] to local astronomer Ormsby M. Mitchel's "The Exact Sciences." Since all of these men apparently spoke without payment, the price of a ticket for the series was only $1, or 25¢ for a single lecture. Ladies, who would have been escorted, attended free.

Although the Association had hoped to make a considerable profit, Dr. Locke's series on fossils and rocks did not do well, barely covering the cost of the "transparencies" used. The winter series fared even worse. "These instructive lectures," lamented the president in the annual report for 1842, "have been listened to by but few of our members, and that noble enthusiasm in the cause of virtue which prompted them [the supporters] to devote time and labor in our service has been dispirited and chilled by the reprehensible conduct of those who, through this Board as their agent, induced them to undertake their gratuitous task." The president then blamed the poor attendance on the large number of lectures in the

25 James Handasyd Perkins, a minister in the First Unitarian Church, was the author of a history of the Old Northwest Territory, first president of the Cincinnati Historical Society, founder of the Cincinnati Relief Union, and a major donor of books to the Mercantile Library. His apparent suicide in December 1849 was greatly lamented in the city.

city—"nearly every evening in each week—and concluded by suggesting some type of coordination with the Society for the Diffusion of Useful Knowledge.[26]

The following year, 1843, the board followed a different path, substituting a series of "Literary Essays or Addresses" by active members. As John W. Ellis ruefully commented some years later, if these lectures "did not enlighten the people on the subjects of which they treated, they at least had the benefit of teaching their authors the subject of composition and delivery."[27] The board also contacted former president John Quincy Adams about giving a lecture before the Association when he visited the city later in the year to dedicate the new observatory. The elderly Adams declined, however.

The board's disappointment with the lectures reflects its continued concern over the Association's financial affairs. Although membership now hovered around five hundred and use of the library had increased, operating costs continued to rise as well. To expand the library's holdings, the board voted to launch a special subscription drive to raise $1,000 to purchase books in London.[28] The initial response brought in pledges totaling $400, but then momentum slowed. This was not the fault of the committee, the board assured the members, but rather a result of "pecuniary pressure" on the community, a reference to the lingering effects of the 1837 financial panic. In October 1840, when the goal had still not been reached,

---

26 Several educational or cultural organizations existed in the city during all or part of the 1830s, and most used lectures to raise money. These organizations included the Society for the Diffusion of Useful Knowledge, the Cincinnati Lyceum, the Western Academy of Natural Sciences, the Ohio Mechanics' Institute, and the Western Literary Institute.

27 See Henry A. and Mrs. Kate B. Ford, *History of Cincinnati, Ohio* (Cincinnati: L.A. Williams & Co., 1881), 259; Ellis, the president at the time, also gave one of the lectures in the series.

28 Because books could be purchased duty-free, it was cheaper to purchase them in London.

Isaac D. Wheeler generously donated the remaining $100. The following spring, however, no doubt because of lapsed commitments, the board had to approve an expenditure of $150 to fulfill the subscription.

To meet the constant fiscal challenges, the board voted to grant honorary membership to resident clergy (for a $3 annual fee). Many took advantage of this offer. The president also used the annual meeting as an occasion to urge the expansion of active membership to include professional men and mechanics. He further stressed the importance of reaching out to the large body of young men, age fifteen to eighteen, who would be the future merchants of the city. Although professional men were eventually granted membership, the Association's ambitions always pushed expenses perilously close to revenues.

Another avenue for generating income was to crack down on those members who neglected to pay dues or fines. Throughout the early 1840s the board minutes reveal numerous attempts by the librarian to collect money owed the organization. On several occasions the board even resolved to bring legal action against negligent members. One such case involved William Parry, "having been fined sundry times and refusing to pay, stating the amount to be unjust." Parry was a charter member and one of the men who had declined to serve as an officer in the imbroglio of 1839; he owed $3.40 in fines.[29] There is no record of payment nor of any legal action.

Concerns over money showed up in other ways as well. In September 1840, Librarian Wildy reported that $43.05 in col-

29 Another case involved a suit against a J. P. Broadwell, initiated in July 1843. The Association's attorneys, the firm of Taft and Key, finally collected the amount due, but not until Broadwell "had thrown the last obstacle within his reach in the way."

lected fines and dues had been lost. According to his account, the money had been stolen "from his pantaloon pocket" while he and his wife slept. After a thorough investigation, the board concluded that the sum was "not lost because of any neglect" on the librarian's part. Given the librarian's later behavior, however, one might well question the "thief in the night" story.

In all fairness to James Wildy and the other early librarians, their lot was not an easy one. Not only did the board expect of them all the librarian's normal duties, but they also had to periodically compile catalogs, collect dues and fines and report delinquent members to the board, handle all janitorial duties, and deal with irritated members—in other words, much like the current librarian's duties except that he has a competent staff. During Holley's tenure, the board had instructed him to pick up newspapers "from the Post Office immediately after the distribution of the mail by which they arrive. All papers and periodicals placed on tables; back issues to be kept in files and made available when requested. He shall be particular in keeping the tables, chairs, papers [?], etc. free from dirt and dust...." During Wildy's service, the committee on the Reading Room reported "the newspaper stands as they are now arranged to be very illy [sic] adapted to the purpose for which they were supposed to be constructed, and [we] recommend that some alteration be made in them, the management of the lamps might also be improved upon as the light now thrown in every direction but upon the papers which are left somewhat eclipsed."

The board apparently did not comprehend the effect of the many demands it placed on the librarian. Although in Wildy's case it increased the annual salary to $500, it had also extended the hours of operation so that the facilities now opened at 8 a.m. As Wildy complained in 1840, in order to collect fines he had to close the library, which led to irritated members and frequent complaints. To address this problem, the board approved closing the library regularly "from 10 to 11½ O'clock A.M. [sic] and from 3 to 5 P.M. [sic] when it is necessary for the purpose of attending to the business of the Association & from 1 to 2 P.M. [sic] for his own convenience." Although this action solved one problem, it also underscores the length of the workday the board expected from its sole employee. The board considered hiring an assistant librarian in 1842 but postponed that decision because of budget concerns.

The board of directors, through its various committees, continued to tinker with the operation of the Reading Room and Library Room. In 1842 it experimented with leaving maps, journals, and newspapers out on the tables without any direct supervision. This step would help free the librarian for his other duties. The board's faith in their fellow members proved unfounded: "After a fair test of this experiment," commented the president, "it was found that the benefits resulting therefrom [sic] were by no means equal to the loss & vexation arising from the inexcusably bad usage and mutilation of the works & the occasional pilfering of some attractive numbers by persons whose cupidity far outweighed their sense of decency or honesty." The president recommended dropping this idea "unless [the board] can procure the services of an Argus-eyed overseer to watch over those whose cravings after literature so remarkably outrun their respect for the moral law."

Apparently Wildy was not that man. Indeed, problems surrounding his behavior began to surface. In April 1843 the new president, John W. Ellis (later the founder and president of the First National Bank of Cincinnati, now a part of U.S. Bancorp), felt it necessary to instruct the librarian in his duties, singling out punctuality "at the hours specified in the bylaws," and "strict adherence to sobriety and personal cleanliness." The newly elected board of 1844 unanimously reappointed Wildy as librarian, but new boards tend to be cautious about making radical changes. Soon, however, the librarian's situation deteriorated further. In October the directors informed Wildy that "the continuance of his present situation is dependent upon obeying to the letter the directions of the Vigilance Committee."[30] It also instructed the Vigilance Committee to report "any and every dereliction of duty on the part of the Librarian."

By year's end Wildy was in serious trouble. A specially appointed committee reported "irregularity" among books on the shelves and continuing poor record keeping, with no records for some missing books. The committee concluded that the librarian was "guilty of great, almost unpardonable, carelessness." A month later the minutes show that "certain information seriously reflecting upon the moral character of the Librarian" had come to light. A "closed letter" was then sent to the incoming board, which promptly fired Wildy and replaced him with Charles E. Cist. Further details about Wildy's behavior emerged later: frequent drinking, failure to open the rooms on time, incomplete records, and a slovenly appearance. He died sometime between his dismissal in

30 Earlier in 1844 the board discontinued the committee responsible for the Library, Reading Room, and Exchange Room, replacing it with a committee of one to serve one month to oversee the "arrangement and cleanliness of the rooms." This position, which rotated among the board members, was called the Vigilance Committee.

January 1845 and April of that year.

In the meantime the board busied itself with the day-to-day affairs of the Association. In December 1841 it announced that a new catalog was available at a cost of 25¢. Free copies went to life members, lecturers in the current winter series, and editors of all the city newspapers. At its annual meeting in January 1842, the president proudly pointed to the acquisition of 1,076 volumes for the Library, 748 of which resulted from the $1,000 subscription levied the previous year. Lest anyone think that the Library had acquired frivolous works, he also emphasized that these books were for "improvement rather than amusement." The annual report a year later made a similar point, noting that "biographies, popular works on science, histories, and philosophical treatises are rapidly displacing the use of ephemeral and almost useless works of Romance."

The board also wrestled with the question of organizing the growing collection more systematically. From the beginning, the librarian had numbered books in order of acquisition (a system surely in need of a Melvil Dewey), but in December 1843 the board introduced a plan to classify books into "departments of Science, History, Natural and Political Philosophy, Theology, Biography, etc. etc." The board members hoped that this would illustrate the library's needs and facilitate compiling future catalogs. The current plan, "if there is any," grumbled the chairman of the committee on the library, is "a blind adherence to numerical progression."

Although the Reading Room demanded less attention than the collection, the board voted to increase the number of foreign newspapers, including several from Germany. This may have been a response to the city's rapidly expanding German population.[31] On the other hand, three board members protested vigorously against acquiring the *New York Herald*. They opposed permitting the "notoriously immoral character" of that newspaper to undermine the morals of the Association's members.

In 1842 the board experimented with new lighting. Following complaints about smell and insufficient light, devices known as Greenough's lamps were given a trial run in the Reading Room. Although the cost would be "enormous" ($300 per year), the increase in patronage, according to the committee, would offset the annual expenditure; if the board rejected the new system, they stated "we can return again to the penumbra of our discarded lamps, & the odoriferous fragrance of camphene oil."[32] Yet despite the committee's endorsement, the board chose not to purchase the lamps. The next year a new board had gas lighting installed.

At its May 4, 1843, meeting, the board, at the urging of the business community, recommended the creation of a "Merchants' Exchange" in a section of the Reading Room. Here one would be able to find registration books for hotel arrivals and records of "Imports & Exports of Produce and Merchandise by the Miami and Whitewater Canals & Little Miami Railroad—and for the arrivals and departures of steamboats and the Exports & Imports of same—Bulletin Boards for advertisements, news & items of Interest to merchants gener-

31 For the Association's first eight or ten years, the great majority of the members' names indicate English or Scottish descent; by the end of the 1840s, Germanic names are more in evidence. In 1842 the Association introduced classes in both German and French, although these were soon discontinued for lack of support.
32 According to an advertisement in the city directory, B. F. Greenough sold "Patent Solar Air Lamps" that could burn a variety of fuels; camphene was a kerosene-based oil that gave off a very pungent odor.

ally...." The estimated cost of $500 per year, which included an employee to collect the information and statistics, would be covered by an assessment of $5 per year on member subscribers. Lewis J. Cist, a son of Charles E. Cist, was hired to manage the Exchange Room, as it was called. In December of that year, the newly established committee on the Exchange Room reported that the area had realized its objectives, although they expressed some irritation that "the merchants have failed to attend very regular [sic] during the hours of 'Change' but this omission is with themselves, and not with the arrangements of the room—But the statistics, mercantile news, and other items of interest to merchants and traders generally have been the means of increasing the number of visitors to the Exchange and Reading Rooms...."

As suited their expanding place in the community, Association members marched in the downtown funeral procession of President William Henry Harrison, a member of the Association when he died in 1841. Two years later the board agreed to send representatives, wearing pink identification badges, to join in the cornerstone ceremony for the Cincinnati Observatory on Mount Ida.[33] The Association also subscribed to four nonvoting shares in the Cincinnati Astronomical Society which allowed Mercantile Library members to attend its meetings. Then, in the early 1840s the board explored the possibility of a "plan of union" with the Society for the Promotion of Useful Knowledge. Nothing came of this venture and the Society dissolved shortly thereafter.

As the Young Men's Mercantile Library Association moved

33 Mount Ida was renamed Mount Adams in honor of former President John Quincy Adams' participation in the dedication. Some months later the telescope arrived from Germany; at that time it was the largest and finest such instrument in the United States.

toward its tenth anniversary, scheduled for April 1845, it could take pride in its accomplishments. Membership had grown to 625. The Association had secured "permanent" quarters in the Cincinnati College Building and had created a Chamber of Commerce. Besides its Reading Room and Library Room, it operated a Merchants' Exchange and presented an annual lecture series. The Association was well established in the community, and its facilities were used by thousands of local citizens as well as visitors to the city. The library boasted a collection of over four thousand volumes; the Reading Room housed more than sixty-five newspapers and magazines, including seven Cincinnati daily papers.

The Association also continued to believe in its lofty goals. As President John Ellis stated in the annual report for 1844, "[W]e can believe that this Institution has already rescued many a noble youth from a tendency to those evil propensities and directed them to refined sources of intellectual enjoyment." Ellis also delivered a cautionary message to all members: "Commercial pursuits have in themselves the elements of good and evil. The great evil is that our love of gain may descend into a devotion or idolatry to Mammon."

"I do not know that I ever saw a town of its size so well provided as Cincinnati with publishers, libraries and reading rooms."

WILLIAM CHAMBERS
Things As They Are in America, 1853

"The Mercantile Library have a Course of very able Lectures in progress, which are attended by a large portion of the first minds of the city."

The Herald of Truth, 1848

CHAPTER 2

Finding Its Place

TWO EVENTS soon shattered the enthusiasm surrounding the approaching tenth anniversary celebration. First, a public dispute broke out over the annual election scheduled for January 7, 1845, when "A Member" (later identified as Richard B. Pullan), writing in the *Cincinnati Daily Gazette*, criticized the proposed officers and directors as narrowly representing businesses located around Columbia and Main Streets. He had a particular dislike for R. M. W. Taylor, the candidate for president and the corresponding secretary of the outgoing board of directors. Pullan accused Taylor of arbitrarily controlling all Library purchases for the past year.

As letters filled the Gazette over the next several days, it became clear that the disagreement had started the previous summer. Pullan believed that the board, in appointing a committee of two (which included Taylor) to oversee book purchases for the library, had relinquished one of its principal responsibilities. In July, Pullan and another director had resigned from the board over the issue, and the board apparently had divided evenly over whether to retain the committee approach.

At the heart of the matter lay Pullan's criticisms concerning the acquisition of a French edition of Voltaire's works and the purchase of multiple copies of Edward Bulwer-Lytton's historical novel *The Last of the Barons* and James Fenimore Cooper's *The Wing-and-Wing.* Thus in December, when new officers and directors were nominated (soon referred to as the "Regular Ticket"), Pullan and other members met to create an opposition slate of names (known as the "Independent Ticket").

All of this discord remained within the organization until Pullan's letter of January 3 was printed. Supporters of Taylor and the Regular Ticket, particularly someone calling himself "A Member of 1835," challenged Pullan's account. This member pointed out that the Voltaire purchase had been authorized by the entire board of the previous year (that is, 1843), and that acquiring multiple copies of the two titles in question merely reflected the high demand by the members. He went on to assert that no committee had usurped the powers of the board; rather, the committee structure facilitated board action. Furthermore, the current board had "invited" members from the canal area to run for office, but none had expressed interest.[1] (According to the 1850 city directory, Pullan's wholesale grocery business was located at 19 East Second Street, but he lived close to the Whitewater Canal terminal in the southwestern corner of the city.)

[1] This whole affair can be reviewed in the pages of the *Cincinnati Daily Gazette,* January 3 to January 8, 1845, usually on page 2. Pullan's angry response to a letter of January 7, 1845, signed by all of the board members except the president, who was out of the city, can be found in the *Daily Gazette,* January 20, 1845, 2. Pullan remained active in the Association, however, contributing to the Perpetual Lease Fund later that year. The *Cincinnati Daily Gazette,* a Whig paper edited by John C. Wright at that time, usually supported the Association and often reported Association lectures and other events.

After all this uproar, the election passed "very quietly." Taylor defeated James Hall of the Independent Ticket for president, 187 votes to 124; indeed, the Regular Ticket swept the election. Clearly embarrassed by the controversy, the new board voted to open the minutes of the Association to any member, but only after deleting the last sentence of the motion stating that no copies could be made "if for the purpose of continuing a controversy before the public."

Even if this seems to modern readers to be much ado about nothing, it illustrates both the prickly personalities of some members and the importance many members attached to the Young Men's Mercantile Library Association. Future elections would also occasionally reflect spirited differences of opinion.

Second and far more disruptive was the calamity of January 19, 1845. On that Sunday morning, fire broke out in the College Building. The flames destroyed the structure, leaving only walls and a small portion of the roof. Fortunately, the members, most of whom lived within a few blocks of the structure, helped save almost the entire collection of books (only seventy-eight volumes were lost), along with full-length portraits of William Henry Harrison and Charles H. Hammond.[2] All unbound newspapers were destroyed, however, and furniture, shelving, and maps suffered considerable damage amounting to an estimated $100.

The Library's collection was quickly housed in temporary quarters. The editor of the *Cincinnati Daily Gazette* believed

2   The fullest account of the fire is found in the *Cincinnati Daily Gazette*, January 20, 1845, 2. This account provides the only mention of these two portraits. The Harrison portrait was eventually returned to a family member; the Hammond portrait has disappeared. Charles H. Hammond (1779-1840) had been the outspoken editor of the *Cincinnati Daily Gazette* before his death in 1840.

that more fire bells (church bells) should have rung, but given the state of firefighting equipment at that time, it is doubtful that the "late arrival" of engines from the nearby community of Fulton would have made much difference.[3]

Over the next several days the board met frequently in the vestry of the First Presbyterian Church, trying to come to grips with the disaster. To begin, the board suspended all Association activities and appointed committees to examine the salvaged books and to secure new rooms. Under somewhat constrained circumstances, the Library soon reopened in a building on Sycamore Street.

In the meantime a third special committee met with the Cincinnati College trustees to explore the possibility of a new building. Just thirteen days after the fire, the Association committed itself to raising $10,000 (roughly $300,000 in 2009 dollars) toward the cost of a new building in return for a perpetual lease, and on February 6 the committee announced that it had already received $8,750 in pledges.[4] The lease that eventually resulted is the Mercantile Library's greatest treasure: "a perpetual right in fee, in and to the grounds belonging to said college together with any buildings that may be erected thereon as well as the use of sufficient and suitable apartments therein." The College would pay all taxes, liens, or assessments "such as paving and lighting the street." The document also permitted the Mercantile Library Association the use of College Hall, with a seating capacity of 2,500 to 3,000, free of charge for up to twenty-five nights per year, although the

---

3 Fulton, a separate community just upriver from Cincinnati, was known for its boat building; today it is the area around St. Rose Church on Eastern Avenue.

4 Eventually more than $11,000 was pledged. Although the Association hoped to retain its relationship with the Cincinnati College, the board was prepared to negotiate for rooms with the Chamber of Commerce if necessary.

Association was required to pay the gas bills and janitorial costs associated with those evenings. The lease was to last ten thousand years (one year for each dollar, perhaps?) with right of renewal. Alphonso Taft, father of the future U.S. president, is credited with serving as the Association's attorney and drawing up the document.[5]

Architect Henry Walter designed the edifice, a four-story neoclassic structure topped by a cupola modeled after the Tower of Winds in Athens. Situated on the site of the former college building, the structure was 140 feet wide and 100 feet deep. The front was covered with Dayton marble, and the full entablature was patterned after the Choragic Monument of Thrasyllus (fourth century BCE). The Association's new quarters on the second floor provided for a Reading Room (45 by 29 feet), a Library (45 by 29 feet), a Directors' Room (16 by 14 feet), and a similar room for the librarian. At the rear of the second story was College Hall, where numerous public programs were held.[6] The Library president described the proposed new College Building as "the fitting home of a great and public spirited Association, and an enduring monument to the taste and liberality of the merchants of Cincinnati."

Repercussions from the fire occupied most of the board's energy during the early months of 1845; still, routine matters had to be handled. Although the fire had caused only $182.05 in damages to Association property, which was paid by the Lexington Insurance Company, it had thrown a scare

5   For a rather humorous account of the lease, see John Fleischman, "The Ironclad Lease," *Ohio Magazine* (July 1992), 26-29. A copy of the lease may be found in the Mercantile Library Association archives, shelf box: "Emery Lease & Related Items," folder: "Lease 1849."

6   Descriptions of the building may be found in an appendix to the Association's twelfth annual report and in Charles Cist, *The Cincinnati Miscellany, or Antiquities of the West* (Cincinnati, 1846), 317.

into the organization. The board quickly voted to increase its coverage to $2,000. At this time it also chose to add a new staff position, that of messenger. This employee would serve as assistant librarian, be responsible for collecting dues and fines, and handle janitorial duties. A Mr. John Huddlesey took the position at an annual salary of $200. To replace the dismissed and now deceased Wildy, the board hired Charles Cist as librarian, at $400 per year. Lewis Cist, originally employed in 1843, was reappointed as news collector for the Exchange Department, at a salary of $700.[7]

Plans moved forward for the tenth anniversary celebration scheduled for April 18, 1845, and J. B. Headley agreed to give an address titled "What Is the Prospect of War?" Headley's talk, as described in the *Cincinnati Daily Gazette*, was "fresh and racy, and free of cant." [8] Despite growing tension with Mexico over the admission of Texas as a state, the war in question involved tensions between the United States and Great Britain over the boundary with Canada. The shock of the fire and the enthusiasm surrounding the tenth anniversary no doubt helped the members to put the election conflict behind them.

The board also sought members willing to participate in

---

7 Charles E. Cist (1793-1868) was well known in the community for his description of the city in his *Cincinnati in 1841: Its Early Annals* (Cincinnati: 1841). Later he wrote *Sketches and Statistics of Cincinnati in 1851* (Cincinnati: Wm. H. Moore & Co., 1851) and *Sketches and Statistics of Cincinnati in 1859* (Cincinnati: 1859), as well as *The Cincinnati Miscellany*, a compendium largely taken from his newspaper, *Cist's Weekly Advertiser*. All of his books, which provide many statistics and valuable descriptions of Cincinnati and its institutions, are basic sources for any history of the city. A Philadelphian by birth, Cist came to Cincinnati in 1827, where he engaged in various businesses and involved himself in the Democratic Party. In 1840, after he had served as a city councilman for several years, the Van Buren administration appointed him the official census taker for Cincinnati, a position that suited his talents well. *Cincinnati in 1841* is based heavily on the information, both statistical and anecdotal, he acquired in that capacity.

8 *Cincinnati Daily Gazette*, April 21, 1845, 2.

the coming winter lecture series; eventually James T. Annan, Association president R. M. W. Taylor, Headley, and others volunteered their services. The Universalist Church on Walnut Street generously provided a room for $5 a night, and John W. Ellis inaugurated the season with a talk titled "The Romance of Maritime Discovered."[9] Attendance was "highly respectable," but overall the numbers were disappointing, quite a frequent lament in the annual reports of the time. Yet despite the small audiences, the Association continued to organize lectures as a way to "advertise" the organization and as evidence of its educational responsibilities.

The operation of the Library and Reading Room continued to occupy much of the board's attention. The move into the new rooms had allowed for an easy transition to the new system of shelving books by subject classification, but some problems persisted. On January 16, 1850, the *Cincinnati Daily Gazette* observed caustically that "the man who spits on floors, we perceive, has arrived in town.... We hope he will soon leave and go where spitting in Reading Rooms is considered genteel." [10] The board minutes also record that theft and vandalism remained particularly troublesome. In November 1845 the board offered a $10 reward for "detection of the persons who have.... mutilated & taken from the Rooms the newspapers of the Association." In February 1846 the cutting-out of parts of New York newspapers remained an issue of "peculiar regret and vexation." Notices offering the reward were

---

9   Annan, a Mercantile director, spoke on "The Early British Dramatists and Poets"; Taylor, a clerk in the commission house of Messick and Walters, provided a look at Oliver Cromwell; and Headley titled his lecture "A Sketch of the History of Banking." The series concluded with William Watts' lecture on "Mahomet." Additional information may be found in Brown, *Brilliance and Balderdash*.

10 *Cincinnati Daily Gazette*, January 16, 1850, 2.

placed in conspicuous locations in the rooms; one board member even suggested that the cut-out pieces "be described and advertised in our city papers." Perhaps some good came from all this effort, for in March A. R. Foote reported no thefts or mutilation.

Another persistent problem involved the collection of dues and fines from certain members. On December 16, 1845 the treasurer recommended discontinuing the membership of twenty-two people and bringing legal action against three others, pointing out that some had not paid dues for more than a year. A week later he sent notes to "six delinquents," five of whom gave oral answers. One asked the collector to return on Saturday, but when he did so, "the money was not ready." Another even challenged the Association to sue him. This was a Mr. Robinson, who said he had informed Mr. Wildy that he was resigning, but the treasurer assured the board that during the previous summer Robinson had "promised to settle in a few days." Another member also tried to use the deceased librarian as an excuse, claiming that Wildy had permitted him to keep Charles Lamb's *Essays of Elia*, "a work of trifling pecuniary value." The board was unmoved, although some of the difficulty certainly could be traced to Wildy's careless record keeping. In the annual report for 1846, because the board had received "much censure" for the abruptness of the librarian's termination, the president listed the many reasons, including unaccounted-for sums of money, for relieving him of his duties.

Whereas 1845 had opened with a divided membership and a calamitous fire, the next year brought the excitement of new facilities in the New College Building; the move was completed in early summer. Membership now soared over 800, and the library held more than 4,400 volumes and 60 news-papers, plus scientific magazines, various journals, maps, charts, and globes.[11] Almost as exciting, the Association was "free from debt," and its future seemed secure, courtesy of the ten thousand year lease. The Mercantile also could boast that many of the city's most respected men belonged, including the Honorable Jacob Burnet, Judge James Hall, the scholarly Edward D. Mansfield, Professor Ormsby M. Mitchel, and the Reverend James H. Perkins.[12]

Board minutes also reflect a new maturity: crisis manage-ment began to give way to normal matters of business. To address the problem of vandalism, supervision of the rooms was now turned over to a board member, "styled 'Director of the Week,' whose name [was] regularly posted on the bulle-tin board." This step apparently reduced vandalism and freed the librarian for other responsibilities.[13] As a reflection of

11 According to the minutes of April 8, 1845, the collection at that time included all local newspapers, virtually every major national newspaper and journal, and several from London and Edinburgh.

12 Burnet (1770-1853) was a former associate Justice on the Ohio Supreme Court and a U.S. senator from Ohio; Hall (1793-1868) edited the *Western Monthly Magazine*, an early Cincinnati literary journal; Mansfield (1801-80) was an author and editor of the *Cincinnati Chronicle*; Mitchel (1805-62), a graduate of West Point, established the Cincinnati Observatory and served as its first astronomer. Perkins (1810-49), a Boston native, was a Unitarian minister and founder of the Cincinnati Relief Union and the House of Refuge. Perkins also represents the importance of the city's Unitarians in the Mercantile Library's early years. Alphonso Taft, attorney William Greene, grocer and later banker Learner B. Harrison, Davis B. Lawler, and William D. Gallagher, the city's best-known poet, are among the many Unitarians linked to the Association; for more on the city's Unitarians, see Walter P. Herz, "Influence Transcending Mere Numbers: The Unitarians in Nineteenth-Century Cincinnati," *Queen City Heritage*, 51 (Winter, 1993), 2-22.

13 Vandalism remained a problem. Almost every year the board made some reference to it, and in 1865 it submitted a bill to the Ohio state legislature making mutilation of newspa-pers in reading rooms a criminal offense. Whether or not such legislation was passed, in 1869 a "General F. W. Lister" was observed by George McLaughlin stealing a copy of the magazine *Temple Bar*. Since only a female assistant librarian was in the room, the janitor went out to secure a policeman, but Mr. Lister left while he was gone. Several days later he returned the magazine but left before he could be apprehended.

the city's growing commercial importance, the current board encouraged future boards to subscribe to more of the leading European newspapers and journals. During the year, several hundred volumes were donated to the library, making up for the lack of money available for purchases, and in 1846 the board voted to print a new catalog to reflect the collection's growth.[14]

The Merchants' Exchange, never meant to be a permanent part of the Mercantile Library, was turned over to the Chamber of Commerce in 1846, although it continued to use the largest room in the new quarters. The information acquired by its director, Lewis Cist – import and export statistics, steamboat schedules, information on market supply and demand, and arrivals at hotels – proved critical to the city's merchants. The Merchants' Exchange also served as the western terminus for the newly strung telegraph system and thus provided almost instantaneous information from East Coast cities.

For the annual lecture series that year, the board again drew on the members' talents, although Senator James T. Morehead of Kentucky opened the series with a talk titled "The Causes and Events That Led to the Establishment of the Political Institutions of the United States and the Means of Preserving Them." A "very large and brilliant audience" listened respect-

---

14 John B. Coram Esq. donated forty-one volumes that year, including a four-volume edition of Charles-Lucien Jules Laurent Bonaparte's *American Ornithology*. James H. Perkins gave 146 volumes to the library that year. In making this gift, Perkins requested several life memberships; the board consented, granting him life membership and two others that he could give "to any two individuals whom he may select."

fully in the new College Hall.[15]

For the next several years the Association enjoyed exceptional growth. Although the annual report for 1846 lamented the slight attendance at quarterly meetings, this comment most likely reflected the general euphoria surrounding the move to new quarters. The board minutes reflect little internal discord and, in general, the members found little to complain about. Membership grew steadily, use of the Reading Room and Library increased, and even the troublesome lecture series now drew larger audiences.

Perhaps some of the euphoria stemmed from Cincinnati's economic expansion as the city secured its position among the nation's primary commercial centers. A return to national economic health and a popular, ultimately successful war against Mexico, launched in 1846, certainly benefited many of the city's merchants, while the cloud of slavery still was somewhat obscure on the horizon. Times were good for the Association.

When the College trustees, perhaps regretting the lease to which they had agreed, attempted to assess the Association in 1848 for use of the furniture and gas fixtures in the Association's rooms, the board protested vigorously, stating "[We] will submit to no infringement of [our] rights." In language more reflective of 1776 than of 1848, they called it a "direct tax" not "provided for in the contract." Confident

15 Other lecturers that season included Gamaliel Bailey Jr. (1807-59), editor of the *Cincinnati Philanthropist*, an abolitionist newspaper, who in 1847 moved to Washington, D.C., to edit *The National Era;* attorney William Greene (1797-1883), the Honorable Bellamy Storer Sr. (1796-1875), who had served in the U.S. House of Representatives and then as judge of the Cincinnati Superior Court; Salmon P. Chase (1808-73), a prominent local attorney and later Lincoln's secretary of the Treasury and Chief Justice of the United States; and Charles P. McIlvaine (1799-1873), president of Kenyon College and Episcopal Bishop of Ohio. The inclusion of Morehead and Ohio Governor Charles Anderson, who spoke on immigration and the West, suggests that the Association was widening its search for appropriate speakers.

in their position but hoping for a peaceful resolution to the dispute, the board even suggested outside arbitration, "binding on both parties." Because the topic is not mentioned again in the minutes, one assumes that either the College authorities backed down or arbitration proved successful.

The board also sought to protect the Association's moral fiber. When several members requested that chess be permitted in the Reading Room, the board voted its disapproval, strongly questioning the "propriety of introducing games...."

Another positive sign was the decrease in unpaid memberships, although the collection of fines remained a problem. In October 1848 the board seized an opportunity to purchase a significant number of books from James T. Annan's personal library (566 volumes for $1,043.05).[16] As library holdings increased, alcoves were created in the room and new shelving was installed. Later that year librarian Charles Cist resigned, although he continued to work on the forthcoming catalog. Thomas G. Forster replaced him, and the faithful Huddlesey remained as messenger and assistant librarian.[17]

The election held on January 2, 1850, proved to be another spirited contest. Four hundred and forty-eight members turned out to vote that year, and the nominating committee's slate of officers and directors went down to defeat. Why the sudden excitement? Unfortunately, the board minutes for 1849 through 1858 have not survived. The only hint at a conflict comes from the fifteenth annual report, covering 1849, which refers to a set of constitutional amendments, supported by the

---

16 Annan's collection was especially rich in English literature.
17 Cist returned as librarian the following year at a salary of $700 and remained until 1853. To ease the financial strain on Forster for his abrupt termination, the board voted to give him $83.34 as the equivalent of a longer notice. No criticism was made of Forster's performance; it was just that Cist was the best librarian the Association had ever had.

board, as postponed indefinitely. As the report dryly noted, the position of the board was "evidently misapprehended."

The conflict, however, can be tracked in the pages of the *Cincinnati Daily Gazette*. On November 6, 1849, the Association held a general meeting to vote on revisions to the constitution. What the *Gazette* referred to as "embodying a few changes" apparently included a new definition of "young man" and an undefined enlargement of the powers of the board. Unable to gain the support of the necessary 75 percent of the membership, the board adjourned the meeting until two weeks later. On that day a member calling himself "1838" complained that the board had given no notice of the changes before the first meeting and had tried to force the amendments on those in attendance. Referring to the board's action as "dictatorial," "1838" feared that older members would take over control of the organization. Leave our "time-honored Constitution" alone, he wrote. Five days later, "An Old Member" rebutted these charges, arguing that "the young men will never give up control" and that the increased board powers merely reflected a necessary executive process; they were certainly not a usurpation of authority.[18] In any event, there is no record that these amendments were ever raised again for discussion. The absence of board minutes leaves the history of the Association during the 1850s dependent on the annual reports, which focus largely on the organization's accomplishments.

During this period both membership and library holdings grew steadily. As the holdings approached ten thousand volumes, the board sought to "re-gain" the room leased to the

18 See *Cincinnati Daily Gazette*, November 6, 22 and 27, 1849, all on page 2.

45

Chamber of Commerce for the Exchange Room. This proved more difficult than anticipated: presumably the Chamber of Commerce knew something about leases too. At any rate, the Association did not take possession of the space until 1851, when the Chamber's lease expired.[19]

Before converting this large room for library use, the board adopted architect William H. Bayless's plan for remodeling "the whole suite of rooms." Graceful iron columns replaced the wooden pillars, and the ceiling was vastly improved. New shelving was installed on all four walls, "a light iron gallery or balustrade" provided access to the upper levels of shelving, and arrangements were made so that alcoves could be constructed in the future. The estimated cost was $3,000, with an extra $1,000 for refurnishing. The board optimistically predicted that the increase in membership would largely offset the cost of remodeling, but expenses soon exceeded the estimated costs by almost $6,000; four years and several subscriptions were needed to retire the debt. The result, however, was space for twenty thousand books and much more pleasant surroundings.

The improvements also brought some unforeseen favorable surprises. President James Lupton took this opportunity to donate several pieces of furniture, including hat and umbrella racks and a "rustic sofa." Another member, recording secretary Lemuel A. Ostrom, a bookkeeper, gave an "elegant and costly barometer," while former president Joseph C. Butler provided nine chandeliers, "the finest and most costly donation ever received by the Society."[20]

19 The Merchants' Exchange (often referred to as 'Change) merely moved into College Hall, so that it remained physically close to the Mercantile Library.

20 Except for the hat and umbrella racks and the sofa, it is assumed that the other items either did not survive the fire of 1869 or succumbed later to the effects of time.

Charles Cist, rehired as librarian in 1850, continued to manage the Library and Reading Room operations effectively, but his assistant, Huddlesey, departed without notice, and George Frazer took his place. The following year, perhaps recognizing the increased work involved in managing the facilities, the board added a second assistant librarian's position to help with the expanding responsibilities.

Even so, in 1853 Cist tendered his resignation, announcing his desire to become a lawyer. In recognition of his many services to the organization, the board granted him life membership. It also hired Reuben H. Stephenson to replace him. Stephenson must have made a quick positive impression: the next year the new board sent "our worthy and accomplished librarian" to the National Convention of Librarians, held in New York City.[21]

The Association continued to purchase books, but the character of the books remained an issue. Either individual library users or board members must have periodically questioned the purchase of certain items, for at one point the board reported that it was "studiously careful to admit nothing corrupting in tendency...." Several years later, in its annual report for 1857, the board announced rather piously, "[W]e should endeavor to direct and elevate the taste of our readers, by placing on our shelves, works of an instructive character, and of a correct moral tendency."

The members seemed to have a different perspective. In 1854 the board had authorized the purchase of 19 copies of Mrs. Anna Cora Mowatt's *Autobiography of an Actress*,

---

21 Although the board minutes mention that Cist expressed a desire to become an attorney, this may be an error because he was sixty-one years old at the time. Stephenson served as librarian until 1859; in 1861 the city directory lists him as an attorney.

by far the largest number of copies of any title purchased up to that time.[22] Given the risqué reputation of the theater in mid-nineteenth-century America, it would appear that many of these merchants and clerks sought something a bit racier than books of "an instructive character." As the board admitted in 1858, "the greatest demand... has been for popular and newly-published books, and our Boards have been compelled, in a measure, to purchase largely of works having a present interest, but of little or no permanent value." It then recommended establishing a collection of noncirculating "approved works" that will "be an honor to our City." In early 1860 the minutes quietly noted the purchase for $1 of Charles Darwin's *On the Origin of Species*, a book more reflective of the board's concerns.

The annual reports reveal some persistent problems as well. In 1854 in a burst of enthusiasm the board reinstituted classes in a variety of subjects: French, German, mathematics, penmanship, and bookkeeping. Two years later, mathematics and penmanship had been discontinued, and the following year the board gave up on the others. Six-day work weeks and ten-hour days apparently did not encourage young merchants to seek formal instruction during their evenings; Mrs. Mowatt was much more entertaining.

The subject of delinquent fines surfaced again, as did the problem of vandalism, especially the cutting of newspapers and the removal of engravings from books. (These problems still plague most libraries.) Reference to the purchase of 24 earthen spittoons (for $7.50) reminds us that the general habit of chewing tobacco constantly threatened library cleanliness.

---

22 Anna Mowatt was probably the most successful American actress of that period to perform in England.

Less problematically, the increase in library holdings led to a new catalog in 1856, the first in almost ten years.

The minutes also note a serious threat to the Association's existence. In 1853 the Ohio state legislature approved a tax to support school libraries. By 1859 that legislation had led to the establishment of the Cincinnati Public Library, a free, public institution housed in the Ohio Mechanics' Institute.[23] In December of that year, a committee of the Mercantile Library board, specifically appointed to study the impact of "the Free Library" on the Association, concluded that there was "no cause for apprehension." While the new facility would compete "as a library," it had no authority to collect periodicals. The two institutions would complement each other: another library would only "increase the circle of readers" and cultivate "a higher taste for knowledge."

Elections continued to be contested. In 1853 the newly reelected President Lupton expressed the "earnest hope that minor differences of opinion and policy be henceforth forgotten... consigning the asperities of a somewhat excited canvass to entire oblivion." Perhaps they were, but three years later the annual election was preceded by several weeks of angry letters published in the *Cincinnati Commercial*. Then, in 1858, more than 1,400 members turned out to vote, despite heavy afternoon rains; the Independent Ticket and the Regular Ticket divided the offices evenly.[24] The following year, again with daily advertisements in the newspapers and large numbers voting, the Independent Ticket swept the election. The

---

23 For a lively history of Cincinnati's public library, see John Fleischman, *Free & Public: One Hundred and Fifty Years at the Public Library of Cincinnati and Hamilton County* (Wilmington, OH: Orange Frazer Press, 2002).

24 *Cincinnati Commercial*, December 10, 1855-January 6, 1856; *Cincinnati Daily Gazette*, January 5, 1858, 2.

annual reports, however, shed no light on the "asperities" involved.

By any criteria the 1850s proved highly successful. Membership reached over three thousand, and the board had even opened honorary membership to women, electing a Miss C.W. Moore in 1859.[25] The Library now boasted of twenty thousand books, by far the largest collection in the region, and the Association's finances seemed secure. In 1858 the board purchased "a handsome rack for magazines and convenient desks for the papers," furniture that still serves Mercantile members. To many residents of the city, however, the most impressive feature of the Mercantile Library was the array of lectures that it provided during the years leading up to the Civil War.

In most years, considerable discussion surrounded the annual winter lectures. Although the 1847-48 series still relied heavily on local talent, the board's vision was expanding. Requests were made to both Senator Thomas Hart Benton (Missouri) and Senator Lewis Cass (Michigan).[26] Both declined, but speakers Robert Dale Owen of New Harmony, Indiana, and the Reverend Robert J. Breckinridge of Lexington, Kentucky, reflected the board's growing national focus.[27] Ohio Governor William Bebb, speaking "to a gratifyingly large" audience at the anniversary celebration in April 1848, elaborated on "Cincinnati: Her Position, Duty and Destiny"—a topic dear to the hearts of the city's

25 This was the "honorary" membership in its older sense: simply a nonvoting membership provided to those who were not merchants.

26 Benton (1782-1858) was a major figure in the Senate and a powerful voice for western expansion; Cass (1782-1866) was the Democratic nominee for president in 1848.

27 Owen (1801-77), a social reformer active in Indiana politics, titled his talk "Labor, Its History and Prospect," while Breckinridge (1800-71), Superintendent of Public Education in Kentucky and a member of that state's politically powerful Breckinridge family, concluded the series with "The Destiny of the American People."

merchants. Reflecting an apparent religious turn of mind, the Association reached out the next season to secure the Reverend John T. Brooke of Gambier, Ohio, home of Kenyon College, the Reverend J. M. Hall of Dayton, Ohio, and the Reverend Matthew Simpson, president of DePauw University in Greencastle, Indiana. Six Cincinnati clergymen also lectured.[28] Although not all spoke on moral or religious issues, the board must have felt an obligation to promote character building, or perhaps the divines simply charged less. In 1849, however, in a major coup the board went outside the region to secure prominent New York editor and lecturer Horace Greeley.

On November 27, 1849, Greeley spoke in College Hall, the large auditorium adjacent to the Mercantile Library rooms. Despite the lingering presence of cholera that year, his audience filled the hall "to every corner," or so the *Cincinnati Daily Gazette* stated in describing the evening. Greeley's topic, "Self-Culture," certainly reflected the Association's purpose. Although a representative from the *Cincinnati Daily Times* had to strain to hear the New Yorker's words over the noise of the crowd, most people who attended found the lecture both appropriate and satisfying.[29] Greeley's visit reflected the expansion of railroads to Lake Erie, which reduced the combined railroad-lake steamer trip from New York City to forty-eight hours rather than the week or so it had taken John Quincy Adams just six years earlier.

In 1850, encouraged by Greeley's reception, the board

28 Other possible speakers considered that year included Senator John C. Calhoun of South Carolina and the poet William Cullen Bryant of New York City.

29 Brown, *Brilliance and Balderdash*, 4-8; Brown's discussion of Mercantile Library lectures during this period is the source for much of the information provided here. For a local account of Greeley's visit, see *Cincinnati Daily Gazette*, December 1, 1849, 2.

invited Senator John Hale of New Hampshire, and in the following year secured Louis Agassiz, the Swiss-born Harvard philosopher and scientist. At that time Agassiz was the nation's foremost scientist, although his later opposition to Darwin's theory of evolution pushed his name into obscurity. Agassiz came to Cincinnati for the annual meeting of the Association for the Advancement of Science, an organization that he had founded. The Mercantile Library managed to obtain his services for a series of five lectures in May 1851. His first lecture, titled "The Plan of Creation, As Shown in the Animal Kingdom," set the tone for the series. Speaking informally, and using a blackboard to sketch examples of animal anatomy, Agassiz captivated his large audiences.

In 1852 the Mercantile, learning that Orestes Brownson was visiting the city, quickly arranged to have him speak. Brownson, formerly a transcendentalist and an advocate for social reform, and currently editor of the *Boston Quarterly*, had moved in recent years towards a conservative view of humanity and had converted from Unitarianism to Catholicism.

Brownson's visit coincided with that of Louis Kossuth, the Hungarian nationalist who had led an unsuccessful revolt in 1848 against Austrian control. Kossuth's American visit in 1851-52 stirred up much excitement in the United States, and Cincinnati newspapers carefully reported on his progress toward the Queen City. He arrived at the Cincinnati, Hamilton & Dayton Railroad terminal on February 8 and, escorted by a volunteer mounted force, walked through cheering crowds to the Burnet House on Third Street. Five days later, a crowd of thirty thousand people descended on the Court Street Market to hear the impassioned Hungarian, and he left to "most deafening and protracted cheering." Most likely some in the crowd wore the "Kossuth and Hungarian Hats" advertised in local newspapers by Dodd & Company.[30]

Brownson's visit to Cincinnati may have been no coincidence, for he had been a vocal critic of the Hungarian since 1850. Whether the Mercantile board was aware of this is not known. In any event, Brownson lectured on "Intervention," a topic emphasizing the wisdom of staying out of other countries' affairs. In extemporaneous comments he denounced Kossuth as a traitor, denied a people's right to revolt against a legitimate government, and stated that Hungary was an integral part of Austria. Speaking at times over a storm of hisses and angry mutterings, as well as the rabid applause of his own supporters, Brownson managed to conclude his address.

The next week an embarrassed James Lupton, Mercantile president, publicly apologized on behalf of the Association, stating that Brownson had "abused the confidence of the Association by traveling outside the proprieties of the lecture hall, to indulge in an indecorous and wanton personal attack." Kossuth left the city on February 25, again walking through a large, cheering crowd at the Cincinnati, Hamilton & Dayton Railroad depot. Two days later, Johann B. Stallo, a leader in the liberal German community, refuted Brownson's arguments, point by point, in a lecture at the Mercantile Library.[31]

30 *Cincinnati Daily Gazette*, February 9, February 14, February 17, and February 25, 1852, 2. Also see David Meade, "Brownson and Kossuth in Cincinnati," *Bulletin of the Historical and Philosophical Society of Ohio* 7 (April, 1949), 90-95. For an overall view of Kossuth's American visit, see John H. Komlos, *Louis Kossuth in America*, 1851-1852 (Buffalo: East European Institute, 1973).

31 Johann Bernhard Stallo (1823-1900) immigrated to Cincinnati from Germany at age 16. He taught briefly at St. Xavier College before turning to law and serving as judge in the Court of Common Pleas. Stallo developed a national reputation as a Hegelian philosopher and contributed greatly to the city's intellectual life. The *Commercial* took a rather favorable view of Brownson's appearance, published some rumors critical of Kossuth, and totally ignored Stallo's lecture, whereas the *Daily Gazette* supported Kossuth strongly.

The 1852-53 season proved particularly noteworthy. During that season the Mercantile hosted New York journalist Park Benjamin; Ralph Waldo Emerson, "the Sage of Concord"; Professor Benjamin Silliman of Yale College; and Horace Mann, president of Antioch College and the nation's strongest advocate of public education. The board also had extended an invitation to Senator Daniel Webster to deliver the Association's anniversary address in April. Webster declined on grounds of poor health, however, and died later that year.

Professor Silliman, one of the nation's leading scientists, spoke on "Vesuvius and Aetna," and three weeks later lectured on "Niagara." Benjamin provided a humorous poem titled "Fashion," while the reformer Horace Mann addressed the topic of "Women." Emerson, the star of the season, had first visited the Queen City in 1850 at the invitation of the recently founded Literary Club. His visit in December 1852 was the first of three he made to the Mercantile Library during the decade before the Civil War; on this occasion he spoke on "The Anglo Saxon." A packed house, including hundreds of young women, sat through the two-hour presentation. Many undoubtedly came to see rather than to hear the tall, slender, popular orator.[32] An impressive year indeed.

Over the next several years, continuing to leaven local talent with prominent national figures, the Mercantile board brought in New York travel writer and poet Bayard Taylor,

---

32 At his second appearance, on January 27, 1857, Emerson spoke somewhat extemporaneously on "The Conduct of Life," a rambling lecture that touched on "travel, conversation, patience, good and evil, and a number of other topics." Three years later he returned to expound on the importance of "Manners" as the glue of proper society. Emerson's visits to the Mercantile Library are described more fully in Brown, *Brilliance and Balderdash*, 18-23.

Dr. Oliver Wendell Holmes, abolitionist Wendell Phillips, Senator Thomas Hart Benton, and Herman Melville.

In 1857, when the economy was suffering from a financial panic, the board considered canceling its lecture series, but finally agreed to keep its prior commitments to four men; one of these was Melville. Better known for his first two books, *Typee* and *Omoo*, than for the more recently published but less popular *Moby Dick*, the thirty-eight-year-old author had a reputation for writing about rugged adventure. Probably many in the audience had hoped for something in that vein, but Melville chose instead to speak, at considerable length, on "Statues in Rome." Whether because of the topic or the delivery, the newspapers gave Melville lukewarm reviews. *The Daily Gazette* found him an observant visitor to Rome but felt that his presentation was "too quiet, common-place and unobtrusive" for a popular audience. The *Commercial* agreed: "Earnest though not sufficiently animated," the editor wrote.[33]

Dr. Oliver Wendell Holmes, father of the Supreme Court justice who served in the early twentieth century, made his first public appearance in the city prematurely. Although scheduled to speak on three consecutive evenings beginning on September 5, he agreed to fill in on September 4 for an ailing James E. Murdoch, the popular Shakespearean actor and elocutionist. Murdoch, citing "nervous irritability," had retired from Smith & Nixon's Hall that evening after finding himself unable to remember his speech.[34] Holmes, known for the poem "Old Ironsides," discussed the poets Lord Byron and Thomas Moore before a sold-out crowd of some two thou-

33 *Cincinnati Daily Gazette*, February 3, 1858, 2; *Cincinnati Commercial*, February 3, 1858, 2.
34 James R. Smith and Wilson K. Nixon, piano merchants, owned a recital hall at 24 West Fourth Street, between Main and Walnut, where Mercantile Library lecturers frequently appeared.

sand people. Unfortunately his three scheduled lectures drew substantially smaller audiences – so small that one newspaper wondered where all the Association members were: "Had there been no ladies present, Prof. Holmes would hardly have been justified in delivering his fine lecture...."[35]

Two other lecturers during these years deserve further comment: Edward Everett and William Makepeace Thackeray. Everett, the most prominent orator in the country, delivered one of his most popular lectures, "The Life and Character of Washington." Menter's Band set the proper atmosphere with patriotic tunes before Everett's appearance, and a full-length portrait of Washington was placed on the Smith & Nixon stage. Speaking before a large, enthusiastic crowd on May 7, 1857, Everett extolled the virtues of the nation's first president: at a time of deepening sectionalism, he hoped that descriptions of Washington and Mount Vernon would rekindle a sense of national unity. The first lecture benefited the Library, while proceeds from the second went to the Mt. Vernon Ladies' Association for the purchase and preservation of Washington's Virginia estate. Although Unitarian minister Moncure D. Conway thought the lecture "more a eulogy than academic," both the Mercantile board and Everett were pleased with the results. Before departing the city, Everett sat for his portrait, commissioned by former Mercantile president Andrew B. Merriam and painted by local artist Joseph Oriel

---

35 *Cincinnati Daily Times*, September 7, 1855, 2.

Eaton. That portrait currently hangs in the Library.[36]

Thackeray's Mercantile appearance was something of an accident. The English author of *Vanity Fair* was in St. Louis, a stop on his six-month lecture tour through the United States, when he heard that Cincinnatians were unhappy that he had bypassed their city. He sent off a telegram offering to speak in the Queen City on the next Saturday and Monday. Thus on Saturday, March 29, 1856, the "broad framed but not fleshy" English satirist lectured on George III. "One of the largest and most brilliant audiences of the season" filled Smith & Nixon's Hall and heard a pleasant but somewhat rambling talk on the third Hanoverian king. Two nights later Thackeray spoke on George IV. As the reporter for the *Daily Gazette* wrote somewhat waspishly, "All departed pleased, the lecturer with what he received, and the audience with what they had heard. We think he got the better of the bargain."[37]

Not every lecture worked out so smoothly. In 1858 the Association engaged New York journalist Park Benjamin. Benjamin had participated in two previous lecture series, and the board anticipated no problems. It turned out, however, that Benjamin had arranged to give the same lecture, titled "Hard Times," to another organization in the city before speaking at the Mercantile Library. This situation would undermine his appeal and reduce the anticipated proceeds from his appearance. The board, believing that the journalist had violated an

36 *Cincinnati Daily Gazette*, May 10, 1857, 2; *Cincinnati Daily Times*, May 8, 1857, 2; Moncure Daniel Conway, *Autobiography, Memories, and Experiences of Moncure Daniel Conway* (Boston: Houghton Mifflin, 1904), I, 286-87. Among those in attendance were Governor Salmon P. Chase, Supreme Court Justice John McLean, and the honorable Thomas Corwin. Everett was also the principal speaker at the dedication of the National Cemetery at Gettysburg, Pennsylvania, in November 1863. His almost-two-hour address was far more typical of the oratory expected on such an occasion than the 2½-minute address delivered by Abraham Lincoln.

37 *Cincinnati Daily Gazette*, March 31 and April 1, 1856, 2.

unwritten rule of public engagements, terminated the contract and refused to pay him. Benjamin filed suit against the Association for $100 plus interest.[38] In Cincinnati's Superior Court, a jury agreed with the Library's interpretation and found in its favor.

Despite the time and energy spent on organizing the winter lectures, they did not always prove profitable. Prominent names brought out sizable audiences, but in most years the series struggled just to break even. "To the general inattention to the Lecture Course, the oration of Hon. Edward Everett formed an exception to the usually dull routine of the season," wryly commented the president in his annual report for 1857. In January 1858 a newly elected board seriously considered eliminating the lectures, noting that the abbreviated winter series for 1857-58 had netted only $9.25. Nevertheless, deeming the lectures "a valuable and attractive means of improvement," the board finally decided to continue the series. In January 1860, in response to "frequent inquiries" as to why "Home Lecturers" were not used more frequently than "Important Lecturers," the Association invited four "prominent citizens" to speak, along with several more nationally known figures. Among the local citizens, however, it seems that only attorney William S. Groesbeck accepted the invitation.

That September the lecture committee again recommended ending the winter series, because, they stated, such entertainment "has lately been viewed by the public as flat, stale, and unprofitable." Again several board members disagreed, advising that the Association secure "more nove[l]ties, celebrities,

38 *Cincinnati Daily Gazette*, January 29, 1858, 2.

magnificent strangers, and endeavor to attract not only those who attend purely from the desire to hear... but also those who will attend the lecture to see our distinguished and celebrated Strangers." After much discussion, invitations went out to the Reverend Henry Ward Beecher, William L. Yancey, Caleb Cushing, and Dr. J. G. Holland, editor of *The Century Magazine*, along with Horace Greeley, Bayard Taylor, and Louis Agassiz. Several local speakers were placed on the list as well. That winter (1860-61) Bayard spoke twice, joined by Holland and two local luminaries, the Reverend E. L. Magoon and James E. Murdoch. The political excitement and the threat of disunion and war may well have affected the response: many of the lectures again proved financially disappointing.[39]

The year 1860 also marked the Association's twenty-fifth anniversary. The celebration, held in Pike's Opera House,[40] began at eight in the evening: the reporter for the *Daily Gazette* noted the "hacks and carriages that rattled over the pavements with twice their accustomed velocity, and wheeling in front of the beautiful temple [Pike's Opera House], and depositing their precious loads, would, like good Genii of fairy note, fly away again to repeat the act." The program included an "oration" by businessman William Hooper, William Fosdick's recitation of a poem he had written for the occasion, and dramatic readings from Shakespeare, Byron, and *The Pickwick Papers* by the always-popular James Murdoch. Musical interludes fol-

39 Beecher (1813-87), son of the Reverend Lyman Beecher and brother of Harriet Beecher Stowe, was the prominent and controversial minister of Brooklyn's Plymouth Congregational Church; Yancey (1814-63) was a secessionist politician from Alabama; and Caleb Cushing (1800-79), attorney general in the Pierce administration, was a Southern-leaning Democrat from Massachusetts.

40 Pike's Opera House, the dream of whiskey manufacturer Samuel M. Pike, was considered the finest auditorium west of New York City. It opened in 1859 and served the city until it burned in 1866. Pike rebuilt it, but on a smaller scale.

lowed each part of the program. The boxes were "filled with gaily attired and beautiful women," gushed the reporter, and the soft light from "a thousand jets of gas... lit up their smiling features with a radiant splendor that seemed... to equal the prismatic hues of the diamonds that flashed upon their heaving bosoms." At 10:30 a "Grand March" led the members to a supper on an "elegant scale." The evening concluded with dancing on the stage, which lasted into the early morning hours;[41] these were, after all, young men. A "brilliant success," concluded the president in that year's annual report. The editor of the *Daily Gazette*, in praising the Library's role in shaping the city's public life, pointed out that it was second in size only to the Mercantile Library in New York.[42]

Proud of their organization, confident of the future, few in attendance that evening could envision the problems that war was soon to bring to the city and to the Young Men's Mercantile Library Association.

---

41 Brown, *Brilliance and Balderdash*, 67-68; *Cincinnati Daily Gazette*, April 19, 1860, 3.
42 *Cincinnati Daily Gazette*, April 18, 1860, 2.

"[The Library] is still green and flourishing...."

"PREFATORY NOTICE"
IN *The Catalogue of the Books of the Young Men's Mercantile Library Association*, 1869

CHAPTER 3

Through War and Fire

J ANUARY 1861 brought nothing but anxiety for most Americans. President James Buchanan sat in Washington, waiting out the last 2½ months of his presidency, while president-elect Abraham Lincoln sat in Springfield, Illinois, pondering the issues of union and slavery. South Carolina had already seceded from the Union, and several other Southern states would soon follow. A crisis loomed.

For the Young Men's Mercantile Library Association, however, the year began rather quietly. Members gathered on New Year's Day for the annual meeting, but given the low turnout, they quickly adjourned until January 5 to hold their election and hear the president's summary of the preceding year. He reported that membership numbers had reached 3,327 and that the library now held more than 21,000 volumes, both indicators of continued success. The treasury, although not robust, showed a balance. The usual accolades to the outgoing board, coupled with best wishes for the newly elected board, suggest that few members found the future troubling despite the passions swirling around South Carolina's recent secession.

Yet these merchants, many of whom had personal or business ties, or both, to Southern states, certainly were aware of the darkening political situation. For almost fifteen years they had periodically brought in prominent men to speak about the problems of slavery and sectionalism. As early as December 1846, just seven months after the outbreak of war with Mexico, William Greene had spoken on "The Problem of the Perpetuity of Our National Union." Greene took that opportunity to address the support of disunion among some Southerners and correctly tied it to the institution of slavery. The (Cincinnati) *Daily Times* called it "the best lecture of the season."[1] Two weeks earlier, abolitionist Gamaliel Bailey, editor of the *Cincinnati Philanthropist*, had spoken on "American Progress." Certainly believing that Southern ardor for the war with Mexico was due in part to the opportunity to annex territory for the future expansion of slavery, he criticized going to war for purposes of expansion. Although not aimed directly against slavery, Bailey's position reflected even then the growing concern among many Northerners.

In January 1849 Elwood Fisher of Virginia, in a lecture titled "The North and the South," offered a statistical argument to show that in "Agriculture, Commerce, and Manufactures, the Southern States are superior to the Northern States." By excluding enslaved people from his statistics, Fisher determined that per capita wealth was greater in the South, and he argued that restricting the expansion of slavery would be the same as restricting manufacturing or commercial growth. He concluded by stating that the greater evidence of poverty and crime in the North proved the superi-

---

1   (Cincinnati) *Daily Times*, December 23, 1846, 2.

ority of the Southern way of life. [2]

Most of Fisher's conclusions would surprise most pres-ent-day historians and must have astonished his Cincinnati audience as well, especially those involved with manufactur-ing. The editor of the *Daily Gazette*, implying that Fisher's statistics were "artfully arranged," called it "a labored dis-course" that "failed to convince his audience." A reply was soon forthcoming: later that year a "Carolinian" responded to Fisher, disputing both his facts and his reasoning. In a statis-tics-filled pamphlet he argued that slavery damaged the South economically; he even managed to compare Fisher to Don Quixote, a man tilting at windmills.[3]

By 1850 the issue of slavery and its expansion into terri-tory newly acquired from Mexico had taken center stage in American politics. Angry arguments over the Wilmot Proviso, the Compromise of 1850, and, increasingly, slavery itself should have made Cassius Clay's appearance on December 3, 1850, a volatile event. Certainly many of the estimated 2,000 people (with hundreds turned away) who filled Smith & Nixon's Hall anticipated just such an evening. Clay, the eccentric abolitionist cousin of Henry Clay, proved a disap-pointment, however. Describing himself as neither a logician nor a metaphysician, Clay criticized the Christian religion for its dependence on the inerrancy of the Bible, arguing that recent discoveries in geology had destroyed the Biblical time-line. On "the physical and moral evils of slavery," he watered down his position by insisting that American slavery was not as bad as slavery practiced elsewhere because it had lifted up

2 *Cincinnati Daily Gazette, December 9, 1846,* 2; *Cincinnati Daily Gazette,* January 18, 1849, 2. Fisher's lecture was published as a pamphlet by the *Cincinnati Daily Chronicle;* it was also published in Charleston, South Carolina, and was read widely in the South.
3 The "Carolinian" was later identified as Daniel Reeves Goodloe, a North Carolinian.

the African. The editor of the *Daily Times* strongly disagreed.[4]

For the next three years, slavery and sectionalism virtually disappeared from the Mercantile Library's lecture topics. Either the various boards of directors thought the subject too inflammatory for Cincinnatians or they assumed that prospective audiences would rather hear presentations on historical figures, science-related topics, or the future of commerce. The issue did not resurface until November 1853, and then only indirectly. The Honorable John McLean, an associate justice of the Supreme Court, titled his talk "Government; more especially our own government, as regards the object of its formation, its relations and tendencies." McLean focused on the threat that "party spirit" posed to the Union, and he singled out the "Young America" element in the Democratic Party for its advocacy of "aggressive wars," especially southward. This latter comment was a reference to the Ostend Manifesto, the Pierce administration's push to either purchase or seize Cuba from Spain in 1853. Many Americans, both North and South, saw this as a way to establish a future slave state.[5]

The following year the Reverend Charles B. Parsons of Louisville, in a "bold and eloquent" lecture titled "The Glory, Shame, and Probable Destiny of the Republic," cited slavery as the great "Shame" in God's plan for the nation, but he argued that it would disappear if left in God's hands. His alleged intimacy with God passed without comment. Then in December

---

4 *Cincinnati Daily Gazette*, December 5, 1850, 2; (Cincinnati) *Daily Times*, December 4, 1850, 2.

5 *Cincinnati Daily Commercial*, November 23, 1853, 2; John McLean, "A Lecture on Government" (Cincinnati, 1854). McLean (1785-1861), a Cincinnatian, was appointed to the Supreme Court by Andrew Jackson and served for thirty-one years. His strong antislavery views pushed him out of the Democratic Party and eventually led him to the Republican Party, and he dissented vigorously from the majority in the infamous Dred Scott decision of 1857. His lecture was published in pamphlet form, with the title using lower case.

1856, the outspoken abolitionist Wendell Phillips lectured on "The Philosophy of Reform." Despite "weeping skies" and muddy streets, Smith & Nixon's Hall filled for the occasion. Once again, however, if the audience had hoped for oratorical fireworks, it was disappointed. Speaking in "a terse and Emersonian" style, Phillips provided only a general examination of reform and its importance to the progress of the nation. He made no mention of slavery.[6]

In February 1857 Thomas F. Marshall, a Kentucky congressman and nephew of former Chief Justice John Marshall, lectured on "The Powers of Congress over the Territories." Given the inflamed situation in Kansas, this topic also drew a large audience. Marshall, in offering a conservative Whig view of the issue, disagreed with the Democratic Party's position of allowing settlers to determine the adoption or rejection of slavery in the western territories (known as popular sovereignty), and he lavished much praise on Henry Clay's compromise efforts in 1820 and 1850. Marshall offered no real insights into this complex issue, however. The editor of the *Daily Times* was not impressed, describing the talk as "rambling, disconnected, fragmenting diction."

Two months after Marshall spoke, Senator Thomas Hart Benton of Missouri provided the address at the Association's anniversary celebration. "Old Bullion" Benton's reputation guaranteed a sizable turnout of members, but in a talk titled "The State of the Union," the aging senator provided only a low-keyed, moderate view of the problem. Benton held that slavery should not be permitted to expand, but that the North must not interfere where it was already established.

---

6 *Cincinnati Daily Gazette*, December 20, 1854, 2; *Cincinnati Daily Gazette*, December 3, 1856, 2.

Although the editor at the *Daily Times* agreed with Benton's central point, he caustically described the two-hour presentation as "long, tedious, discursive, soporific, and superlatively egotistical."[7] One wonders what he might have said if he had disagreed.

In 1859 the Reverend Parsons returned to the Mercantile. In an address titled "The American Union," the antislavery Parsons called for limited government interference in the matter of slavery and stated that the peculiar institution was destined to die out as part of God's noble plan for the United States. He expressed no sympathy for either Southern secessionists or Northern abolitionists, concluding that they all should be placed into "one vast funeral pile, and after shooting them with Yankee bores and Kentucky grooves, set fire to them." (No waiting for God's plan for them.) In the process of attacking slavery, Parsons managed to denounce the Pope, Jesuits, the Devil, and "pulpits of the Brooklyn make." This last comment, a reference to the fiery Henry Ward Beecher, brought hisses from some in the small audience. The *Daily Commercial* described the talk as an "odd combination of rhetoric, sense, fustian, argument, abounding in magniloquent periods, possessing merit as a Fourth of July oration, graphic some times... with – once in a while – a dash of brilliant word-painting, occasionally dramatic, somewhat ingenious, and altogether, the most tremendous, rip-staving, Union Saving, Spread Eagle accumulation of patriotic, oratoric [sic], dramatic, and theocratic conceits we ever took to comprehend and digest."[8]

---

7 (Cincinnati) *Daily Times*, February 11, 1857, 2; *Cincinnati Daily Gazette*, April 20, 1857, 2; (Cincinnati) *Daily Times*, April 20, 1857, 2.

8 *Cincinnati Daily Gazette*, March 25, 1859, 2; *Cincinnati Daily Commercial*, March 25, 1859, 2.

The Reverend Henry W. Bellows, pastor of the First Congregational Church (Unitarian) of New York City, followed Parsons a month later and expressed a stronger anti-slavery view. Speaking in Pike's Opera House, at one point he referred to those who seemed content to enjoy the slaves' songs but did not hear the clanking of their chains. "Why ignore the fact," he remonstrated, "that it was the clanking that tuned the melodies!" He urged his audience to hold onto the dreams of youth and become "apostles of Human Rights, demanding Liberty everywhere under all circumstances for everybody...."[9] His two other lectures during that visit focused on crime and individual responsibility.

In November of 1859 Francis P. Blair Jr., a thirty-nine-year-old Congressman from St. Louis, presented an intriguing lecture titled "Colonization and Commerce." His dubious thesis was that the United States should purchase parts of the "tropics in America" (Central and South America) as colonies and place free Negroes there. This action would reduce the "problem" of "mongrelization" in the United States and would create economic centers where free Negroes could civilize and Christianize the tropics. Blacks would benefit from living in a climate more agreeable to them, and the nation would benefit from the trade that would flow naturally between the two areas. The *Daily Gazette* was so strongly impressed by this address that it printed it in its entirety on the front page.

Three days later, on December 1, the eve of the execution of abolitionist John Brown, Henry S. Foote, former senator and governor of Mississippi, delivered a lecture. Foote, one

9 *Cincinnati Daily Gazette*, April 21, 1859, 2. During the Civil War, Bellows (1814-82) was the principal planner and first president of the United States Sanitary Commission, the leading aid society for Union soldiers.

of the more moderate Southern voices at the time, explored "The Idea of a Patriot President." He expressed his concern for the future of the Union and argued that the country now needed a "patriot president" in the mold of George Washington. Peppering his lecture with "quotations from Latin, poesy included," the Mississippian failed to impress one local reporter: "No permanent instruction and little content," grumbled the *Daily Gazette*. Foote's aim apparently "was to utter as much as possibly could be said in an hour and a half, with the sublime intention and result of saying nothing." Perhaps by the end of 1859 there was little more to be said about the political rift in the nation, but certainly a ninety-minute plea for a new George Washington couldn't have provided much sustenance for the sparse crowd at Pike's Opera House.[10]

As the nation spiraled towards disunion and war, the Mercantile Library Association sought less controversial topics. Perhaps the presidential campaign that led to Lincoln's nomination and election in November 1860 provided sufficient excitement; at any rate, the 1860-61 winter lecture season included no topics that reflected the political issues of the time. Instead audiences heard a variety of speakers address such compelling subjects as "Man and Climate," "Laziness," and "Paul Considered As a Man and Not As an Apostle." The season ended on January 24, 1861, with a lecture on "Self-Help" by Dr. J. G. Holland, editor of *The Century Magazine*. With several Southern states having seceded by then, the title might well have served as a *cri de coeur* for the nation.

The months that preceded the opening shots at Fort Sumter

---

10 *Cincinnati Daily Gazette*, November 29, 1859, 1; *Cincinnati Daily Gazette*, December 2, 1859, 2.

struck hard at Cincinnati's mercantile community. Coming on the heels of the financial contraction of 1857, the imminent possibility of secession and war further constrained business arrangements. Cincinnati, as a border city with strong river connections to the South, suffered early. By late November 1860, Association membership had fallen. "Owing to the disastrous state of affairs now existing in business circles," the board called on each member at its December meeting to recruit new members. For a few weeks, membership levels rose. By the following February, however, the membership committee, "with feelings of unfeigned alarm," reported a net decline of fifty during the previous month. The committee attributed some of the loss to the glut and subsequent departure of new members brought in by the recent, heatedly contested election of officers, but it also pointed to "the almost paralyzed conditions of all branches of business, caused by the political troubles of the country...." At the same meeting the board voted to cancel the remainder of the lecture series. With only a few exceptions, the Mercantile Library Association did not resume the lecture business for about ten years.

Meanwhile, the board continued to manage the organization's regular affairs. It raised the librarian's salary to $800 per year and ordered books for the library. Board minutes continue to reflect concern about use of the facilities by unauthorized persons. The nagging problem of mutilation also persisted, particularly in illustrated magazines such as *Punch*. Routine matters, however, could not shield the Association from concerns created by war. On April 16, 1861, just days after the attack on Fort Sumter, the scheduled quarterly meeting of the Association was adjourned for lack of a quorum. The city's newspapers reflect the excitement and confusion of those days, and apparently few Association members had thoughts for the Library. At the same time, the Library's facilities grew more important. Attendance in the Reading Room increased dramatically, but not because of the new spittoons. Members and guests descended on the room to read the latest news, although the "derangement of the Southern mails" had disrupted delivery from that region: in April, President Lincoln had ordered stoppage of all mail to and from the seceded states. The Adams Express Company offered its services, but that soon proved impossible, and for the duration of the war, the Association received no newspapers or journals from states in the Confederacy.

The overriding concern for the board continued to be loss of members and its impact on the budget. The "general stagnation of business matters" had caused a large number of young men to leave the city, and the war would soon take many more. John M. Wilson, the treasurer, resigned in June, "having enlisted for the war"; other members soon followed. By November 1861 the Association faced a net loss of 115 members for the year, and in that month the new treasurer "enlightened the Board as to the condition of the finances, making some statements rather startling to weak nerves and sensitive feelings." The board empowered the treasurer to take out a short-term loan to meet current bills.

Searching for ways to increase revenue, the board contacted Charles F. Brown (the humorist Artemus Ward) and the always-popular James Murdoch to give lectures or readings. In January 1862 Brown attracted a large audience for his entertaining "burlesque upon modern lectures and lecturers, which was heartily enjoyed and applauded throughout."[11] Murdoch, who had delivered three readings the previous January, agreed to appear, but there is no record that he actually spoke that winter on the Library's behalf. The board also invited William H. Russell of the *London Times* to give two lectures in the fall of 1861, but we find no record that he did so. Money was tight: when Mr. Smith (of Smith & Nixon's Hall) sought reimbursement due to the failure of an unidentified lecturer to keep his appointment, the board politely declined. The board also authorized the librarian to dispose of extra copies of books (half price was suggested), a process that brought in a small income and also cleared space on the crowded shelves.

For the most part the war years passed in a fragmented blur. Without a lecture series, the Association lost much of its public presence, and the war itself reduced interest in traditional Mercantile Library activities.[12] The usually faithful *Daily Gazette* failed to report the Association's annual anniversary meeting in April 1861; its pages were filled with news, rumors, and the general excitement generated by the recent attack on Fort Sumter. Information about the home guards and volunteer units such as the Guthrie Grays and the Washington Guards filled newspaper columns.[13] In such a climate, what interest was a library's celebration?

Even the Association's board minutes reflect the organization's stagnation: meetings were less frequent, with less

---

11 *Cincinnati Daily Gazette*, January 30, 1862, 2.

12 Apparently the Library did sponsor a number of lectures during the war years but with little success. In the 1864 annual report, President C. Taylor Jones, after referring to the "distracted condition of the country," lamented the lack of support for lectures over the past several years. He wrote, "Either our people have surfeited of lectures, or we have been peculiarly unfortunate in our selection of lecturers."

13 *Cincinnati Daily Gazette*, April 19, 1861, 2-3. The Mercantile Library did not hold an anniversary celebration again until 1885, its semi-centennial year.

discussion and briefer committee reports. To reduce expenditures, the board approved a cutback in the number of magazine subscriptions and discontinued the binding of journals. It also reduced book orders, although frequent requests by members for "popular works of fiction" continued to annoy the library committee chairman's sense of moral propriety.[14] Yet despite his concerns, in 1865 the board approved $1,000 for the purchase of current literature in the hope that it would increase membership. In addition, the board continued its attempts to raise money through occasional lectures, usually by inviting some local person. These generally drew small audiences and produced little profit, if any.[15]

A partial solution to the Mercantile Library's financial troubles came in an unusual way. In March 1863 Julius Dexter, president of the Cincinnati Insurance Company, inquired about a permanent Library membership that apparently would be assigned successively to each incoming president of the company. The board rejected his suggestion. As one board member argued, the intent of the constitution was not to create "a class of transferable and portable memberships." Another member pointed out that Dexter was "in no sense a person" but rather "a part of a corporate body." A month later the board reconsidered the situation. Seeing an opportunity to increase revenues, it chose to amend the constitution in order to permit perpetual, transferable memberships. It even sent out a circular that encouraged life members to convert to such memberships (for a $5 transfer fee). Dexter was among the

---

14 For example, in March 1865 the librarian reported that out of 1,408 book requests from members, 1,028 were for novels; no doubt many of those requests were for the popular fiction of the day.

15 One of these sporadic lectures, delivered by a Professor Richards and titled "The Atmosphere," resulted in a deficit of $42.25.

first to respond.[16]

As membership continued to erode, the board continued to direct much of its attention to that problem. Almost every year, at least one of the directors or officers called for a personalized membership drive and sometimes offered a prize, usually a book, to the person who submitted the most names. In 1863 no one recruited enough new members to claim the prize. In addition to membership drives, the board, concerned that those who had joined the army might lose interest in the Association, passed a resolution to place those individuals' names on an "Ineligible List." This would exempt them from any charges other than book fines after the date of their enlistment. In 1864 the board finally dropped its opposition to chess tables in the Reading Room; it extended the privileges of the Association to members of the Chess Club, another way of drawing in new members.

That year also saw a serious division within the Association. The board brought to the October general meeting several constitutional amendments that would change the definition of membership and, it hoped, would attract more members from non-mercantile groups. The amendments did not receive sufficient support, however. President C. Taylor Jones, in the annual report for that year, somewhat bitterly referred to a "captious and inconsiderate opposition of a small minority" that was holding back the organization.

Even as increased membership proved elusive, the board renewed its efforts to collect delinquent fines and dues. In fall 1862 the minutes include a long list of names of members

---

16 Other early perpetual members were former presidents Andrew B. Merriam, Theodore Cook, and Joseph C. Butler, along with William Powell, A. S. Winslow, and D.T. Woodburn.

in arrears, but collection remained a problem. The "Action" column of the list makes clear that many of these individuals could not be located, and others acidly refused to pay. Alongside one name the secretary simply wrote "Good for Nothing."

Tragedy also visited the Mercantile Library. In October 1862 both the librarian and his assistant resigned; whether to join the army or simply to seek greater opportunities is not known. The board then hired Sylvester Taylor as its eighth librarian. Six months later it increased his salary to $1,200 per year, probably more a reflection of wartime inflation than of the librarian's abilities. Taylor's health proved fragile, however. In February 1864 the minutes note that he was improving and "hope[d] soon to be at his post," but one month later the secretary somberly recorded the death of "our esteemed and faithful librarian." Death came to the Mercantile more indirectly as well. In January 1865, upon learning of Edward Everett's death, the board called for his portrait, which hung in the Library, to be trimmed "with mourning for two months."

As the war absorbed Cincinnati's energy, it also absorbed much of the Mercantile Library's vigor. By January 1865 membership had slipped to 2,161, a decline of thirty-five percent since January 1, 1861. Annual elections, often so spirited before the war, became placid affairs that often ended in the election of an uncontested Regular Ticket. With the decline in membership and the collapse of the winter lecture series, the Association continually faced annual budget constraints. This situation was compounded by a financial burden imposed by the unfortunate purchase in 1858 of the infamous "Christy

Cabinet," a large collection of minerals and fossils.[17]

The war may have accelerated the Library's acceptance of women, though only as nonvoting honorary members. The earliest recorded female member is a Miss C. W. Moore, elected on February 1, 1859, followed a week later by Mrs. Sarah Ernst.[18] A barrier of sorts had been broken in 1855, however, when the board had invited the prominent actress Eliza Logan to present readings at Smith & Nixon's Hall. She became the first female to speak at a Mercantile Library program. To be sure, Miss Logan was recruited only when the scheduled speaker, General Sam Houston, the "grim senator from the southwest," could not reach the city. Logan's "pure and powerful elocution," however, charmed her audience, many of whom followed her to Wood's Theater for her performance later that evening as Pauline in *The Lady of Lyons*.[19] Three years later the board considered inviting another well-known actress, Miss Fanny Kemble, to give a presentation, although nothing came of that.

Women had been permitted for some time to use the Library facilities as guests. In 1859 a special committee appointed to suggest ways to improve attendance had recommended that two hours each day be set aside "for ladies to occupy the Reading Room." Apparently the board approved this recommendation. The acceptance of Miss Moore and Mrs. Ernst as members did not ruffle any male egos, and in the next

---

17 For more on the Christy Cabinet, see Chapter 4.

18 In 1854 the New York Mercantile Library had opened membership to "all people of good character," including women, and this no doubt helped persuade Cincinnatians that they might risk the same step; see Noreen Tomassi with Mary Collins, "The Mercantile Library Center for Fiction," in Richard Wendorf, editor, *America's Membership Libraries* (New Castle, DE: Oak Knoll Press, 2007), 202.

19 *Cincinnati Commercial*, December 11, 1855, 2; December 12, 1855, 2; *Cincinnati Daily Gazette*, December 11, 1855, 2.

few months several more women became honorary members, including Mrs. W. D. Flagg, Miss M. A. Todd, Miss Sarah Harbeson, Miss Emma Wertheimer and Miss Clara Nourse.[20]

The following year another pair of women, including poet Alice Cary, joined the Association, and the trickle continued for the duration of the war. The librarian reported in May 1865 that seventy-three ladies had visited the Reading Room the previous month (in comparison to 5,362 men during the same period). By the close of 1878, 207 women belonged to the Mercantile Library, out of a total membership of 2,325.[21] The next year a woman, Mrs. Caroline Addy, became a life member. In 1880, although women were still a long way from enjoying gender equality, a Miss Kate Westover received one vote (out of 289 cast) in a special election to fill a directorship.

Another gender barrier fell during the late stages of the war. In October 1863, when the library committee made several recommendations, the board approved all except "as to the employment of women," but this soon changed. Sometime in 1865 Miss Alice McLean of Covington, Kentucky, was hired as an assistant librarian, perhaps because few men applied or because women could be paid less. In keeping with proper Victorian decorum, however, the board instructed that the "lady assistant" was to be relieved from "evening duty at present."

No doubt the war's end in May 1865 brought both great relief and renewed hopes. Looking forward to reviving the

---

20 Although Sandra Geiser, curator of the Mercantile Library's Niehoff Center for Elizabeth Nourse, has not been able to identify this Clara Nourse, she was probably related to the artist, as the name Clara shows up in later generations of the family.

21 Among these early female members are several names connected to the city's importance as a center for the arts: Florence Carlisle, Clara C. Newton, Agnes Pitman, and Mary Spencer.

Mercantile Library's place in the business community, the board voted to restore subscriptions to leading newspapers in principal cities of the South.[22] It also sought information from members as to what they wanted in their organization. Accordingly the board placed petitions in the rooms to ascertain interest in opening the Reading Room on Sundays, and placed a "Want Book" in the library in which members could recommend books for purchase. The Want Book remained, at least for a while, but the more disruptive issue of Sunday hours failed to gain sufficient support. The board also attempted to restart the public lectures by inviting General Benjamin F. Butler to deliver an address, but the controversial Civil War officer declined. In January 1866 the lecture committee recommended a winter lecture series, but nothing resulted from this.

Above all else, however, these cost-conscious merchants wanted to balance the books. Indebtedness frightened them. In January 1866 the newly elected board resolved to make payment of the entire debt "the paramount object of the Board" and to "restore to the Association the prestige of former days ...." A new membership drive was initiated for that purpose, but with only modest results. A special subscription launched to raise $15,000 in contributions proved more successful. The funds were targeted: $2,000 for "fitting up and furnishing the rooms," $3,500 for the purchase of books, and $4,500 to be applied to the debt.

Within two months—that is, by April 1866—the subscription had reached its goal, a tribute to the Association's

22 Current events, regardless of their importance, rarely found their way into the Association's minutes; this reference to the restoration of subscriptions to Southern newspapers is the only hint that the Civil War had ended.

reputation and to the city's economic growth during the war.[23] At its quarterly meeting that month, the president credited "those generous friends who responded to our efforts." Even more remarkable, however, was that only one donation of the $15,000 total exceeded $100.

Suddenly prosperous, the library committee requested a special appropriation for books in the fine arts, especially illustrated works, bibliography, and the history of printing and engraving. Subscribing to the Victorian era's faith in art as morally uplifting, the board approved a $2,000 expenditure, quickly amended to $3,000, for purchases in Europe, with not more than one-fourth for "illustrated works of art." All of this activity must have made the position of librarian more attractive; in September 1866 M. Hazen White took the post, for a salary of $1,800 per year.[24] One of White's first duties was to supervise the printing of a new catalog, assisted by a group of young ladies, and no doubt by Miss McLean, who received a raise and a $50 bonus "for faithful services" at the end of the year.

Another pleasant development in the library was due to Andrew McArthur. He was never a member of the Association, but his son, who died in 1864, had thoroughly enjoyed his membership. Thus, when the English-born bookseller died just two years later, he left his estate to the Mercantile Library Association with the stipulation that the entire amount be

23 The loss of Southern markets and the decline of river transportation harmed many Cincinnati businesses, but military spending and the rapidly expanding railroad network brought increased profits to many others.

24 Moses Hazen White (1817-78), who had taught for many years at the Cincinnati Female Seminary, was usually referred to as Major, a reflection of his military service during the Civil War. He also had given a lecture at the Mercantile in 1848. His twelve-year tenure as librarian provided the Association with both professionalism and continuity in the Association's day-to-day operations.

spent on books "of the most useful standard works commonly known as 'light fiction'...." The bequest was quite specific in other ways as well. The money was to be spent "gradually over time." Each acquisition was to bear a neat label identifying it as part of "The McArthur Library," and the books were to be kept together in a special place in one of the rooms. The board then resolved to limit this newly established McArthur Library to the best editions of American and British authors, and to keep them as reference works. A McArthur committee was established, and by the end of 1867 it had authorized the purchase of 599 volumes at a cost of over $1,500. The committee also requested the purchase of special cases to house the new works.

In February 1867 the board again proposed several amendments to the constitution. Most were routine: raising membership dues to $5 per year, replacing "honorary membership" with "non-voting membership," and introducing a new honorary membership for people who "merit the distinction."[25] These changes inspired little discussion, but the language describing eligibility for membership caused a protracted debate at one board meeting. The idea of opening active membership to virtually all males was resisted for several reasons, but for the first time race became an issue. H. W. Brown, a railroad agent, proposed that the word "white" be inserted before "young man" and before "persons" in the proposed amendment. After considerable conversation (and we can only guess what issues were raised), Brown retracted his motion; apparently he failed to receive much support. He had

25 Elected in 1871, Bellamy Storer Sr. became the first honorary member under this new classification; he was soon followed by Henry Probasco, Alfred T. Goshorn, Robert Clarke, Reuben Springer, Professor Daniel Vaughn, Theodore Thomas, Charles W. West, Judge Moses F. Wilson, and James E. Murdoch, all prominent public-spirited citizens.

made his point, however, and that particular amendment did not pass.

Later in 1867, the lecture committee, still seeking to pump life into the Association, tried again to revive the lecture series. It invited Louis Agassiz to present a "course" of six lectures, much as he had done in 1851. The committee also contacted Henry Ward Beecher, Henry Bellows, Senator Charles Sumner of Massachusetts, Alexander H. Stephens (former vice-president of the Confederacy), Indiana Congressman Schuyler Colfax, and Oliver Wendell Holmes Sr., Agassiz, Bellows, and Colfax declined. There is no mention of replies from the others, but none appeared at the Mercantile that winter.

More disturbing to the board were membership figures: new books and refurbished rooms had not brought the anticipated new members. The membership committee chairman lamented the "great lack of interest on the part of young men of the city in the Association." He believed that a city as large and important as Cincinnati should provide at least five thousand members. No doubt the public library reduced reliance on a membership library, but we also find some suggestion that young merchants and clerks no longer felt any need to belong to an organization that held onto traditions which may have become outdated.

Many members of the Association, as in 1864 and 1867, believed that the organization's future lay in loosening the rules of eligibility. In 1869 these men argued again that extending voting privileges to professional men would increase membership and bring new energy to the Association. If "something isn't done soon," they predicted, "the library association will eventually pass into other hands."

Traditionalists remained unconvinced. They suspected that such a change would alter the very nature of the organization. They also feared that members of the professions would change book-purchasing policies to the disadvantage of mercantile interests, and, implicitly, that they would make the Association no longer a mercantile organization. The traditionalists defeated the motion.

Again, the race issue was implicit in the discussion. After James Laws grumbled that the Association was "fast losing its distinctive character," H. W. Brown, already on record as opposed to any changes that might permit African-Americans to join, cautioned against "haste." "Damage may be done that can't be repaired," he declared ominously. In support, C. W. Rowland, a former president and current life member, and a gadfly at meetings, expressed his concerns. Active membership already had been given to manufacturers, he pointed out, and the wording of this amendment "would end restrictions on Negroes and women." Later in the heated debate he commented, "[I]f right of voting is extended to all, including women, what will hinder the having of a woman for President?" Others predicted that for every ten new members, the Association would lose fifty, but John F. Adair remained unconvinced. He did not believe that anyone would leave "because a few mechanics should be allowed to come and vote, and thought the fear of women and Negroes to be all talk." At the April quarterly meeting the proposed amendment received twenty-three of the forty votes cast,[26] but it was declared "lost" because it failed to receive the required seventy-five

26 Because this was a quarterly meeting of the Association, the small number of voters suggests that the issue was not important to many members. The next year, 1872, the number of votes cast again remained small.

percent.

The issue reappeared the next year, when the new board brought before the membership essentially the same amendment. As the president argued, "[T]he most liberal views should be expressed in all matters referring to education.... Let us give a hand of welcome to every man, woman, and child who loves to read." Noble sentiments, but the motion failed to gain even a majority this time.

In 1871 the amendment failed again, but the board of directors persisted and a revised constitution, apparently approved late in the year, extended active membership to "men of pursuits and professions." Although this decision ended the exclusively mercantile nature of the Association,[27] women still were not included as active members. However, there is evidence that women were being permitted to vote: the ever-vigilant Rowland complained that the election held in January 1872 was "illegal," and alluded to voting by women and children. His remark led to no further discussion.[28]

Two months later a motion was made to approve twenty-nine names for membership, "including that of Peter H. Clark, a colored man." An amendment to approve all the names except Clark's was defeated, but after lengthy discussion the original motion was tabled for one week. On March 9, 1872, again after considerable discussion, the original motion was approved,

27 Although the Regular Ticket in 1872 placed three attorneys among its nominees for office, a point sharply criticized by the Independent Party, it was not until 1891 that Joseph Cox Jr., also a lawyer, became the first professional person to serve as president of the Association; see *Chic* 2 (January 10, 1891), 16.

28 The board minutes do not record when female members were granted the right to participate in elections, but in April 1873 the board approved a separate ballot box for lady members, supervised by the two female assistant librarians. No source explains why this was felt to be necessary, but it may have been related to the fact that for several years women voted in a separate location; perhaps this arrangement reflected on the atmosphere surrounding the men's voting area.

and Peter H. Clark became the first African-American in the Young Men's Mercantile Library Association.[29] The forces of reaction, however, sought the last word, pushing through a motion stating that Mr. Clark's election was "not to be regarded as a precedent for action upon any application for membership that may be made hereafter by colored persons."

Also at the January 1871 annual meeting, as other constitutional changes were being discussed, James J. Hooker moved to have the Library rooms opened on Sundays.[30] The board minutes reflect the continued sensitivity of that issue. Julius Dexter quickly spoke in favor of the proposal, pointing out that access to the Library's rooms would help offset the growing influence of places of "immoral tendency."[31] Hugh Colville, the just-elected president, countered that Sunday hours would desecrate the Sabbath. William P. Anderson favored the expanded hours, believing that the "usefulness of the Library and Reading Room demanded such a course." C. W. Rowland, true to his conservative views, responded by calling it a "very dangerous step." James H. Snodgrass offered a compromise amendment: open the Reading Room on Sunday afternoons, but leave the Library closed. Others added their comments; Rowland's motion to table the whole issue was defeated, and Snodgrass's amendment then passed, thirty-nine to twenty-nine. Rowland objected that an amendment to the constitution required a three-fourths majority to adopt, while

29 Peter H. Clark, a leader in the city's black community, had long advocated improved public schools for the city's black youths. At the time of his election to the Mercantile Library he served as principal of Gaines High School, a segregated public school. Ironically, he lost his position when the Cincinnati Public Schools integrated in 1887. On March 16, 2004, Walter Herz spoke at the Mercantile on the subject of Peter Clark.

30 This issue had also been discussed at a board meeting in January 1868, but was "indefinitely postponed."

31 Dexter probably was thinking of places such as saloons, theaters, and the increasingly popular baseball games.

Hooper argued for a simple majority. Lewis Seasongood, a native of Bavaria and a highly successful clothing manufacturer, then suggested that the matter be postponed to a later meeting, but in vain. Finally, after the board decided that a three-fourths vote indeed was required, the amendment was declared defeated.

After the board had disposed of all other business, Hooper made one last attempt. He moved that the bylaws be changed to permit Sunday hours for the Reading Room only. Fatigued by the lateness of the hour, the board tabled this motion. The issue was raised next at the April quarterly meeting of the membership, when it was approved.[32]

Keeping the rooms clean proved as difficult as increasing membership. Open windows, the common use of coal for heating, and dirty streets had made cleanliness a constant struggle from the Mercantile Library's beginning. By the 1860s the problem had intensified. In 1860 the board secretary reported how inconvenient to members the annual cleaning was, when the library closed for a week or more. The process also damaged the collection. Yet he understood clearly the central problem, as he humorously phrased it, of "damaging atoms belched forth by our factory furnaces and thickly packed chimneys."

Nine years later the situation had worsened. An increase in manufacturing, coupled with the geographical effect of an enclosed basin, made Cincinnati one of the dirtiest and most compact cities in the country: "[o]ld and valuable books" were being "ruined with the soot and dirt from the furnace." And that comment referred to the Library's own furnace, which

---

32 In January 1872 the issue of Sunday hours again highlighted the election, but the Regular Ticket, headed by William P. Anderson, proved too strong.

pushed dirty air through the ventilation system, not to the widespread soot that entered through the windows during the warm months. No solution was found, but at this time lady members requested that "a suitable wash stand be placed in the rooms."[33]

All of these concerns faded when the Mercantile Library Association again confronted a fire, this time in October 1869. Ironically, in February the president had mentioned that a fireplug near the building would be most desirable. It is doubtful that the city responded to this, or whether the Library even made an official request. Nor would a fireplug have prevented the fire, although it might have helped reduce the damage.

On October 20, shortly after one o'clock in the afternoon, smoke began pouring out of the roof at the north end of the building. Hundreds of spectators quickly gathered along Fourth, Fifth, and Walnut Streets. With church bells sounding the alarm, Fire Company 14 and the Hook and Ladder Company responded first. As smoke "bound the building like a garland of storm-clouds," more alarms brought every fire company in the city to the blazing structure. While the firemen struggled to reach the roof—the department's longest ladders reached only to the cornice of the building—dozens of public-spirited citizens, including some members, climbed through windows on the south end and brought out the Library's books, including the recently purchased McArthur collection, and carried them across the street to the lobby of the Gibson House.

When the fire was extinguished, about three hours later, the roof had collapsed and a large portion of the building

---

33 One can still find coal residue in some of the Library's older volumes.

had been destroyed. Fortunately, although 622 books were declared a total loss, the bulk of the collection was saved, along with most of furniture, statuary, and pictures. The iron safe remained in the ruins: it was considered "best not to remove it at present."[34] Just as Association members were congratulating themselves on their good fortune, however, word slowly spread through the community that Captain Mathias Schwab of the Hook and Ladder Company had died in the inferno.[35]

Although the Mercantile Library rooms had largely escaped intact, the collection had suffered considerable water damage and the rooms were now unusable. The board had to deal instantly with problems of temporary quarters, salvaging books, filing insurance claims, and planning for a none-too-clear future. The James M. Clark Company on West Third Street immediately offered space for the rescued books, while badly damaged volumes were left in the rooms until insurance losses could be calculated.[36] Furniture and other property found a temporary home in the warehouse of the American Express Company on Fourth Street, and the statuary took up temporary residence at Charles Rule's marble yard near Broadway and Fifth.

In the meantime, the board met over the next few weeks in a series of special meetings to deal with fire-related issues. Most pressing was the need to salvage damp books before mildew set in. In addition, to avoid losing members, the board opened a temporary Reading Room at 137-39 Race Street. By early December these prompt actions had saved most of the collection and membership losses were held to just thirty-five.

34 This is not the safe presently used by the Association.
35 *Cincinnati Daily Gazette*, October 21, 1869, 2; *Cincinnati Commercial*, October 21, 1869, 8.
36 According to the annual report for 1869, 622 volumes were destroyed in the fire, and another 907 had to be rebound. Insurance companies paid for all of this.

Furthermore, a special committee had been created to hold discussions about rebuilding with a similar group from the Cincinnati College Building trustees.

The first joint meeting was held at Pike's Opera House in the administrative offices of Spring Grove Cemetery. These discussions did not start well: the College Building trustees rejected all plans to rebuild unless the Young Men's Mercantile Library Association advanced $20,000; the representatives of the Association, which did not have that kind of money, rejected that notion. When Alexander H. McGuffey,[37] president of the Cincinnati College Building, asked if the Mercantile Library had any plan to propose, President Colville responded sharply that they were there "not to propose but only to listen...." Furthermore, if no plan could be agreed upon, he stated that the Library would extend the "simple demand... that the Library Rooms should be placed in the same condition they were before the fire" (There's that lease again!). The Association minutes then noted tersely, "[T]he joint conference terminated."

In December the College Building trustees proposed an architectural plan that greatly reduced the size of the public hall. Frank H. Baldwin, on behalf of the Mercantile, protested that this was "a serious encroachment upon our rights and privileges."[38] At this time the Association board explored the idea of selling its lease rights to the College Building and using the funds to construct a separate, fireproof structure for itself. Economic considerations soon dashed these ambitions.

Even so, President Colville and representatives from the

---

37 Alexander H. McGuffey (1816-96) and his brother William Holmes McGuffey (1800-73) were the authors of the widely used readers that bear their names.
38 F. H. Baldwin to Robert Buchanan, December 31, 1869; copies of the correspondence are in the minutes of the Association, January 3, 1870.

College Building continued to look into solutions, and eventually plans moved forward to rebuild on terms acceptable to the Association. On the evening of September 28, 1870, just eleven months after the tragedy, the Mercantile Library Association celebrated its return with an open house for the general public. A liberal supply of tastefully arranged flowers, a "promenade concert" by Courier's String Band, and elegant ladies in "gay dresses" made for a scene "unknown to the old past." The broad well-lighted entrance, new carpets, freshly painted walls, and re-bronzed chandeliers impressed all who visited the rooms. The *Daily Gazette's* reporter described the Reading Room as "more sightly [sic] and beautiful," and praised the spiral staircase that led up to the Directors' Room and "Consulting Library" on the second floor. Despite the attraction of the city's first Industrial Exposition at Twelfth and Elm Streets, hundreds of Cincinnatians visited the new Library facilities that evening, and sixty new members enrolled.[39]

"Has the association, like the Phoenix, come out of the fire better and stronger in the affections of the community?" asked the president in the annual report at the end of that year. Certainly on that September evening, most members would have responded with a resounding "Yes!"

---

39 *Cincinnati Daily Gazette*, September 29, 1870, 4; *Cincinnati Enquirer*, September 29, 1870, 4.

"No other city of the Union, cœteris paribus, has produced so many artists, reckoning among them, too, some of the brightest names in the art of the country."

Charles Cist, 1859

CHAPTER 4

More Than Books

THE FIRE had been a tragedy for the Mercantile Library Association, but quick action by many people had saved most of the books, always the heart of the institution. Many of these books remain on the shelves today, but the same cannot be said for many of the art objects that found their way into the Association's rooms. At a time when few institutions existed for collecting what we would call museum-type material, subscription libraries such as the Mercantile, by default, became custodians for a wide array of artistic and cultural items. Of course, literature of all types remained paramount in the members' minds, but any object that fit the nineteenth-century concept of self-improvement might be judged worthy of acquisition. This included paintings, sculpture, and much more.

Just 6½ years after the Mercantile Library's founding, the Association acquired its first painting. In October 1841 member R. H. Parry offered "to send Kellogg's portrait of General Jackson to be placed in the Reading Room." Although Parry intended this to be a loan, it is not clear what motivated him.

Perhaps he had no place or no desire to hang this portrait in his home, or perhaps it reflected his political leanings. The previous spring the Library had permitted a portrait of the late William Henry Harrison to be exhibited in its rooms. Of course, Harrison was considered a Cincinnatian and was a member of the Association at the time of his death, but it is quite possible that Parry was an ardent Democrat who sought to balance the Association's usual Whig political views. Five years later the Association purchased the painting.[1]

The Jackson portrait apparently triggered within the organization a more ambitious approach to collecting, for in a few months the board recommended establishing "a gallery or museum which should contain specimens of the fine arts, such as paintings, engravings, etc.; specimens of geology and mineralogy, as well as curiosities of all kinds." Although this suggestion was made in the annual report for 1841, the incoming board of directors chose not to act on it. The next year, however, in their own annual report, they recommended the acceptance of a collection of minerals, rocks, and "rare curiosities" offered by a J. G. Anthony on the condition that the Library would provide adequate display cases.[2]

In 1843 the Association happily accepted an "excellent time piece" given by Messrs. McGrew and Beggs.[3] As the secretary noted in the minutes, with pun no doubt intended, this was "a most timely present." The annual report for that year also men-

---

1 Unfortunately this portrait has disappeared, as have so many of the Association's art works. See Appendix C for a list of the art and other collectibles that are present today or have passed through the Library.

2 In the 1844 city directory, J. G. Anthony is listed as an accountant. In the annual report for 1842 the material that came to the Library was described as just part of Anthony's collection.

3 Although city directories do not include these names, in 1844 a J. P. Beggs became a director of the Association.

tioned the acquisition of a painting, "Hamlet and Ophelia," by a Miss Martin. This would have been an early work by Lily Martin, a young artist who had come from Marietta, Ohio, to study with James H. Beard.[4] The following year the board negotiated with a Mrs. Douglas for the purchase of three busts, probably plaster casts of prominent people. Although no action was recorded, these may have included likenesses of Henry Clay and a Mr. Guthrie of Louisville, which are mentioned in later board minutes as "ornaments for the hall."

In early 1845 a movement was launched in the city to raise $500 for the purchase of a marble bust of William Henry Harrison, the work of Shobal V. Clevenger.[5] Clevenger, one of a group of talented young sculptors who came out of Cincinnati in the 1830s and 1840s, had died two years earlier while returning from study in Italy. His widow, financially pinched, hoped to sell some of his work. The bust was exhibited at Burt & Greene's on Third Street, where anyone who wished could subscribe $1 towards the purchase. The subscribers then would determine the final disposition of the sculpture. Just how this would be accomplished was never made clear, but the intent was to keep the bust in the city as a gift from its citizens. Just two days before the fire that destroyed the Library's rooms in the (old) College Building, the board pledged $25 toward the bust, "provided it be placed permanently in the Library

---

4 Lily Martin, after marrying Benjamin Spencer, took her talent to New York City, where she established a considerable reputation as a painter of coyly sentimental genre scenes. Several of her works are in the collection of the Cincinnati Art Museum.

5 Charles Cist, in his *Cincinnati in 1859*, spelled Clevenger's first name "Shubael," although most modern works have spelled it Shobal. The bust of Harrison probably was rendered first in plaster in 1838 while the sculptor was still in Cincinnati and then was carved in marble in Florence, Italy.

rooms of the Association."[6] Today it still rests comfortably in the Reading Room. In the same year, in the *Cincinnati Daily Gazette's* account of the fire, the reporter mentions that two portraits were rescued, one of William Henry Harrison and the other of Charles H. Hammond, the outspoken editor of the *Gazette* who had died in 1840.[7]

In February 1845 the board received notice that the American Art Union of New York City[8] was sending it a "painting by Bingham" as part of its annual distribution by lot. At some point the Association apparently had taken out a membership in the American Art Union, and one of the benefits of membership was an engraving of an American painting, distributed annually to members. In this case the "painting" may have been an engraving of *Fur Traders Descending the Missouri,* one of George Caleb Bingham's best-known paintings and the first of his narrative frontier scenes. Several months later word arrived that the Association was to receive a second work from the American Art Union, this time "a view on the Hudson from the pencil of Cole." This also was probably an engraving, although later references in the minutes continue

6 *Cincinnati Daily Gazette,* January 6, 1845, 2; Charles Cist, *The Cincinnati Miscellany, or, Antiquities of the West, and Pioneer History and General and Local Statistics* (Cincinnati: Caleb Clark, 1846), I: 119. After the fire of January 18, 1845, the board reduced its pledge to $10, no doubt concerned about the Library's uncertain financial future.

7 These two portraits were painted by James H. Beard (1811-93), considered the city's finest artist at that time. The Hammond portrait originally was only loaned to the Mercantile by Stephen S. L'Hommedieu, Hammond's son-in-law, but apparently it remained with the Library. Both portraits were loaned to the Cincinnati Art Museum in 1906.

8 The American Art Union (1839-51) was established in New York to promote American art; in subsequent years other cities, including Cincinnati, established their own art unions. Each member received an engraving of an original work by an American artist, while other original works, usually oil paintings, were distributed by lottery. Since the American Art Union had about fifteen-thousand members in 1845, it is highly unlikely that the oil painting came to the Mercantile Library.

to mention a landscape painting by Thomas Cole.[9]

Beginning in 1846 a steady stream of interesting items flowed into the Library's new quarters. Nicholas Longworth gave two framed engravings, one of the Cincinnati-trained sculptor Hiram Powers, whom Longworth had supported financially, and the other of a Truman H. Safford.[10] Later that year, Crafts J. Wright, co-publisher of the *Cincinnati Daily Gazette*, donated "rare specimens of Minerals from Lake Superior." John Kennet, one of the city's many wholesale grocers, gave George Washington's autograph, provided the board would promise "its careful preservation" and place it in an "appropriate and conspicuous position." (This may be the autograph currently kept in the Library's safe.) A portrait of Andrew Jackson by Miner K. Kellogg is also mentioned in the minutes, although it is not clear if the portrait was actually given to the Library.

The year ended with the arrival of several government documents presented by former Kentucky Governor and now Senator James T. Morehead. These included "Nicollet's Topographical Map of the Basin of the Mississippi," which the board placed on rollers for public viewing.[11] At about the same time, three more items entered the collection: John B. Coram, another grocer, donated "a splendid and costly copy of "Buonaparte's [sic] Ornithology," a four-volume study of birds in the United States, with many engraved illustrations;

9 Thomas Cole (1801-48) was the nation's foremost landscape painter before the Civil War and is credited with founding the "Hudson River School" of painting. If this was an engraving, it was probably based on Cole's *Scene on Lake George*, that year's "gift" to members.

10 I have been unable to locate any information about Truman Safford.

11 Joseph Nicollet (1786-1843), a French mathematician and geographer, led several expeditions into the upper Mississippi Valley on behalf of the United States government. Shortly before his death in 1843 his map of the hydrographical basin of the Upper Mississippi was printed.

William W. Scarborough gave a chart executed "by an officer of Captain Cook's last voyage"; and Albert G. Day, publisher of the *Cincinnati Enquirer*, donated an "Anastatic fac-simile" of the Declaration of Independence.[12]

During 1847 Lewis J. Cist added Benjamin Franklin's autograph to the Library's growing collection of historical items, and Day donated a facsimile of the warrant issued for the beheading of England's King Charles I. In May 1848 the Association agreed to loan both Clevenger's bust of Harrison and the painting or engraving of Cole's *Scene on Lake George* to an exhibit mounted by the Western Art Union, the Cincinnati counterpart of the American Art Union. The board also authorized the purchase of plaster casts of public men to be placed in additional alcoves planned for the Library's rapidly expanding book collection. These practical merchants placed a $20 limit on each bust. Two months later the Association announced its purchase of a bust of the recently deceased John Quincy Adams. In 1849 another engraving arrived from the American Art Union, this time Thomas Cole's *Youth* from his *Voyage of Life* series.

The display of various art objects and the increasing number of items in the Library's "art collection" encouraged more people to make contributions. No other institution in the city had the facilities or the inclination to collect such disparate items as autographs, mineral samples, busts, and engravings, and the new, supposedly fireproof building also proved attractive to potential benefactors.

The gifts kept coming. In 1851 Dudley Hall, a commission

12 Charles Lucien Bonaparte (1803-57), a nephew of the Emperor Napoleon, was a French naturalist who spent considerable time in the United States in the 1820s. His major work, *American Ornithology, or, The Natural History of Birds in the United States*, was published in Philadelphia between 1825 and 1833.

merchant, contributed "Views from Pompeii," and then the United States Commissioner of Indian Affairs sent a copy of Henry R. Schoolcraft's *History, Condition, and Prospect of the Indian Tribes of the United States*, a "magnificent work," with illustrations by Captain Seth Eastman. Stephen S. L'Hommedieu, president of the Cincinnati, Hamilton & Dayton Railroad, presented the Association with a signed letter from George Washington; John B. Russell, superintendent of the Job Department at the *Daily Gazette*, matched that with a letter written by John Adams to his son Thomas. Both documents were framed and placed in the Reading Room. These letters were soon followed by two more: another letter by John Adams—"of singular interest and value"—came through the generosity of Andrew J. Reynolds, while Charles D. Drake donated a letter from Thomas Jefferson to Drake's father, Dr. Daniel Drake. This letter was particularly important to Cincinnati because in it Jefferson acknowledged receipt of Daniel Drake's *Natural and Statistical View, or Pictures of Cincinnati and the Miami Country*, published in 1815.

Other items that arrived in the early 1850s included a 16th-century French dictionary, a collection of Latin pamphlets bound in sharkskin—"a great curiosity," noted the board secretary—the Gospel of Matthew in Persian, and a German Bible printed around 1500.[13] Charles Stetson, president of the Ohio Life Insurance and Trust Company, donated a "costly clock—a Geneva Regulator,"[14] while Henry D. Huntington, senior partner in a firm that imported china and glass objects from

13 *Cincinnati Daily Gazette*, April 21, 1852, 2. The editor of the *Daily Gazette* found at least one engraving in the German Bible of considerable interest: the illustration of "Eve chuckling her nude lord [Adam] under the chin, while she persuades him to take the 'forbidden fruit,' is peculiarly edifying."

14 Most likely, this is the wall clock that hangs behind the staff work area.

Europe, contributed "beautiful and valuable" embossed maps of London, Paris, Vienna, and other European cities.

This period also saw the "one that got away." The Library made an effort to purchase John J. Audubon's book on ornithology, but abandoned the project because the available copy was no longer on the market. This was probably the double elephant folio edition of *Birds of America*, now worth millions of dollars.[15] Having missed the opportunity to purchase an original Audubon, in 1859 the board looked into buying the later (and smaller) edition scheduled to be published in forty-four numbers and issued monthly. The total cost, including binding, would have amounted to an estimated $800. The board postponed any decision until the work was completed; we find no record that the Library ever made the purchase.

In 1853 the Mercantile Library Association joined the rest of the nation in its desire to memorialize its first president. The idea for a commemorative structure to honor George Washington had originated in 1832, the centennial of his birth, and construction of the 555-foot obelisk in the nation's capital began sixteen years later. By 1853, when sectional politics and rising costs had slowed the process, the idea of states and various institutions contributing single memorial blocks was launched. This effort would make the structure truly a citizens' commemoration. Association President James Lupton spearheaded the Mercantile Library's fund-raising drive; as a result, a block of "fossiliferous marble" was taken from the bed of the Ohio River and prepared by David Bolles, owner of a local marble yard. The inscription on the stone reads:

15 A copy of this remarkable work may be seen in the Public Library of Cincinnati and Hamilton County. Audubon lived in Cincinnati in 1819 and 1820, and worked as a naturalist and taxidermist for the Western Museum, the predecessor of today's Museum of Natural History, Cincinnati Museum Center.

The Young Men's Mercantile Library Association, of
Cincinnati, Organized A.D. 1835; A.D. 1853, 2,400 members,
proud to honor Washington, contributes its humble quota to
the swelling tide of National gratitude. Ohio—first born of the
Ordinance of '87, every pulsation of her heart beats high, beats
strong for Liberty and for the Union.

Wordy and grandiose language to be sure, but heartfelt none-
theless. One suspects that Lupton had much to do with the
inscription, and the reference to the Union held great significance during the troubled 1850s. The cost to the Association
was $500: $100 to Mr. Bolles and the remainder to the committee in Washington. All of the money came through
voluntary contributions from Library members, and President
Lupton generously paid for the installation of the stone in the
monument.[16]

In 1852 an eight-foot marble statue of *Cincinnatus*, the
product of Cincinnati-born sculptor Nathan Flint Baker,
was placed temporarily in the Mercantile. It rested there for
two years and then was moved to the Chatfield and Woods
Building on Fourth Street.[17]

The placement of the *Cincinnatus* in the Library may have
led directly to one of the Mercantile's most prized possessions.
On November 25, 1855, Davis B. Lawler wrote a remarkable

16 Those wishing to view this four- by two-foot "piece" of Cincinnati will find it on the
   23rd-floor landing, about midway up the stairs inside the monument.
17 Baker (1820-91), a grandson of Hezekiah Flint, had gone to Florence, Italy in 1842 to
   study with Hiram Powers and Shobal Clevenger. The following year, he and fellow sculptor Henry Kirke Brown moved to Rome, where Baker soon began work on *Cincinnatus*
   and another life-size statue, *Egeria at the Fountain*. Both statues came to Cincinnati
   in 1847. In 1894 *Cincinnatus* was moved from the Fourth Street building to the newly
   constructed City Hall, but it has since disappeared. *Egeria* was eventually purchased by
   the Western Art-Union, and in 1862 it was placed on Strauch Island in Spring Grove
   Cemetery. See David R. Hanlon, "Arts and Letters: The Baker Family Papers," *Ohio Valley
   History*, 9(Summer 2009), 89-93.

letter to the president and directors of the Mercantile Library. Lawler (1786-1869), a native of Philadelphia, had moved to Cincinnati in the early 1820s. After amassing a considerable fortune in wholesale dry goods and other business ventures, he traveled extensively in Europe.[18] Visiting Paris in 1855, Lawler had come across a statue that seemed appropriate for the library, a work of American sculptor Joseph Mozier and titled *Silence*. He ordered a marble copy made and offered it to the Mercantile.[19] Lawler would pay all costs to have the work shipped to the East Coast if the Association would take charge of it at that point. He also asked that a pedestal be provided: "ought to be solid & 28 to 30 inches high, square if you do not wish it to turn round, circular if you do, but I would not advise the latter," he cautioned. Lawler went on to describe the figure as "full life size, being 5 ft. 3 in. in height." *Silence* joined the Library on Thanksgiving Day, 1856, when it was placed on a pedestal designed by architect James McLaughlin. McLaughlin also donated a drawing of the statue, from which Gibson & Company made lithographs.

Along with *Silence*, several other sculptures entered the Library's collection in 1856. The Association purchased a marble bust of Senator Daniel Webster and a plaster bust of Louis Agassiz, one of the most popular speakers sponsored by the Association during the decade. John C. King, a Boston sculptor, created both. About the same time, Samuel M. Murphy,

18 I want to thank Rick Kesterman of the Cincinnati Historical Society Library (Cincinnati Museum Center) for tracking down personal information on Davis B. Lawler.

19 Joseph Mozier (1812-70) was born in Vermont, and after a successful career as a merchant in New York City turned to sculpting. He spent most of his life after 1845 in Italy, and in 1867 his romantic work, *Undine*, earned a grand prize at a Rome exhibition. Mozier studied with Hiram Powers in Florence, but the two men soon fell out. Mozier eventually became quite critical of Powers' work; see Richard P. Wunder, *Hiram Powers, Vermont Sculptor*, 1805-1873, Volume I: Life (Newark: University of Delaware Press, 1989), 153-55.

identified in the 1856 city directory as a bookkeeper, gave the Association a bust of Daniel Drake. This was the work of the French-born Charles Bullett, another of Cincinnati's young artists.

In its annual report for 1857, the board included a list of "Statuary and Paintings," and it mentions two paintings for which no record exists in either the minutes or the annual reports.[20] These are a portrait of Hezekiah Flint, painted by Miner K. Kellogg and donated by John Baker, and "A Portrait" by Brannon [sic], purchased in 1849. The Brannan portrait has disappeared. The Flint portrait now hangs in the entranceway to the twelfth-floor meeting room.[21]

The gifts and purchases continued. In 1857 the Association received "the beautiful 'Statue of Sabrina,'" which was placed in the Library room. Although this statue is mentioned in the annual report for that year, neither the sculptor nor the donor is named and its present location is unknown. Also in 1857, Association president C. W. Rowland, a partner in the firm of Moulinier and Rowland, presented a bust of John C. Breckinridge, the Kentuckian then serving as vice-president of the United States. Finally, in that year A. B. Merriam commissioned the portrait of Edward Everett by J. Oriel Eaton. The next year brought additional riches. Thomas Gallagher, a prominent local attorney, donated a bust of the Honorable

20 The board minutes from 1849 to 1857 are missing, although annual reports for those years are available.

21 Hezekiah Flint (1774-1843), a cousin of the well-known Timothy Flint, had come to Cincinnati from Marietta, Ohio, in 1795; Charles T. Greve mentions that Flint grew corn from 1795 to 1800 in the area that was later directly across Walnut Street from the Mercantile Library; see Greve, *Centennial History of Cincinnati*, 348. John Baker was Flint's son-in-law and the father of sculptor Nathan Flint Baker. Brannon is probably William P. Brannan (1825-66), a portrait artist who moved to Cincinnati in 1840 and shared a studio with Thomas Buchanan Read, Almon Baldwin, and Thomas Worthington Whittredge. The subject of this portrait is later identified as a Mr. Abbey.

John McLean,[22] and Charles Rule, of the Steam Marble Works, gave a bust of Senator Stephen A. Douglas, the powerful Democratic senator from Illinois.

By this time the Mercantile Library Association owned an impressive collection of paintings, engravings, and sculptures. Yet it lacked anything from the city's best-known artist, sculptor Hiram Powers. A native of Vermont, Powers had come to Cincinnati in 1818. He worked with Luman Watson, a clockmaker, and eventually studied sculpture under the Prussian-born Frederick Eckstein. In 1838, aided by Nicholas Longworth, Powers left the city, first to work in Washington, D.C. and then in Florence, Italy, where he spent the rest of his life. *The Greek Slave,* completed in 1843, firmly established his reputation.

In March 1858 corresponding secretary Thomas Biggs wrote Powers inquiring about a work appropriate for the Library. In his reply Powers suggested either a bust of Franklin or of Washington, modeled after those done by the Frenchman Jean-Antoine Houdon, "with drapery added by me." His fee was £75 sterling (about $12,000 in 2009); if the Library desired an original work, the cost would be substantially greater.

The board opted for a marble bust of Washington, and the cost was paid by a private subscription headed by Learner B. Harrison. Although the bust was not given immediately to the Library, Harrison assured the board that it would be left permanently in the rooms. The bust finally arrived in 1861, a fitting symbol of the nation at the onset of its greatest test.[23]

---

22 John Frankenstein sculpted this bust.

23 C. Wesley Cowan, in his paper delivered at the Library's annual meeting in 2006, estimated the market value of the Powers bust at $100,000 to $150,000.

While the Mercantile Library negotiated with Powers, another local sculptor, Thomas D. Jones, accepted a commission to create a plaster bust of Salmon P. Chase, formerly a Cincinnatian and currently governor of Ohio. This piece also found its way into the Library's collection in 1858 as a gift of Library president S. C. Newton, a bookkeeper with the pork-packing firm of Evans & Wright.[24] In 1859 Davis Lawler, the donor of *Silence*, presented a plaster bust of John P. Foote, one of Cincinnati's most distinguished civic leaders and the author of *The Schools of Cincinnati and Its Vicinity* (1855). By the late 1850s, then, the Association had acquired a significant art collection, certainly the finest in the city. Busts of local and national figures decorated its alcoves; portraits and engravings hung on its walls; and two full-sized sculptures – *Silence* and *Sabrina* – greeted users of the rooms.

Indeed, the Library's reputation brought an inquiry from the "Ladies' Picture Gallery" (The Ladies' Academy of Fine Arts), an organization founded by Mrs. Sarah Worthington King Peter to provide art instruction to young women and to cultivate public taste. She had personally assembled a large collection of copies of European masterpieces, both paintings and sculpture. By 1859, however, the Ladies' Academy was struggling financially; Mrs. Peter contacted the Mercantile Library Association about taking the collection "in perpetual trust," along with the Academy's current debt. She also raised the possibility that the Association might use the artwork to carry out Charles McMicken's aim of establishing a school of design for young women. The Library wanted the collection

<hr>

24 *Cincinnati Commercial*, April 19, 1858, 2.

but, not unreasonably, balked at absorbing the debt.[25] In that year as well, the Association expressed interest in acquiring the approximately two thousand volumes in the collection of the struggling Cincinnati Historical Society. Although nothing materialized from either of these opportunities, they reflect the Library board's ambitions.

Much of this philanthropy resulted from the general prosperity of the decade, but times were about to change. The national economy began to weaken in 1857, and the slide toward civil war further affected Cincinnati's merchant class. Yet nothing caused greater financial distress for the Mercantile Library than the acquisition of the Christy Cabinet, a collection of shells, minerals, and fossils. In October 1858 Professor David Christy, identified with Miami University but in 1858 a resident of Cincinnati, offered to sell to the Association his entire collection of specimens, then housed in the Ohio Mechanics Institute. He proposed a price of $4,000 to be paid "at any time within twenty years," with an annual interest rate of eight percent. That year's board, overcoming questions about cost, space, and the possibility of weakening the organization's primary mission, approved the purchase in November. By year's end a portion of the collection was on display in the Library Room, "where it attract[ed] the studious attention of a large number of members." The board justified the expense on the grounds that the collection was worth the $4,000 and quite probably much more, and that "the time of payment [was] placed at so remote a period, that any probability of embarrassment to the Association

25 The collection of pictures and casts remained with the Ladies' Academy of Fine Arts for several more years, but eventually it went to the recently established McMicken School of Design, an institution stipulated in McMicken's will.

[was] completely removed." In one quick action the Mercantile Library had acquired a "scientific department."

For members who questioned how shells, fossils, and minerals fit into the Association's objectives, the board argued that the study of the natural sciences had made great strides in recent decades, and that the Christy Cabinet was not "a collection of mere curiosities, but rather many volumes of God's own writings... where there can be no interpolations... and no mistranslations."[26] The board also anticipated that the collection would support itself by attracting bequests from members. In other words, what was there not to like about the acquisition?

Just what had the Mercantile Library received for its efforts? An appendix to the twenty-fourth annual report describes the collection: about thirteen thousand to fourteen thousand specimens of shells, which included three-fourths of the known genera of mollusks. These were contained in 189 cases, arranged and classified. The Lower Silurian fossils filled twenty cases, with many duplicates that could be exchanged with other institutions. Twenty-eight cases of classified minerals and about six cases of unclassified items rounded out the collection. Brimming with enthusiasm over its coup, the board quickly opened correspondence with several people to exchange the duplicate items for additions to the Christy Cabinet.

The new board that took office in January 1859 was far less enthusiastic about the collection's value to the Association. Viewing the purchase as a grave departure from the founders'

26 Much of the recent work in the natural sciences was setting the stage for Charles Darwin's explosive book *On the Origin of Species*, which the Library purchased in 1860 for $1. This volume is no longer in the collection.

intentions, it balked at having been saddled with such a burden on the treasury. At one of its first meetings, this board called on the "friends" of the Cabinet to come up with the money so as to remove the debt, but no friends came forth. In April the board made a direct plea to the previous board to raise the necessary funds; this action was "met with a positive refusal of assistance." The election held in January 1859 had been more than spirited, and one suspects that personal animosities carried over to poison the relationship between the two boards. At a general meeting of the Association in April, a large majority of the membership gave the board the authority to dispose of the collection.

In its annual report at the end of that year, the board affirmed its position in an appendix devoted entirely to the Christy Cabinet. It pointed out that the previous board had approved the purchase "just before the expiration of their term of office, when the practical value of [the collection] had not been fairly tested by experience, and its anticipated benefits were matters of mere conjecture." "No effort has been lacking, on our part," the report continued, "to rid the Association of this INCUBUS without suffering pecuniary loss." The board closed its review with the hope that the next year's officers would succeed in disposing of the collection.

The next year proved equally frustrating, however. The $4,000 debt was a millstone around the Association's neck. The $320 annual interest ate away at the operating budget, aggravated by the general economic contraction resulting from the political uncertainties in 1860. The INCUBUS remained. Attempts to sell the collection to a scientific institution in the United States failed, and a revived attempt at a private subscription fund met a similar fate. During that year, several members put forth a constitutional amendment that would establish a department of science and art within the Association. After prolonged discussion, the motion was "indefinitely postponed." One amendment, however, received strong support: future boards of directors were prohibited "from making purchases, or creating liabilities, for matters foreign to the legitimate purposes of the Association...."

In early 1861, with war threatening, the Association stepped up its efforts to dispose of the Christy Cabinet. At one time it had hoped that Christy would buy back his beloved specimens; instead he asked that the Association pay the bond,[27] but the board did not look kindly on this request. The next year the Association corresponded with various institutions in Europe, although a motion to extend the search to South America and the Feegee [sic] Islands was defeated. By 1863 a tone of desperation had crept into the board minutes. That year the Association borrowed $5,000 at six percent interest to redeem the original bond (now renegotiated down to $3,500), and it began advertising "our collection of shells" in British and French scientific journals.

In 1864, since no one was willing to buy them sight unseen, all of the specimens were packed and shipped to London; now storage and shipping costs could be added to the Association's burden. The following year, just after the Civil War ended, Trubner & Company of London[28] informed the Association that the collection had been valued at £100 to £150, "with no offers at any price."; apparently Europeans were not interested in God's writings. Finally, disappointed and disillusioned, the

---

27 At this time Christy was involved in a tangled legal suit and had turned over the bond to a Reverend Mr. Wright.
28 Trubner & Company was a bookseller and publishing firm.

board directed the London firm to sell "to the best advantage either at auction or otherwise." The last reference in the board minutes indicates that the collection was finally gone. All that remained was a bill from Trubner & Company for £38/11s/2d. With that, the Mercantile Library ended its short career as a scientific institution.[29]

The war years did not completely end the generosity that marked the previous decade. John D. Caldwell donated a bust of the Honorable Thomas Ewing; a bust of Abraham Lincoln arrived, courtesy of a Dr. Hamlin; J. S. Pugh donated a signed letter from Andrew Jackson. In 1863 the board resolved to make the Association "a depository of autograph letters or manuscripts bearing upon the history of our country, or of prominent individuals." It even distributed "return envelopes" to encourage donations. In 1864 the Library proudly loaned its "autographs, shells, relics, etc." to the Great Western Sanitary Fair exhibition held in the city that year to raise money for support of injured soldiers.

Three significant gifts entered the Library's collection during the war. Lewis C. Hopkins, a wealthy dry goods merchant, donated a "Colossal head and Bust of Napoleon by Canova, formerly in the collection of Joseph Bonaparte." This marble work is currently on display in the twelfth-floor meeting room.[30] Later in 1864, a John W. Owens bequeathed oil portraits of "two pioneer women," Geanette Cummins and Susan

---

29 There is no record of the eventual disposal of the collection, although it may have been sold piecemeal in Europe. In 1870 the Mercantile Library gave another, smaller collection of minerals to the Cincinnati Society of Natural History.

30 Antonio Canova (1759-1822) was an Italian sculptor who worked in the neoclassic style. The bust may be a copy of one that the artist made in Paris in 1802 at Napoleon's personal request.

Ludlow, grandmothers of his wife.[31]

After the war the Mercantile Library entered a period of gradual decline. Membership that had surpassed 3,300 in 1860 dropped to 2,188 by the end of 1865. This attrition continued for several years: by 1870 the Association numbered only 2,051. In the early 1880s, however, membership briefly increased rapidly. In 1882 it reached an all-time high of 4,555 members, an increase of 1,142 over the previous year. There is no recorded reason for this sudden growth, but it was probably due to pre-election recruitment to obtain votes in the annual elections. After 1883 the elections cooled off, and in a few years membership had dropped to 1,174; by 1900 it was sliding toward 1,000.

In many ways this decline mirrored the city itself. Cincinnati had lost some of its prewar economic energy. The conclusion of the war had brought an end to military contracts, and Southern markets, so important prior to 1861, were slow to revive. Once the sixth largest city in the nation, with grand (even grandiose) hopes of becoming the country's largest inland commercial and manufacturing center, Cincinnatians now watched with some alarm the rapid growth of Chicago, St. Louis, Pittsburgh, Cleveland, and Milwaukee.

Then, too, mercantile libraries themselves had become somewhat antiquated. Public libraries offered the latest books without requiring a membership fee, and public universities offered increased opportunities for ambitious young men to

---

31 According to the donor, Cummins and Ludlow are credited with being the mothers of the first white male and female children born in Cincinnati. Charles Greve, however, in his *Centennial History of Cincinnati*, reports that the first white male child born in Cincinnati was a William Moody, although Greve does mention that Dr. Daniel Drake had given that honor to David Cummins and that Charles Cist thought Daniel Gano deserved the distinction. All three children were born in the spring of 1790. See Greve, p. 352.

improve themselves. Lectures as public entertainment and self-education had become passé. Young men turned to the many new forms of entertainment: musical concerts, vaudeville performances, amateur and professional baseball, and the newly constructed hilltop entertainment venues. All of this translated into fewer members for the Association and less interest in the Mercantile Library as a public institution. It also meant that the Library received fewer gifts.[32]

The well was not completely dry, however. In 1867 William Powell Jr., a commission merchant, donated "a large and elegant marble medallion of Washington Irving"; in the 1870s the minutes record the gift of a steel engraving of Washington, a large engraving of Lincoln,[33] "three large chromos representing the crucifixion," and a framed engraving of George Peabody Esq.[34]

More interesting to twenty-first-century readers are several volumes that fall into the category of art books. David Sinton contributed Luigi Canina's *Gli Edifizi Antichi dei Contorni di Roma*, a lavishly illustrated set of six volumes depicting ancient Rome; Alphonso Taft, attorney general of the United States in 1876, presented the Library that year with Lt. George M. Wheeler's *Explorations*, including a folio volume of photo-

32 After 1881 the Cincinnati Art Museum began receiving its own assortment of gifts including mineral collections, fossils, and paintings.

33 This engraving by Henry Gugler, based on a John Littlefield's portrait of Lincoln, was given by a group of Library friends that included librarian M. Hazen White and his assistant, Miss Alice McLean. Lincoln and Washington currently hang on the west wall of the Library.

34 George Peabody (1795-1869), a Massachusetts-born merchant and financier, made his fortune in Baltimore but lived in London as an international banker after 1837. One of the world's first great philanthropists, he founded the Peabody Institute in Baltimore and gave much of his wealth to educational institutions.

graphs[35] and one hundred card photographs "illustrating the descriptive volume."[36] Two years earlier the Association had purchased the two-volume "variorum edition of Shakespeare." This acquisition was meant to strengthen the recently created "Dramatic Department";[37] printer Robert Clarke soon added a facsimile reprint of the 1623 quarto Shakespeare. Finally, in 1880, Charles H. Justis donated a copy of Auguste Racinet's *Le Costume Historique*.[38]

The Library received perhaps its most unusual gift in 1868. Isaac J. Miller, an attorney and a former member of the Association, presented a Chinese translation of the Declaration of Independence, accompanied by "a phonograph [sic] in our Romanic letter, intending to give some idea of the pronunciation of the Chinese characters." At a time when interest in Asian cultures was growing rapidly, the gift seemed appropriate. As Miller described the item, the document was written on silk "by one of the most distinguished of the Cantonese literati," and while being written it had attracted so much interest "among this apathetic race" that ten copies were made. "But should our 'Great Declaration' come to be an Evangel of political faith to their Race of 350 millions, all reading the same written language," he solemnly continued, "the translation... would have tendencies of unconceivable

35 This volume of photographs by Timothy O'Sullivan apparently was sold to Walter Burton, of Burton Gallery in the city, in 1983 for $7,500; see board minutes for April 19 and May 4, 1983.

36 This is a reference to part of Lieutenant (later Captain) George M. Wheeler's *United States Geographical Surveys West of the One Hundredth Meridian* (Washington, D.C., 1869-83). Wheeler's work helped establish the U.S. Geological Survey.

37 The board created the Dramatic Department within the collection in 1872, funded initially by an "[e]ntertainment given by the Shakespeare Club... before our Association...."

38 Auguste Racinet (1825-1893) produced a magnificent world history of human clothing. Charles Justis would have donated one volume, as the entire work was not completed until 1888. In its complete edition it ran to six volumes, with five hundred chromolithographs. Justis, was a partner in Pappenheimer Hardware.

importance." There is no record, however, that these ten copies launched a democratic movement in China.

Despite the gradual decline in philanthropy toward the Mercantile Library, 1877 proved particularly beneficial. In February, Robert Clarke presented the Mercantile with a "very rare and valuable folio-sized Bible written in Latin." Published in Nuremburg, Germany, in 1479, the volume was described in the board minutes as being in "splendid" condition, with "the illustrated letters... as brilliant as newly painted work." Eight months later, David Bolles donated a plaster bust of Joel Barlow, author of the late eighteenth-century epic nationalistic poem *The Columbiad*. Also in 1877 Calvin W. Thomas gave a full-length oil portrait of his father, E. S. Thomas, former editor of the *Cincinnati Commercial and Advertiser* and later of the *Cincinnati Evening Post*. The picture, painted by John Frankenstein, was quickly placed "alongside the portraits of the other distinguished and eminent men that now adorn the walls of the Library."

In 1879 a Mr. Leaman[39] presented the Association with a "beautifully illuminated design containing the names of the Board and of the committees," the work of local artist Henry F. Farny.[40] Later that year the board discussed purchasing a bust of Emanuel Swedenborg, the eighteenth-century Swedish philosopher and religious writer, but could not solicit sufficient funds from members. In 1880 Thomas J. Wheatley, one of the city's more successful commercial pottery makers, donated a "beautiful vase"; whether this was a product of his own kiln is not known. Four years later, in 1884, George A. Bowen con-

---

39 In all likelihood this is Robert F. Leaman, described as a businessman with literary tastes who served as president of the Mercantile Library in 1880.

40 There is no record explaining why Farny created the design, nor does any record exist to tell what became of it.

tributed an "ornamental stained glass window"titled *The Three Arts*. First placed in the College Building, it was reinstalled on the south wall of the present building in 1904. There it was joined by a second stained-glass window, *Woman with a Book*, given by Augustine ("Gussie") Ogden to memorialize her late husband, Frank McGee Ogden.[41] Both windows were loaned or given to the Cincinnati Art Museum after the 1968 construction of the Formica Building (now the Mercantile Center Building), which blocked the Library's view to the south (see Chapter 8).

The twentieth century proved far less generous. In August 1906 the Library, with less wall space in its new quarters, loaned its large portraits of William Henry Harrison, Charles Hammond, and Mr. Ernst to the Cincinnati Art Museum.[42] Despite the reduction in wall space, in 1907 Emery Barton, a local dealer in picture frames and artwork, gave "oil portraits" to the Library; nothing is known about the artists or the subjects. Four years later the Library accepted four more pictures from Barton; these were identified as portraits of Charles Dickens, Robert Burns, Oliver Wendell Holmes (probably Senior), and "Whistler's portrait of Nicholson." Although these might have been engravings, in all likelihood they were framed reproductions. Along with various other works of

---

41 Frank M. Ogden (1850-1901), a Cincinnati native, and his wife, Augustine, were both ardent members of the Mercantile Library; see Lewis Alexander Leonard, editor, *Greater Cincinnati and Its People: A History* (Chicago and New York: Lewis Historical Publishing Co., 1926), III: 100.

42 In October 1919, after determining that the several portraits at the Art Museum "were [not] of any value to the Library," the Library board gave the Harrison portrait to a Mrs. Hendricks, a descendant of the former president, who had inquired about it. At the same time, the board voted to offer a "Hunt portrait to some colored institution, it being the work of a colored artist...." This intriguing comment is the only reference to this particular portrait, but it may have been one of the unidentified oil portraits donated in 1907 by Emery Barton.

art, the Mercantile received a "Symmes Land Grant" from Lawrence Mendenhall, a generous collection of photographs from Herman M. Moos, and several picture frames from the A. B. Closson Jr. Company.[43] In 1915 Judge Max B. May presented a portrait of Rabbi Isaac M. Wise, who established Reform Judaism and founded Hebrew Union College in Cincinnati.

The 1930s brought several more notable items. In 1930 the Misses Gallagher donated a portrait of their ancestor Thomas Gallagher, painted by Thomas Buchanan Read, a prominent artist in the city during the mid-nineteenth century. The following year, as a result of John Galsworthy's visit to the Mercantile Library, W. T. H. Howe presented a sketch of the noted author, made by Rudolf Helmut Sauter, Galsworthy's nephew and illustrator. In 1935, at the Mercantile's 100th anniversary celebration, Moses Ranney's granddaughter gave a miniature portrait, the only known image of the Association's first president. Five years later Mrs. David May provided the Library with the handsome Duhme "grandfather clock" that presently graces the Reading Room. Then for almost five decades the board minutes go silent, except for a daguerreotype of Morgan Ewing, an early member, donated in 1983.[44]

Over the past twenty years, however, the Mercantile has received a rich assortment of art objects, probably a result of

43 Except for the Burns, which remains in the Library, the whereabouts of these portraits is unknown. As for the "Symmes Land Grant," this was probably a land certificate issued by John Cleves Symmes, who in 1788 had purchased from Congress an approximately one-million-acre tract of land in southwestern Ohio, known as Symmes' Purchase or the Miami Purchase.

44 Morgan Ewing joined the Young Men's Mercantile Library Association in 1835 but was not among the "founders." The daguerreotype was sent by a man in North Carolina whose signature appears to read "E. Remelin."

energetic programming and expanded membership. During the 1990s Patricia and H. C. Buck Niehoff, underwriters of the annual Niehoff Lecture, presented a bronze bust of poet Robert Frost[45] as well as a fine edition of the works of Octavio Paz, with illustrations by Robert Motherwell. In 1995 Patricia Niehoff commissioned local artist Stacey Davidson to paint a portrait of her husband seated in the Library. Virginius Hall gave a bust of Henry Wadsworth Longfellow in 1998, a handsome addition to the Library's collection. Brad Wigor, a Cincinnati native and Hollywood screenwriter, contributed a first edition of Charles Dickens' *Our Mutual Friend*, while Mr. and Mrs. Joseph Andrews presented the Library with a first edition of *Dombey and Son*, also by Dickens. Perhaps in support of these gifts, Charles Fleischmann donated a wax bas-relief of Dickens himself, which later was stolen.[46]

In 2003, as part of the inaugural Harriet Beecher Stowe Festival, the Library commissioned local sculptor Walter Driesbach to create a bust of Stowe, the city's most famous author. Then, in the following year, Patricia Niehoff gave a number of sketchbooks and other material that had belonged to nineteenth-century Cincinnati artist Elizabeth Nourse. This included her lovely watercolor *Portrait of a Married Woman* and an oil-on-linen banner titled *Seven Owls*.

All of the Nourse material had come perilously close to being destroyed. When Elizabeth Nourse died in 1938, her possessions, including a number of her paintings and a trunk full of sketchbooks and French period clothing, were shipped

---

45 Director and future Mercantile president James Wellinghoff constructed a bracket and base for the Frost bust.
46 For the Wigor gift, see Albert Pyle to Brad Wigor, May 15, 2003, in Mercantile Library archives, box: "Miscellaneous," folder: "Wigor Gift." The board minutes mention the theft of the Dickens bas-relief, but with no details.

to Cincinnati. Eventually the paintings were sold through Closson's Gallery. Patricia Niehoff's grandmother purchased several of the paintings, and Closson's threw in "the trunk of stuff," apparently considering it not worth selling. The trunk, rarely opened, eventually passed to Patricia's mother. Buck and Patricia knew about the sketchbooks but had never seen them, so when her mother died they asked the people emptying out the house to keep an eye open for some sketchbooks. Nobody thought to check the contents of the trunk, until it was being carried out as trash.[47] The Nourse sketchbooks, housed in a special cabinet constructed by Wellinghoff, now occupy a central place in the remodeled Reading Room. Sandra Geiser serves as administrator and curator of the collection.

Unfortunately, a significant number of these objects acquired over the years can no longer be located. Some surely were lost to fire, theft, or carelessness. Apparently neither librarians nor board members before 1969 paid much attention either to the proper care or to the security of art objects. They were simply part of the Library's furnishings. Some of them have attained real value only in recent years. It is also quite possible that various boards of directors sold some items without any mention in the minutes. For most of the last century boards did not meet during the summer months, and other meetings ended prematurely for lack of a quorum, so some business matters were handled by the officers or even by the president alone. Given the constant problem of adequate funding, selling certain art works or books would have been an easy way to bring in some much-needed cash.

To balance these losses to the Mercantile, the Library also

---

47 Author's interview with H. C. Buck Niehoff, October 27, 2009.

contains several objects of note for which there is no acquisition information. These include the four Rookwood pieces, three probably designed by Kataro Shirayamadani, the outstanding Japanese-born designer, and the other by Matt Daly, which are displayed in the twelfth-floor meeting room; a Thomas Buchanan Read portrait;[48] a large engraving of Benjamin Franklin; and the large Sèvres vase (or urn) formerly in the Members' Lounge. The collection also includes an attractive watercolor by an artist named Drisler, about which little is known. (Appendix C documents the comings and goings of the Mercantile Library's collection of art and art objects.)

The works discussed in this chapter span the Association's history from the earliest years to the present because they represent a special aspect of Mercantile history, but now we return to the timeline of events following the rebuilding of the Library in 1870.

---

48 This is the portrait hanging on the east wall of the Reading Room. It may be the portrait of Thomas Gallagher.

"Has the public interest in literature and art so died down that it is a struggle to keep alive an institution like ours? If so, let it be spoken to our shame."

PRESIDENT WILLIAM P. ANDERSON
ANNUAL REPORT, 1873

"The library and a book are better than a bar-room and a drink, or an aimless lounge by a hotel stove."

INDEPENDENT TICKET SLOGAN, 1872

"Our dear old Young Men's Mercantile Library Association; may it live a thousand years."

JAMES LUPTON
FORMER MERCANTILE LIBRARY PRESIDENT, 1885

CHAPTER 5

A Change in Focus

WITH A RECONSTRUCTED College Building, completely refurbished rooms, and a new sense of excitement, the Mercantile Library Association had skirted disaster once again, and its accommodating lease opened the way to a promising future. Membership increased, from just over 2,000 members in 1870 to more than 2,800 by 1872. Financial worries as expressed in the board minutes, although never far from the directors' thoughts, appeared less frequently.

At the same time, Cincinnati shook off the despondency that had come with the onset of the Civil War. In 1869 the city hosted a highly successful Exposition of Textile Fabrics, followed a year later by the first of a long series of popular industrial expositions. In just 4½-weeks during the fall of 1870, more than three hundred thousand people attended this display of the city's commercial and manufacturing prowess. In 1872 the Liberal (anti-Grant) wing of the Republican Party convened in Cincinnati to nominate for president Horace Greeley, whom the Mercantile had proudly secured as a lecturer in 1849. Four years later a reunited Republican Party assembled in the city to nominate former Cincinnati resident Rutherford B. Hayes as its presidential candidate; in 1880 the Democrats arrived to select Winfield S. Hancock as their candidate for president. In October 1871 the magnificent Tyler Davidson Fountain was unveiled; in the following year the Mount Auburn Inclined Plane was constructed, the first of five that accelerated the process of moving people from the basin area to the surrounding hilltops.

In 1873 a combination of events and circumstances led to the first May Musical Festival, held in the recently constructed Saengerfest Hall. Five years later, Music Hall opened its doors as the permanent home for the nation's most polished (and now oldest) choral festival. Theodore Thomas, the leading music director in the country, came from New York to head the College of Music and to establish the city as the music capital of the nation. Meanwhile, young women turned their talents first to art-carved furniture and later to ceramic decoration, and their success led to a special Cincinnati exhibit room at the 1876 World's Fair in Philadelphia. Local boosters modestly referred to Cincinnati as the "Paris of America."

In the midst of all this activity, the Mercantile Library attempted to restart the lectures that had been its public face before the war. In January 1872 the board of directors turned to local talent, believing that if these were successful they would seek "the most popular lecturers in the country" for the next year. Alphonso Taft, Richard Smith, and S. Dana Horton answered the call, and collectively earned a profit of $237 for the Library.

The following year the board invited the Reverend Henry Ward Beecher to make two appearances. Beecher, the brother

of Harriet Beecher Stowe and the son of Lyman Beecher, former president of the city's Lane Seminary,[1] had graduated
from the seminary before eventually becoming the pastor of
Brooklyn's Plymouth Congregational Church. An active anti-
slavery advocate during the Civil War era, he was at the height
of his popularity when he returned to the Queen City as the
nation's most celebrated clergyman. Eloquent, popular, considered quite handsome by many women, he used his pulpit
to address numerous moral and social causes. It is not known
whether the Mercantile directors were aware of the adultery
charges that had surfaced in late 1872 and eventually would
lead to a highly publicized trial in 1875. At that trial the jury
failed to reach a decision, but any rumors current in early 1873
could only have enhanced Beecher's appeal as a speaker.

The Mercantile paid Beecher an astounding $1,500 per
night plus expenses, and the directors anticipated large audiences for his two-lecture visit in February. They were not
disappointed. Long before the first lecture on February 20,
scheduled for 8 p.m., people began streaming into Pike's Opera
House until every seat was taken. Latecomers stood along
the walls. Shortly after 8:00, an announcer explained that
Beecher's train had been delayed and requested the audience's
indulgence for a half an hour. At 9:20 the Mercantile Library
president, Samuel B. Warner, read a dispatch from Beecher:
"We are struggling to get through; hope to reach the hall by
9:00." This announcement brought considerable laughter
from the patient crowd.

Finally, at 9:50, Beecher arrived on stage to hearty applause

---

1   Lane Seminary was located in Walnut Hills. The Lyman Beecher home, where Harriet
    lived before she married Calvin Stowe, is now known as the Harriet Beecher Stowe House
    and is located on Gilbert Avenue.

and great anticipation. After opening with humorous remarks about his late arrival, he launched into his advertised subject, "Manhood and Money." He walked a fine moral tightrope, arguing that wealth was not inherently bad, but greed was. Then, in a prescient moment, considering the reputation of the "Gilded Age," Beecher expressed serious concerns about the future direction of the country. Two nights later, with considerably less drama but before an equally large audience, he spoke on the virtues of compulsory education. The Library netted $320.55.[2]

Ten months later Harriet Beecher Stowe followed her brother's path. Mrs. Stowe had lived in Cincinnati for almost eighteen years, arriving as a young woman with her father in 1832 and departing for Connecticut in 1849 as the wife of Calvin Stowe and the mother of several children. Although she didn't complete *Uncle Tom's Cabin* for another two years, her experiences while living in the city shaped much of the book.

An eager audience arrived, despite the formidable December weather, and sat attentively, sometimes laughing, sometimes in somber silence, as Mrs. Stowe read from her works. Dressed mostly in black, sitting dramatically on a stage lit only by an oil lamp, she entertained with readings from *The Minister's Wooing*, "Sleeping in Church," and of course *Uncle Tom's Cabin*. To commemorate this occasion, and because she is the best-known writer associated with Cincinnati, the Mercantile Library holds an annual Harriet Beecher Stowe Lecture to recognize authors "writing to change the world." Joan Hedrick, Pulitzer Prize-winning author of a biography

---

2 *Cincinnati Enquirer*, February 21, 1873, 4. Much of the information concerning this lecturer and those discussed in the rest of this chapter is taken from Dale P. Brown, *Brilliance and Balderdash: Early Lecturers at Cincinnati's Mercantile Library* (Cincinnati: The Mercantile Library, 2007), 39-46.

of Stowe, inaugurated the series in 2003.

In 1873 Cincinnatians also had an opportunity to hear Bret Harte. Although his reputation had faded somewhat after he burst onto the literary scene in the 1860s, the thirty-four-year-old former writer for *The Atlantic Monthly*, the country's most prestigious literary journal at that time, still drew "a fair house." With "a quiet, candid manner, a clear enunciation, and a pleasant delivery," Harte described the experiences of "The Argonauts of 1849," the famous forty-niners who had gone to California in search of gold. Using colorful anecdotes and dialect, he sketched vivid characters from the western frontier.[3]

The Mercantile also brought in several other lecturers during the 1870s: Charles Bradlaugh, a leading English atheist of the time; English poet Gerald Massey; and Cincinnati's Dr. Isaac M. Wise. Wise, born in what was then Bohemia, had arrived in the Queen City in 1854 at the age of thirty-five. He soon became the leading voice of Reform Judaism, helped establish the Plum Street Temple (now the Isaac M. Wise Temple) at Eighth and Plum Streets, started *The American Israelite*, and founded Hebrew Union College.

During late February and early March 1874, R. A. Proctor, a British astronomer and "a pioneer of popular science writing," presented a five-part series on the solar system. The reporter for the *Cincinnati Daily Gazette* described Proctor as "a man of medium height, but a little above the medium weight," who parted "his glossy black locks in the middle, and [wore] the typical English side whiskers." "He cannot be regarded as a great orator," the reporter continued, for "he has not the art of emphasizing the leading points of his discourse, and also

---

3 *Cincinnati Daily Gazette*, April 14, 1873, 8. The previous December, Harte had given the same talk at the New York Mercantile Library.

perhaps flatters his hearers too much by presuming upon their familiarity with certain matters of science, not as plain as a pike staff to all creation."[4] In other words, the reporter struggled to understand the lecture but had to write something.

Lectures, however, never really came back into vogue. Until very recently, they virtually disappeared from the Mercantile Library's social calendar. The Massey lecture in 1874 proved particularly disappointing. As noted dryly in the board minutes, the poet "was greeted with so sparse an attendance as to decide the committee to discontinue other lectures already negotiated for." Another attempt, made during the winter of 1875-76, proved equally frustrating. After local physician P. S. Connor's lecture on "Pain and Its Relief" attracted only twenty listeners (ten of whom had complimentary tickets), the board canceled scheduled talks by Judge Johann Stallo and the Reverend Thomas Vickers, head of the Cincinnati Public Library. They offered ticket refunds but "earnestly hoped... that no person will avail themselves of that privilege." The cash-strapped organization wanted to hold on to every penny.

Even so, significant anniversary celebrations still required keynote speakers, usually local men of prominence. For the Association's fiftieth anniversary in 1885, seven former presidents of the organization worked with the present board to plan "a proper celebration of the semi-centennial," and several other former presidents, who could not attend, wrote strong letters of support. At the Odeon Theatre, the setting for the affair, Association officers and the planning committee sat on the stage, "all in full dress." Evergreen wreaths decorated the walls, and from the proscenium hung a large banner with

---

4 Brown, *Brilliance and Balderdash*, 69-70.

"Young Men's Mercantile Library Association 1835-1885" in red and blue, the colors of the two factions that annually competed for the organization's offices. President James L. Foley provided the usual "appropriate remarks," followed by attorney Samuel Hunt's "historical and literary address." The ever-faithful James Murdoch, now seventy-four years old, gave a short recitation, and Dr. A. C. Kemper read his original poem titled "In the Library."[5] Nothing special, nothing expensive was offered; the annual report described the evening as "a most pleasant and entertaining one." (In contrast, the Association's seventy-fifth anniversary, held in 1910, was marked by a more elaborate celebration: an opportunity to invite President William Howard Taft to attend the occasion proved irresistible.)

Various boards also explored other forms of entertainment. In December 1872 the Mercantile invited the Shakespearean Club of Cincinnati to present an evening of readings in College Hall. The *Cincinnati Enquirer* reporter described it as a "somewhat exhaustive programme." Four years later Library members were invited to Melodeon Hall for an evening of music and the reading of two farces, one in German. In January 1877 the Mendelssohn Club of Boston inquired about presenting a concert for a fee of $200. After some discussion the board concluded that it "would be unadvisable and inexpedient." Apparently the board soon reversed its position, for on March 1 the Mendelssohnians, accompanied by vocalist

---

5 *Cincinnati Enquirer*, April 19, 1885, 8. Other Cincinnati newspapers made little note of the Mercantile's fiftieth anniversary. Several gave more space to the "grand Spring opening" of the Alms & Doepke store at Main and Canal; see *Cincinnati Graphic*, 3(April 11, 1885), 242.

Ella C. Lewis, performed at Melodeon Hall.[6]

On November 13 of that year, the Association sponsored a concert by several prominent local musicians: pianist George Schneider; Miss Fannie Manetti, a vocalist who came from Columbus, Ohio, but was advertised as "lately from Berlin, Paris, and London"; and the Cincinnati Choral Society. Given the local enthusiasm for the May Festival, the directors must have concluded that choral music was a safe bet. The concert was held at Pike's Opera House. Although the reporter from the *Cincinnati Daily Gazette* praised Schneider's strong rendition of Schubert's "Fantasie Sonata," he found Manetti's voice not strong enough for the size of the hall. The concert left a deficit of $128.97; the Association board absolved itself by blaming the poor attendance on competition from a testimonial concert for Miss Julie Rive-King, scheduled for the following evening. Board minutes described that performance as "an array of talent seldom found together."[7]

To help the troubled Library, the Cincinnati Choral Society offered $100 for the Library's list of subscribers; this, plus the $29 raised by special subscription, left the Mercantile Library with "a credit to the Lecture fund of $.03." In the annual report for 1877, the president concluded sadly "that the era of library entertainment has passed and that future

6 Although Dale Patrick Brown lists this concert in her book, it is not clear that the Mercantile Library actually sponsored this performance or a performance given two days earlier at Robinson's Opera House; see Brown, *Brilliance and Balderdash*, 155.
7 *Cincinnati Daily Gazette*, November 12, 1877, 5; November 14, 1877, 8. Also see Brown, *Brilliance and Balderdash*, 71. Julie Rive-King (1857-1937), born in a Cincinnati suburb, was taught by her mother, Caroline Rive, and she later studied piano in Europe with Karl Reinecke. She made her American debut with the New York Philharmonic Society in 1875 and went on to a distinguished concert career. Miss Rive-King is buried in Spring Grove Cemetery. The testimonial concert on her behalf included Myron W. Whitney, Anna Drasdil, and Emma Thursby, three vocalists well known to Cincinnati audiences, and the event packed the house.

The first Cincinnati College building was the Library's home from 1840 to the fire of 1845. The lovely Federal-style structure stood on the site of the present Mercantile Library Building in what was then the Public Square.

The second Cincinnati College building featured commercial spaces on the ground floor that are echoed in the present structure.

A second fire in 1869 resulted in major modifications to the second Cincinnati College building.

A

The Library's miniature portrait on ivory of first president Moses Ranney is the only known image of the industrious grocery clerk who stood first among the founding forty five.

Poet and artist Thomas Buchanan Read wrote a commemorative piece for the Library and painted one of the two major portraits in the reading room.

Portrait of T.B. Read courtesy of the Philadelphia History Museum at the Atwater Kent, The Historical Society of Pennsylvania Collection

Alphonso Taft, the shrewd lawyer who devised the Library's 10,000-year lease.

By permission of the William Howard Taft National Historic Site.

Thomas Emery's Sons commissioned a design for the Mercantile Library Building that features a Beaux Arts front on a clean, industrial-age structure, with shops along Walnut Street.

*The Annual Meeting of 1913. The Library continues to serve
an afternoon tea for this event.*

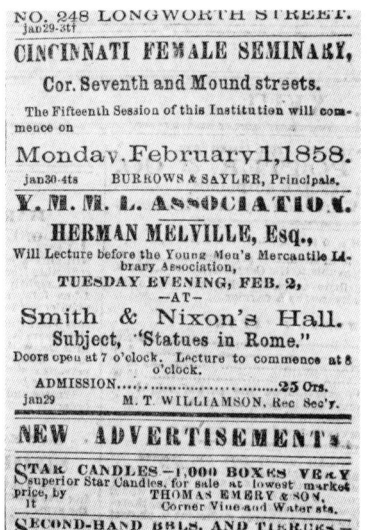

NO. 248 LONGWORTH STREET.
jan29-3t†

CINCINNATI FEMALE SEMINARY,

Cor. Seventh and Mound streets.

The Fifteenth Session of this Institution will commence on

Monday, February 1, 1858.

jan30-4ts   BURROWS & SAYLER, Principals.

Y. M. M. L. ASSOCIATION.

HERMAN MELVILLE, Esq.,

Will Lecture before the Young Men's Mercantile Library Association,

TUESDAY EVENING, FEB. 2,

—AT—

Smith & Nixon's Hall.

Subject, "Statues in Rome."

Doors open at 7 o'clock. Lecture to commence at 8
o'clock.

ADMISSION..............................25 Cts.

jan29   M. T. WILLIAMSON, Rec Sec'y.

NEW ADVERTISEMENTS.

STAR CANDLES—1,000 BOXES VERY
superior Star Candles, for sale at lowest market
price, by   THOMAS EMERY & SON,
1t   Corner Vine and Water sts.

SECOND-HAND BBLS. AND TIERCES.—
1,000 good Second-hand Barrels and Tierces, for
sale by   THOMAS EMERY & SON,

*A modest advertisement
for a literary giant.*

D

*Thomas Ernst Huenefeld, Honorary Member, walked away
with the Snappy Attire Award at the party to celebrate the 175th
anniversary of the Library's founding.*

The Mercantile Library
presents
Niehoff Lecture XVIII
with
Salman Rushdie

November 5, 2005

*Political cartoonist Jim
Borgman contributed a
caricature for the invitation
to Sir Salman Rushdie's
2005 Niehoff Lecture.*

E

Buck and Patricia Niehoff flank three Pulitzer Prize winners, playwright Edward Albee, author John Updike, and political cartoonist Jim Borgman on the night of Mr. Updike's Niehoff Lecture.

Nobel laureate Saul Bellow's sesquicentennial visit became the model for the continuing Niehoff Lecture series.

F

The 2000 reconstruction of the Library's 12th floor clubroom gave the club a handsome and flexible lecture space. Architect Frank Russell borrowed decoration from the building's street façade.

President Vere Gaynor and past president Hope Taft formally opened the new lecture hall.

Distinguished Librarian John Marshall Newton died at his desk at the Mercantile.

Jean Springer and her board revived the Library's fortunes in the mid-twentieth century.

Modifications in 2010 created new stacks and a performance stage at the south end of the reading room.

Photo of John Marshall Newton courtesy of Cincinnati Museum Center-Cincinnati Historical Society Library. Portrait of Jean Springer and south wall of the Mercantile Library by Robert Flischel.

H

Boards would do well to hesitate before embarking in these enterprises."

Future boards heeded this advice. Except for notable anniversary events, the Mercantile Library retreated from all public programs for more than a half-century. The exception was a full "season" of lectures and music in 1890-91, organized by J. L. Shearer, a professional planner, and intended to "revive the old-time interests." Miss Kate Field, a celebrated journalist, led off with "a very entertaining and instructive talk" on "Despised and Neglected Alaska."[8] In subsequent weeks James A. Green, city editor of the *Cincinnati Times-Star*, presented an illustrated travelogue on Ireland, and Kentucky author James Lane Allen addressed "The Literature of the New South." A Dr. W. L. Davidson, using a stereopticon, took his audience on a tour "In and About the Home of Shakespeare." In February 1891 Sergius Stepniak, a Russian radical whose real name was Sergius Mikhailovich Kravchinsky, explored the revolutionary currents in Russia, and Professor Richard G. Moulton of the "University of England" spoke on English literature.

Interwoven with this diverse group were musical performances by the Philharmonic String Quartette, the Harvard Quartette, and the Lotus Glee Club of Boston. James Murdoch concluded the series with readings from *King Lear* – altogether a considerable contribution to Cincinnati's cultural and intellectual life. A season ticket cost $2.50, and individual evenings cost 50¢. However, we find no record as to whether the series turned a profit, and it was not repeated.

Even though lectures and other entertainments were

8 *Cincinnati Enquirer*, November 23, 1890, 4. Details of the entire series may be found in Young Men's Mercantile Library Association, "Course of Lectures and Entertainments: Odeon – Season of 1890-91" (Cincinnati: Armstrong & Fillmore, 1890).

discontinued, the Mercantile Library remained a popular destination for visitors to the city. Resting on top of the Library's iron safe is a musty visitors' sign-in ledger, covering the period from April 1872 to early 1918. If there was an earlier volume, unfortunately it has disappeared. Nevertheless, the existing ledger provides a window into one aspect of the Library. The majority of visitors came from Ohio and adjacent states, but every state and territory in the Union is represented. Ohio River commercial connections brought a substantial number of people from places stretching from Pittsburgh to New Orleans, but more recent rail connections made it easy to reach Cincinnati from Indianapolis, Chicago, St. Louis, and Baltimore. The city's economic importance also ensured that numerous businessmen from New York, Boston, and Philadelphia visited the Queen City. Occasionally an important event in Cincinnati is reflected in the ledger: the 1875 May Festival drew music critics from Chicago and Boston; the opening of the Cincinnati and Southern Railway in 1880 led to a sharp increase in visitors from Chattanooga; and national political conventions increased the number of visitors to the Library in 1876 and 1880.

Among the thousands of names are several of significance, although most were better known then than now: Henry Demarest Lloyd, a muckraking progressive journalist who worked for the *Chicago Tribune* and later wrote *Wealth Against Commonwealth*, a serious criticism of the emerging industrial capitalism; Edward L. Godkin, the Irish-born reform-minded editor and publisher of *The Nation;* Frederick W. Root, a composer of popular songs; and General Henry Heth, who led Confederate forces in the attempt to attack Cincinnati in 1862. Union General George H. Thomas, the so-called

"Rock of Chickamauga" during the late war, stopped by in 1875; the next year the Reverend James McCosh, Scottish-born philosopher and president of the College of New Jersey (now Princeton University), visited. Ralph Waldo Emerson made his last visit to the Library in 1877. The following year, William Graham Sumner, Yale professor, polymath, and ardent champion of laissez-faire economics, came calling, as did Horatio Alger Jr., author of a popular series of "rags-to-riches" juvenile books. The Library also welcomed two sculptors of the period: Preston Powers, son of Hiram Powers, and Edmonia Lewis, daughter of an African-American father and a Native American mother, who worked in the neoclassical tradition. In 1882 Arthur M. Sullivan of London signed the ledger. The composer, known best as the collaborator with W. S. Gilbert, had come to the United States as part of a touring company performing his operetta *Patience*.[9]

The ledger also records the names of visitors from dozens of other countries. England, Scotland, and Ireland are mentioned most frequently, but virtually all of Western Europe is represented. More exotic locations also catch the eye: Jamaica, San [sic] Domingo, South Africa, Brazil,[10] Chile, India, Australia, and Japan.

Several visitors used the ledger to make personal comments. R. C. H. Dumahut of Tromsø, Norway which sits almost 200 miles inside the Arctic Circle, proudly inserted "North Pole"

9 The opera company followed the path of Oscar Wilde, who was in the country to promote Gilbert and Sullivan's *Patience* and, of course, himself. Wilde spent several days in Cincinnati but did not appear at the Mercantile, speaking at Pike's Opera House instead. Besides his work with Gilbert, Sullivan was an accomplished conductor and the composer of operas and songs, including "Onward, Christian Soldiers" and "Nearer My God to Thee."

10 The visitors from Brazil in 1876 were surely part of the contingent traveling with Dom Pedro, Emperor of Brazil, who was touring the United States after assisting in the opening ceremony of the Philadelphia World's Fair that year.

and "71 North Latitude" next to his place of residence, and a Jonathan G. Burns of Cleveland wrote rather cryptically, "Love to the Human Race. Good by [sic] Good Blues to You and Yours." One wag even signed in as George Washington from Mount Vernon, with his sponsor listed as B. Franklin. This entry was dated October 31, 1888, perhaps as a Halloween prank, but was placed in the ledger at the bottom of the page for January 1883.

The visitors' ledger also reveals a disturbing trend after 1880. As the Library's and the city's importance declined in the last years of the nineteenth century, fewer visitors came to the Mercantile rooms. In particular the number of guests from Europe and East Coast cities diminished. By the end of the century, the total for an entire year might fill only two or three pages, and the last 8½ years required only two pages.

On February 19, 1918, with perhaps forty pages remaining blank, the librarian closed the book for the last time. By then, of course, the Mercantile Library was only a shell of its former self. Board minutes reflect this decline as well. Except for the years 1881 through 1883, membership during the last several decades of the century dropped steadily, and a surprising number of board meetings failed to draw a quorum.[11]

Despite the overall decline in membership, the 1870s and early 1880s often witnessed very active elections, a reminder that to be an officer or director of the Mercantile Library

11 In 1882 membership climbed to 4,413; in 1883 it reached 4,555, the highest total ever recorded. By 1885 the number had dropped to 1,874, and it continued to decline. The temporary spike reflected the very closely contested Association elections, with candidates recruiting new members in order to gain their votes. In the election of 1882, for instance, 2,001 members voted; the victorious presidential candidate won by only fifty-one votes. In 1885, however, the Regular Ticket ran uncontested, and only 201 members bothered to cast ballots. Further evidence of the rapid increase in board ennui is the *Cincinnati Graphic's* wry comment in its "Funny to See" feature: it would, indeed, be funny to see "a full meeting of the Directory of the YMMLA." See 3 (April 11, 1885), 242.

carried considerable social prestige. When issues such as membership eligibility or Sunday hours surfaced, both tickets—the Regular and the Independent—placed advertisements in major newspapers, put up banners and posters in shop windows, and canvassed for votes. Supporters often wrote letters to the newspapers touting their favorites or deriding the position of those they opposed. According to one newspaper account from around 1900, "bribing of voters was general."[12] Rather than causing internal bitterness, these lively elections helped maintain the Association's profile in the community.

As membership decreased, financial concerns again dominated Association board meetings, and throughout the final decades of the century various boards introduced plans to bring in new members. None was very successful. The ensuing financial pinch, especially during recession years such as 1874[13] and 1894, was relieved by various gifts that the Association received during this time. These sometimes came in the form of cash, such as George T. Harrison's bequest of $500 in 1892 and Fred T. Lincoln's gift of $5,000 in 1897.

More important, because they extended funds over longer periods, were the donations of property that brought in rental income. In 1869 Timothy Crane Day left to the Mercantile

12 Unidentified newspaper clipping in the scrapbook "Libraries of Cincinnati, Volume 3: Mercantile Library," p. 10, in Cincinnati Historical Society Library, Cincinnati Museum Center. The 1891 election brought a brief renewal of election spirit when Joseph Cox Jr. narrowly defeated Fred M. Stimson for the office of president. Cox, a lawyer, was the first professional man to head the Association. Following his brief address to the members, his predecessor as president, Joseph T. Carew, received "three cheers and a tiger... given with a vim."

13 Plans to establish an endowment fund of $25,000 had to be scrapped in 1874 because of the effects of the financial panic that had started the previous year. A fund was established the next year.

one-third interest in two downtown lots;[14] in 1876 John F. Dair's will provided half of any proceeds from a lot at the corner of Sixth and John Streets. Dair, formerly a life member, specified that the property was to be sold one year after his death and the income to be spread over a three-year period. Part of the McArthur bequest of 1867 (his will was probated in 1871), designated for the purchase of books, also came in the form of real estate. Timothy Kirby, who died in 1875, gave "certain real estate" to the city of Cincinnati, but any rents or profits from the property were to go to the city's two principal libraries for "the purchase of scientific books and books on the subject of industrial trades...." This bequest eventually brought about $5,000 to the Association. Various treasurers' reports mention other rental income as well, although the source of these properties is not always made clear. Eventually all of this property was sold with most of the proceeds going into a general endowment fund that provided annual interest to help cover operating costs. Thus the Mercantile Library Association limped along.

The board minutes reflect the usual internal operations of the Library, although directors now spent less time on day-to-day affairs. The librarians, beginning with M. Hazen White, brought a more professional touch to their duties, particularly acquisitions and cataloguing. The Reading Room is hardly mentioned, which suggests that the mercantile community had become less reliant on newspapers and journals for commercial information. The book collection, however, continued to grow. Even during financially troubled years,

14 One of the lots given by Timothy C. Day was on the southwest corner of Seventh and Walnut Streets; in 1903 it was finally sold for $51,000, one-third of which came to the Mercantile Library. Day also bequeathed funds to provide annual tickets for meritorious Cincinnati public school students to use the Library. This program is still maintained.

the board authorized the expenditure of $50 every month for new books. In 1882 the Ex Army and Navy Officers' Society loaned its collection of military books to the Mercantile, with the proviso that it would be shelved with the Library's own military books in a special carved wooden case. The Society's badge was to be placed on the books it contributed. When the Society "expired," its books would remain permanently with the Mercantile. In the meantime, Society members would have free use of the Library room.[15]

In 1882 the ninth edition of the *Encyclopedia Britannica* included the Mercantile among some twenty significant libraries in the United States–high praise indeed. Two years later, Library members must have taken great pleasure in a *Cincinnati Enquirer* article on local libraries that described the Mercantile before mentioning the city's larger but younger public library. In 1897 the board of directors almost scored a coup when two members met with pharmacist John Uri Lloyd about "securing his valuable Botanical Library." Unfortunately nothing came of this effort; eventually the collection became the basis of the Lloyd Library and Museum, presently housed at 911 Plum Street.[16]

Although the Mercantile failed to acquire Lloyd's wonderful collection, its own holdings continued to grow. To make room for this expansion, in 1899 the board agreed to send duplicate books "of no further practical use" to Berea College in Kentucky and to the Axtell Circulating Library

15 The Ex Army and Navy Officers' Society would have been made up primarily of Civil War veterans, and its collection would have consisted of many personal memoirs; these men assumed that with their deaths the Society would cease to exist. The Library no longer possesses a military history collection.
16 John Uri Lloyd (1849-1936) came to Cincinnati in 1864 and apprenticed with a local pharmacist. He became a pioneering pharmacist and, with his two younger brothers, established the Lloyd Library and Museum.

in Buckingham County, Virginia.[17] Three years later, a large number of surplus books went to the chaplain at Fort Thomas for use by soldiers stationed in the Philippine Islands.[18] Mercantile Library boards also dealt with the organization's various material needs, particularly changes in technology. In 1878 an ad hoc committee looked into a proposal from the Cincinnati Gas, Light & Coke Company to supply gas for the next 10 years. The committee reported that it would be "unwise... to enter into any binding agreement... for so long a term of years." The committee's report continued by pointing out that "scientific investigations in the subject of light [probably a reference to the work of Thomas Edison] are now being made...." Although commercial electric lighting was not far off, the Mercantile did not switch from gas for another ten years; perhaps the board should have accepted the company's offer.

In 1879 the Bell Company "agreed to place one of their instruments, in connection with a microphone, for one year free of charge in the Library Rooms." Cutting-edge technology had arrived! Some twenty months later, when the telephone company asked for an annual fee of $72 for the instrument ("and then only for offices"), the board balked. The telephone was removed. In 1888, the year when elec-

---

17 Berea College, a liberal arts college in Berea, Kentucky, was founded in 1855 by abolitionist John G. Fee and enrolls low-income students from southern Appalachia. There is no record that the Axtell Circulating Library still exists. The Mercantile donated 307 volumes to Berea and 230 volumes to the Axtell Library.

18 Fort Thomas, named for Civil War General George H. Thomas, who visited the Mercantile Library in 1875, was an army recruiting and training post and served for many years as the home of the Sixth Infantry Regiment. The post was formerly called Newport Barracks and was located at the junction of the Licking and Ohio Rivers in Newport, Kentucky, an area prone to flooding. In 1890 the post was moved to the higher elevation known as The Highlands, just south of Newport. The city of Fort Thomas takes its name from this installation.

tric lighting was installed, the board revisited the telephone issue and again voted against it. Finally, in 1895, the Library took the step: a line was installed and a "postal" went out to all members "informing them of the new arrangements." Somewhat curiously, in October 1901 the board, in the midst of rumors about a possible new structure to replace the College Building, spent almost $300 on painting the walls and installing "new electrical lighting." Although it was important to modernize the facilities, the building was torn down less than a year later.

Non-technological needs also came before the board. In 1892 the Association approved the purchase of a desk for the Library. At the same time it authorized the acquisition of a new safe, probably the one that currently stands near the base of the spiral staircase.

Even though new purchases gradually found their way into the Library, old problems remained. Conflicts with the College Building trustees ruffled feathers on both sides. The first year in the reconstructed College Building proved particularly exasperating. In 1870, when the College trustees failed to pay "certain bills incurred by reason of the fire," the Mercantile directors filed a lawsuit. This dispute lingered into the next year, until the Library board finally agreed that the College's position was correct: the Mercantile had to pay for its new carpeting and shelving. Earlier that year the College trustees had brought their own suit against the Library for taxes they claimed should have been paid by the Association. This case eventually went before the Ohio Supreme Court, which ruled against the Library. Two other disputes involved the installation of a new "Ladies Dressing Room," which was submitted to arbitration, and control of the space formerly occupied by the Chamber of Commerce. There is no record showing how these were resolved.

By 1871, relations between the College trustees and the Library directors had deteriorated so far that the Mercantile board appointed a committee "to adjust the misunderstandings and differences now existing...." Relations apparently improved, but in 1893 the minutes again reflect considerable irritation when the Library directors wanted to improve the electrical lighting in the rooms but felt thwarted by "the improbable conditions imposed by the Trustees of the Cincinnati College who controlled the building outside our rooms." These and other nagging issues might be dismissed as typical renter-landlord conflicts, but they certainly complicated later attempts by the College Building trustees to buy out the Library's lease rights.

Personnel issues also engaged the Library's board of directors. In May 1878 M. Hazen White (1817-78), the well-respected librarian who had served since 1866, died unexpectedly at his Mount Auburn home. White, a native of New Hampshire and a graduate of Dartmouth College, had come to Cincinnati in 1845 and taught at a girls' school for a number of years. During the Civil War he attained the rank of major with the 23rd Ohio Volunteer Regiment and, in the fashion of the day, was frequently referred to as Major White.[19] The Library closed for his funeral, and the directors attended the services

19 *Cincinnati Daily Gazette*, May 2, 1878, 4. In 1849 White, along with 11 other men, founded the city's Literary Club, which remains active at its East Fourth Street quarters. Another founder of the Literary Club, Reuben Stephenson, served as librarian of the Mercantile in 1851; John Marshall Newton, who followed White at the Mercantile, was another Literary Club member. During the long history of the Mercantile Library, many men have been actively involved in both institutions, including Robert H. Allen, Robert L. Black, John D. Caldwell, Herbert F. Koch, George McLaughlin, Ainsworth R. Spofford, Alphonso Taft, Charles B. Wilby, Stephen H. Wilder, Henry C. Yergason, current Mercantile executive director Albert Pyle, and the author.

at the First Unitarian Church. Funeral expenses, amounting to $34, came out of the Association treasury, and a one-month salary was sent to White's widow.

After placing a long memorial tribute in the board minutes, the directors appointed Alice McLean as acting librarian until a replacement could be found. By September they had selected John Marshall Newton, who had received "unqualified endorsement from a large number of citizens."[20] Because all five candidates considered by the board were men, it is doubtful whether the directors even thought of Miss McLean as a possibility. She resumed her duties as assistant librarian.

Gradual inflation during the next few years led to a salary increase of $200 per individual in 1883, leaving $2,000 for the librarian, $1,000 for McLean, and $800 for Miss Caroline Gaither, the second assistant librarian. In 1889, at Newton's request, the board hired a canvasser, Mr. J. E. Foley, "to solicit new memberships." His salary was lower, but he received a twenty percent commission for each new member he brought in. Apparently success eluded Foley: he soon left and was replaced by a Mr. Bridge. Bridge found the position unsatisfactory and soon departed as well. The board then made canvasser an assistant librarian position and increased the salary to $1,000, but still retained the twenty percent commission for securing new members. A Mr. H. Shockley next tried his hand at the job. Shockley may have performed better than his predecessors, but he had difficulties with librarian John Newton. In 1890 the board authorized the Library Committee to instruct the new assistant that he was "subject to the orders of the Librarian," and if necessary the committee

20 Before his employment with the Mercantile Library, Newton had served as secretary of the Adams Fire & Marine Insurance Company.

was "to make a change in the position of Assistant Librarian." Four months later Shockley resigned; the position was not refilled.

On December 9, 1897, John Newton (1825-97) died suddenly at his desk in the library. Legend has it that he died "so quietly that the glasses did not fall from his nose." A shocked board of directors placed crepe on the front door and closed the Library for the remainder of the day.[21] At their next meeting, the directors outlined Newton's many contributions to the Association in a long memorial: he had created the card catalog (the one recently digitized), had arranged a manuscript catalog, in 1879 had established a course of lectures on American history by one of the city's leading educators, and in many other ways had encouraged "the study of American History among our citizens." To perpetuate his memory, a special history alcove was dedicated to him. Although the alcove no longer exists, a bronze plaque near the librarian's office remains from that tribute. The board also agreed to compensate his widow by paying his salary up to March 1, 1898; the directors then placed the faithful Alice McLean in charge again.

White and Newton combined had given the Mercantile Library more than thirty years of distinguished service. (The Association was less fortunate during the next several decades.) The board immediately hired William J. Holden, at $100 per month, to serve as librarian for the remainder of the year, and Miss McLean once again returned to her regular duties.

Holden cast only a faint shadow as librarian. Indeed, it

21 *Cincinnati Enquirer*, September 10, 1897, 4.

seems he was not considered for the permanent position, although he was kept on for an additional year. In October 1900 the board instructed its president to contact library schools in order to secure a new librarian, "a male being preferred." Alice McLean might have received consideration except that earlier in the year the board minutes had noted somewhat ominously the assistant librarians' "lack of ready attention" to the wants of some of the members, and the board reminded the two women – McLean and Gaither – about "uniform courtesy." Given Alice McLean's thirty-five years of faithful service at that point, it is difficult to picture her as discourteous; more likely any lack of courtesy was initiated by members. Nevertheless, the situation could not have strengthened her chances, if any, of becoming the librarian. The official list of Mercantile librarians, however, shows a gap between 1900, when Holden left, and 1904, when William B. A. Taylor was hired. Although not mentioned in the board minutes, it would appear that Alice McLean served as acting librarian during this period.

In 1900, when Alice McLean turned sixty-five, she had spent almost her entire adult life caring about the Mercantile Library Association. She must have enjoyed the work; certainly she enjoyed the confidence of virtually every board member and librarian with whom she worked. In many ways she had become the heart of the organization, known to every member and virtually indispensable to the operation of the Library. She continued as assistant librarian for another nine years, until she suffered an accident in February 1909. The board's immediate response was to extend her salary through her convalescence. In May, placing the Association's best interests before her own needs, Miss McLean thanked the directors for their kindness but requested that her salary lapse at the end of that month. Noting that her improvement was very gradual, she still expressed a desire to return to duty when she was fully recovered – at age seventy-four!

The board used McLean's situation to look into the matter of "pensions for older assistants," but the Association's financial condition worked against that possibility. A few months later, the inevitable occurred. On November 5, 1909, Alice McLean submitted her letter of resignation, although it caused her "a painful wrench to do so." Her letter is our clearest view into her character and feelings:

> The Library seemed a part of myself for so long; we came into
> existence the same year, the Library in April and I in June,
> 1835; I have given forty-four years of my life to its faithful
> service and five years of that time I fulfilled the position
> of Librarian,[22] doing all the Librarian's work, except the
> bookkeeping, which Mr. W. W. Brown faithfully attended to;
> taking the extra work to my home, and burning the midnight
> oil to coax the truant members back, in which effort I was very
> successful. Neither Miss Gaither nor myself ever received a
> dollar for the extra work done during all these years, nor did
> we expect it. We were glad to hold things together during
> the transition from the old to the new quarters [1904], and
> the figures will, I think, show that the membership and
> the circulation were not much below the present showing,
> although we did not have an up to date card catalogue, but we
> managed to supply the wants of the members.

22 She is probably referring to the years from 1900 to 1904.

After venting some of her frustrations, McLean thanked the directors for all "the courtesy and kindness shown to me." She singled out "dear Mr. [Charles] Wilby" as "a faithful friend in every trying hour." All "have been most kind, as have all with whom I have been connected at the Library since the days of Adolph Wood's Presidency." "I have never asked a favor," she continued, "whatever came to me was the voluntary offering of the Board." She concluded her letter by informing the board "that as a result of a letter of mine to President [William Howard] Taft last June–written without a suggestion from anyone–at that time–I have received the announcement that Mr. Carnegie has placed me on his personal pension list, which relieves me of anxiety regarding the future."[23] True to her character, her parting thought was for the Library's welfare: "As 1910 will be the golden jubilee of the Library, I trust something may be done to increase the Endowment Fund."

The board accepted McLean's resignation with "regrets" and "appreciation of her services." They also made her an honorary member. In replying to her resignation letter, board secretary Edward S. Ebert kindly informed her that the directors "wished that we, and not the Carnegie Fund, had it in our power to relieve your future of anxiety. Could you have heard the kindly expressions on all sides I am sure you would feel that the Board of Directors of the Y.M.M.L.A. were your friends."

Slightly more than two years later, on February 1, 1912,

---

23 Andrew Carnegie spent a considerable part of his fortune on building libraries for communities around the country. Apparently, as part of that philanthropic endeavor, he established a "pension list" for deserving librarians such as Alice McLean. In 1918 the Carnegie Foundation established the Teachers Insurance and Annuity Association, a retirement program for educators.

Caroline Gaither, the other assistant librarian, resigned. She had devoted almost forty years of her life to the Mercantile. Again the board expressed its regret at being unable to provide a pension, although it did grant her a life membership. We have no evidence that Mr. Carnegie placed her on his pension list.

These two women, virtually unknown today, helped carry the Mercantile Library through some of its most difficult times. Their departures, along with the relatively short tenures of the next four librarians, left a serious void in the operations of the Association.[24]

A major event in the Library's life was the move into the present building in 1904. Long before this occurred, however, various boards of directors had explored the possibility of obtaining a separate building for the organization. As early as 1861, Charles Kilgour, running for president of the Association on the Regular Ticket, proposed that the Library give up its lease and move into Pike's Opera House. He lost the election, and the Library remained in the College Building. In 1864, when a "wealthy merchant" offered a lot on Fourth Street, the Mercantile board started a subscription fund for a new building. The merchant then changed his mind, however.

In 1870 a special committee of the board met with representatives of the College Building to discuss the possibility of the College trustees' purchasing the Mercantile Library's interest in the building. Nothing came of that, but seven years later Alexander H. McGuffey, secretary of the College Building Board of Trustees, presented the Library board with an offer

---

24 Caroline Gaither, almost always referred to as "Miss Gaither" in the Association minutes but known to her friends as "Carrie," lived another twenty-seven years. She died in 1939 at age ninety-two.

to purchase its lease for $36,000. At the next general meeting of the Association, the membership "unanimously rejected" the proposal.

Five years later, in January 1882, a newly elected board of directors established a subscription fund to construct "a permanent building for library purposes." In conjunction, the directors contacted the College Building board regarding the value of the lease, with the idea of selling it. The trustees, somewhat annoyed by the Mercantile Library's rejection of its earlier offer, stated bluntly that it was now up to the Library to make "a counter proposition." When the Mercantile directors discussed the situation at their March meeting, they first settled on a value of $50,000, and then raised it to $75,000 in hopes of obtaining as large a return on the lease as possible. The College Building trustees were not impressed: they replied that the offer was "too extravagant to require serious consideration."

Concerned that negotiations might break down, the Library board arranged for a joint conference in late May. After a prolonged discussion, each person at the meeting wrote down his estimate of the lease's value. The average within the joint committee was $44,000, and eventually they agreed to a fair market value of $40,000. Each group then took that figure back to its board for approval. The Mercantile board approved, contingent on a vote by the membership; the College trustees, who quickly approved, found the inevitable delay "not satisfactory" and wanted a "definite settlement" before August 10. At this point a Mr. Donahue of the Mercantile board, expressing reservations about selling the lease, moved to have the proposal reconsidered; except for Donahue all either voted against his motion or "voted blank."

In December, in preparation for the annual meeting the following month, President Foley explained the issue in a letter to the membership: if the lease could be sold for $40,000, then this, plus the sum raised by a special subscription, would allow the Mercantile Library Association to construct a building specifically designed for and controlled by the Association. He neglected to mention where such a building might be located or the estimated cost of construction. At the January meeting the members voted 48 in favor of selling the lease and 1,724 opposed. If the board did not understand the true value of the lease, certainly the members did.

In the summer of 1885, another board tried a different approach: it decided to look into purchasing the College Building for itself. The College Building trustees declined to meet with the Library directors, and this idea faded quickly.

The vision of owning their own building did not die, however. In March 1890 the Library board met with the Library's Real Estate board (a separate entity established to oversee the various properties owned by the Association) to discuss once again the possibility of a new building. This time the members supported the general idea of a new building complete with elevators, toilet rooms, chess rooms, and "all the modern improvements." Yet despite membership support, apparently nothing further came from this initiative. Two years later the board minutes reveal that another attempt was made to "investigate relations of the Library to the College Building." That investigation also led nowhere.

In 1895 and 1896 the vision of a new facility continued to tantalize the directors. Then in 1897 the board sketched out another proposal stating "that the Library Board will convey its interests to any party who will extend the lot to the corner of 4th and Walnut Streets – and erect on same – a suitable building – us[e] of the top floor of such building – $10,000 per annum – with proper service of all kinds secured – the ceiling of the top floor not to be lower than 22 feet." In other words, the Mercantile would be happy to move into a new building on the lot to the south of the present site, if such a building was constructed. Later that year, the board approved another resolution supporting a move to new quarters – of "similar space" – "on the top floor of any building erected on the present site." Clearly something was in the air.

To counter the various rumors about the Association's future, in December 1897 the Mercantile board and the Real Estate managers passed a joint resolution that they made public. In it they assured everyone that the organization was in sound financial health, that the Library's location could "not be improved upon," and that they had no plans to sell their lease. They stated, however, that should the trustees of the Cincinnati College desire to sell, build, or repair the building, "we will meet with them or those to whom they wish to sell fairly.... " The College Building, constructed in 1845 and rebuilt in 1870, occupied increasingly valuable real estate, and new construction technology demanded more efficient use of that space. No doubt Mercantile board members had learned of plans for developing the east side of Walnut Street, and they wanted to assure Association members that they would look after the Library's interests.

For a number of years various Mercantile boards had felt that the College Building quarters were inadequate. In February 1899 the board of directors offered to exchange the lease with the Cincinnati College for a new lease that would retain the same basic conditions but would provide space on the top floor of any new building to be erected by the College trustees. Should the College trustees sell the property, those provisions would extend to the new owner.[25] Whatever the future might bring, the Mercantile Library Association had established its position.

In spring 1900 the Union Central Life Insurance Company considered purchasing the College Building as the site for its planned new structure. The Mercantile directors quickly sent the company their ideas on how the Library's needs should fit into any building scheme. Because these amounted to a rephrasing of the original lease provisions, the Union Central found them unsatisfactory to its interests. John Pattison, president of Union Central, rather bluntly informed the Library directors that "it [would] not be worthwhile to make any further attempts at negotiation." The complications posed by the Mercantile Library lease may have kept Union Central from purchasing the property; eventually the company constructed its new skyscraper along the south side of Fourth Street.

Finally, late in 1901 William Buckner, on behalf of the Thomas Emery's Sons Company, inquired if the Mercantile Library Association would take the top floor of a new twelve-story building being planned for the site. The Emerys needed this assurance before they would purchase the property. The Library directors responded immediately, "inviting a proposition from [Buckner]." The Emery proposal called for the Mercantile Library to occupy the entire top floor, with elevator service. In addition the Emerys would pay for temporary storage of all books and other possessions during construction. The letter also made clear that the Library would be

---

25 This proposition, clearly written by a lawyer, spelled out in considerable detail what the Mercantile Library Association would expect in any new building.

responsible for all moving expenses associated with both vacating the old building and occupying the new one; that the Emerys would not pay for rental of any temporary facilities; and that the Library would have to employ its own elevator operator. To sweeten the offer, the Emerys stated that they would name the structure the Mercantile Library Building.[26]

Because previous boards of directors had outlined what the Mercantile Library expected in any new quarters, the newly elected board found the Emerys' offer unsatisfactory. President John E. Bruce responded to Thomas J. Emery on January 15, 1902, pointing out that many members of the Library preferred the convenience of remaining on the second floor, but that the Association would accept the top floor if extra space on the floor below was included. Furthermore, the board insisted that the Emerys must pay for both removal and storage costs, and that a temporary reading room must be provided as well. The Library could not simply close while construction took place. In an attempt to depersonalize the situation, Bruce concluded by pointing out that the board of directors had a legal responsibility to protect the Library's interests as expressed in its lease.

The Emerys found the president's reply "disappointing." They had hoped that their "accommodating spirit would have been reciprocated." The Emerys suggested that the Library, in which "membership has fallen off largely," would certainly benefit greatly from having its name on the building. Yet, however flattering the use of the name might be, the Library directors were far more concerned about expenses associated

---

26 The correspondence relating to the Emery-Mercantile Library negotiations is housed in the Library archives, shelf box: "Emery Lease & Related Matters," folder: "Originals: Correspondence with Emery Brothers, 1901-1902."

with any move. They dug in their heels.

Negotiations continued, and from this point plans moved forward quickly. By the next summer, the Library membership had ratified an agreement that included continuance of the original lease provisions; rooms on the floor second from the top and certain rooms on the top floor; exclusive use of one elevator, with operating expenses to be paid by the Emerys; and certain provisions concerning ceiling height and utilities. In addition, the Emerys were to pay moving costs and any costs associated with establishing a temporary reading room. In other words, the Emerys eventually conceded on every significant point of contention. Once again, Alphonso Taft's lease had prevailed. Late that summer all of the Library's possessions were moved out, and a temporary reading room was established in the Emery Hotel Annex (now the site of the Carew Tower).

The construction of the Mercantile Library Building was part of a major building boom in Cincinnati, with the corner of Fourth and Walnut as its epicenter. In the first decade of the twentieth century, Cincinnatians watched as almost a dozen new structures pushed skyward, including the First National Bank Building (now the Fourth and Walnut Centre), the Fourth National Bank Building, the eighteen-story Union Trust Building (now the Bartlett Building), the Sinton Hotel (since destroyed), the Textile Building at Fourth and Elm, the German National Bank Building, the Traction Building (now the Tri-State Building), and the Ingalls Building at Fourth and Vine.[27]

In 1904 the Mercantile Library Association proudly opened its new facilities on the eleventh and twelfth floors of the Mercantile Library Building, where they remain today. While a few traditionalists in the Association may have grumbled about taking an elevator to the 11th floor, most of the members enjoyed the increased light from the many windows and the superb view of the river to the south. Although there would be periodic disputes over aspects of the new arrangement, particularly over shelving and the furnishing of the Ladies' Lounge, the Emerys gave ground whenever the Library board threatened legal action.[28]

Six years later, in 1910, the Mercantile Library prepared to celebrate its seventy-fifth anniversary. Upon learning that William Howard Taft, now President of the United States, would be attending the opening of that year's May Festival, the Association directors asked if he would be able to take part in the Association's festivities. In April, word arrived that he would join the Mercantile members at midday on May 3. The board quickly obtained permission to use a second elevator in order to handle the anticipated crowd. Tables and newspaper racks were pushed to the sides of the room, and a speaker's platform was placed in the southwest corner. Plants, donated

27 The First National Bank Building, the Fourth National Bank Building, the Traction Building, and the Union Trust Building were all designed by prominent Chicago architect Daniel Burnham. With the exception of the Textile Building, which is located at Fourth and Elm, all of these structures are within a block and a half of the Mercantile Library Building. Construction must have made for a messy decade for pedestrians trying to navigate through the area. For further information on this construction boom, see John Clubbe, *Cincinnati Observed: Architecture and History* (Columbus: Ohio State University Press, 1992).

28 Some of these disputes involved placement of shelving, an extra room on the eleventh floor, and cash payments tied to the Library's move to temporary quarters when the old building was torn down.

by local florist Julius Baer, added to the festive atmosphere.

President Taft, who arrived in the city by train at 10:25 that morning, was met by Mayor Louis Schwab and was driven immediately to the Pike Street home of his half-brother, Charles P. Taft (now the Taft Museum of Art). From there, Mercantile president Charles Wilby escorted him to the Library.

Taft gave a chatty, humorous talk (what the Enquirer reporter described as a "heart-to-heart neighborly talk") to the some 650 members and guests who amply filled the Reading Room.[29] "When a man comes home," rumbled the good-natured Taft, "he wants to go where he will feel the most at home. I don't know any place which holds the memories of old Cincinnati to me more than the Mercantile library." He recalled how, as a youth, he had enjoyed spending time at the library, but primarily as a place to meet girls. He commented that the staff from those days surely would have had "some secrets which would have made good reading."

After spending a little more than an hour at the Library, the President departed to visit with friends, attend two other receptions in the city, and then conclude his day at the opening concert of the May Festival, where he helped dedicate sculptor Clement Barnhorn's memorial statue to Theodore Thomas. By midnight he was on a train headed for St. Louis.[30]

29 See "Home-Like," unidentified newspaper clipping in Library archives, flat file, drawer #6; Brown, *Brilliance and Balderdash*, 73-76.
30 *Cincinnati Enquirer*, May 4, 1910, 1. Biographer Ishbel Ross, in a presentation to the Friends of the Cincinnati Public Library in 1963, quoted a note from Taft to Miss Nellie Herron (his future wife), written in 1885: "If a young lady whom I know should happen in the Mercantile Library after half past three this afternoon she would find a young man burning to show her the material magnificence of the United States in our city."

*"So long as the Mercantile Library remains
with us we are sure to have the ideals
of an intelligent community."*
MAYOR RUSSELL WILSON, 1935

*"In these degenerate days, we rejoice to buy
any kind of dirt people may like, if only they will
come to us to get it."*
ROBERT L. BLACK SR., *Annual Report*, 1943

CHAPTER 6

The Doldrums

ITH ITS SPACIOUS new rooms, a private elevator, and a magnificent view of the Ohio River, it would appear that the Mercantile Library Association had a great jump on the new century. Instead it entered the doldrums, a long period of listlessness as it struggled to redefine itself. No longer young or particularly mercantile, it had lost its direction, its reason for being. Unable to compete with the rapidly growing public library and no longer a necessary educational institution for young merchants, it had become merely a subscription library without a public face, supported by a loyal but shrinking membership. Despite the glowing confidence that had surfaced at the Association's seventy-fifth anniversary celebration, the people most directly involved with leading the now venerable institution recognized its central problem: without increased membership, financial instability would plague the organization.

As early as 1906 the librarian, who now took on increased executive duties, urged board members to recruit fifty new perpetual memberships as a way to obtain a quick infusion of cash. Whether they attempted that is unknown, but four years later he notified the board that an anonymous donor had offered to give $5,000 to the Association if the Library could secure $10,000 through perpetual memberships. That proved too difficult, however. About that time the board started selling advertising space on the covers that were wrapped around circulating books, a tradition that continues today. That first year the Smith Book Company paid $100, and the telephone company provided free service in exchange for its advertisement.

In 1908 the membership committee devised a plan for increasing the Association's general membership. Its primary suggestion was to "extend the courtesies of the library" to twenty selected people, each for one month, in hopes that this favor would awaken them to the advantages of membership. There is no evidence that any of these "visitors" joined the Library. The board also sent letters of invitation to various business-connected organizations, and in one year each director sent personal letters to people whom he recommended. At Christmas in 1910 advertisements touting the Library's many advantages were distributed through bookstores, with "For a Christmas Present" stamped diagonally in red across the notice. In 1920 former president Charles B. Wilby personally attempted to persuade life members to become perpetual members by paying an extra $50; again, there is no indication that any of these efforts worked. Membership remained stagnant, and annual deficits continued to plague the organization.

In 1913, in an attempt to recapture the spirit of earlier years and attract new members, a committee of ladies served tea at the January election. Because only ninety-two members cast votes, it is unlikely that "the flavor of the old time election"

generated much enthusiasm. If anything, it may have rein-
forced an image of antiquarianism unappreciated by a younger,
progressive-minded generation. A financial crisis loomed. The
newly elected president that year, Thomas C. Powell, sent a
letter to each board member calling for fiscal retrenchment.
He noted ominously that during the past year the organization had run a deficit of almost a $1,000.

Several months later, Librarian Robert M. McCurdy recommended a number of cost-cutting measures including the
reduction of Sunday afternoon and weekday evening hours
and the elimination of one assistant librarian position. This, he
stated, would save a total of $700 per year. After thirty mem-
bers protested the cut in hours, the board relented; the rest of
McCurdy's recommendations were approved. By December,
however, with the budget still bleeding, the board announced
that the Library, but not the Reading Room, would be closed
on Sundays and all evenings.[1] McCurdy, who had proposed
the cutbacks, even offered to have his own salary reduced by
$25 per month, although he did "not urge immediate action on
the last clause." A resolution made at this time to raise annual
dues to $7 also failed. The board feared that such action might
result in a further loss of membership, but McCurdy was given
permission to cancel subscriptions to seveteen magazines and
two newspapers. The following year, four more subscriptions
were dropped.

---

1 The board minutes of June 12, 1913, provide a breakdown of the Association's financial
situation for 1911 and 1912. The bottom line shows a deficit of $2,700 for the two-year
period, which could not be ignored. Thomas C. Powell, a vice-president with the Queen
& Crescent Railroad, pushed for these retrenchment efforts, and in his annual report
for 1914 he proudly announced that income had exceeded expenses for the year. Robert
Black, in his 1943 annual report, referred to Powell as "Napoleonic" in his handling of
the financial issues; see Robert L. Black, "President's Report 1943," 5, in Mercantile
Library Association archives.

Money matters were only one of the Mercantile Library's problems as the new century moved forward. Problems with the Emerys continued. Library members complained about the elevator operator's rudeness, and several refused to use the library "until assured of receiving civil treatment from the employees of the building."

A more serious conflict arose in 1913. After a fire in the Gibson Hotel across the street, representatives of the Emerys presented a plan to extend the building's main stairway from the tenth floor to the twelfth floor as a fire safety improvement. This measure would require removal of the spiral staircase so that the enclosed stairs from the tenth floor could be extended. To compensate the Mercantile Library for the lost space, the area where the elevators now open and the adjacent stairway would become part of the library's main room. Initially the board rejected this proposal, but six months later, in October 1913, it reversed its position. In doing so, however, the directors forwarded to the Emerys a set of conditions, some of which the board expected the Emerys to fulfill as part of the existing lease arrangement. One of these conditions was that all of the work must be done without inconveniencing the Library, an unrealistic request given the need to remove the spiral staircase. The Emerys, confronted by this inflexibility, decided not to make any changes, and the spiral staircase remains a part of the Mercantile's charm.

Dissatisfaction with elevator service surfaced again in 1918. To deal with this and other issues, a special committee was appointed to meet with representatives of the Emerys. The Association's complaints were "constantly being disregarded," grumbled one board member, and the special committee was authorized to take legal action if the situation was not resolved. Because we find no record of a lawsuit, we can assume that the Emerys eventually did respond. If they had a strategy during this period, it seems that it was to ignore and delay, in hopes that nagging issues would go away. But if the Library directors pushed, the Emerys almost always came around.[2]

Even while problems with the Emerys persisted, as well as concerns about membership, the board of directors still had to oversee the general operations of the Association. The board itself also underwent a change. In 1910 board minutes mention a Miss Fanny Field as a new director, the first woman to achieve that position. She attended board meetings irregularly and resigned in 1913, to be replaced by a Miss Fanny E. Turner. Turner also played an insignificant role on the board, and one suspects that male board members viewed both her and Miss Field primarily as token female representatives. That was not the case with the next woman to be elected, Miss Johanna Hochstetter, who took her place on the board in January 1916. She served for twenty-some years and became a strong voice in many areas, even serving as president pro tem for one meeting in 1923. By this time, unlike boards in the previous century, directors were being elected to three-year terms, with one-third standing for reelection each year. As a result, directors often remained on the board for ten years or more, providing some much-needed continuity to the Association.

Staff changes also took place. During the late nineteenth century, the tenures of M. Hazen White and John Newton, plus the long service of Alice McLean and Caroline Gaither, had brought stability and continuity to Library operations.

---

2   I have presented only the Mercantile Library's view of this relationship; various Library boards may well have been responsible for many of the disputes.

With Newton's death in 1897 and the retirements of McLean in 1909 and Gaither in 1912, constant staff changes weakened the Library's operations. In 1904, just in time for the move to the new quarters, the board hired William B. A. Taylor at an annual salary of $1,500. Taylor had spent the previous seven years at the St. Louis Public Library.[3] Less than seven years later he informed the board that the Public Library of New York had offered him $1,800, and he wanted "to go east and look over the ground." The Mercantile Library board matched the New York offer in hopes of keeping him. Apparently Taylor found "the ground" to his liking, however, for the next month, in January 1911, he submitted his resignation.

For a short time Caroline Gaither served as acting librarian without increased compensation, but the extra work may have been too much for the aging assistant because president Charles Wilby, after discussing the situation with several other directors, replaced her with a Miss Boswell, another assistant. By May the board had recruited Robert McCurdy of the University of Illinois to take charge of the organization.

McCurdy lasted just slightly more than four years. Although there is little to indicate why he departed, in July 1915 the board was forced to reprimand him. Apparently on his own initiative, he had opened negotiations for an assistant librarian "from the East." The board of directors saw this as bypassing its authority and instructed him to stop. McCurdy resigned the following month.

Miss Alice Coy, a native Cincinnatian and formerly on the staff of the Cincinnati Public Library, then took the top posi-

3 *Cincinnati Enquirer*, August 13, 1904, 11.

tion, at a salary of $1,200, the first woman hired as librarian.[4]
Coy served just over three years, resigning on January 1, 1919;
virtually nothing is known about her. Caroline Blanton, who
became the new librarian, also remains a shadowy figure. Her
resignation in March 1922, along with that of assistant librarian Miss Buckner, was "accepted with regret." A Mrs. Anna
E. Sechrest next accepted the challenge, with Mrs. Natalie
B. Dohrmann as her assistant. Sechrest was paid $1,500.
Disharmony prevailed, however. Apparently Mrs. Sechrest
lacked interpersonal skills. By May 1924 the situation had
become "an impossible one," and the board notified her that
"her resignation would be accepted." Dohrmann, a native
Tennessean but a resident of Covington, Kentucky, since
1896, then accepted the position at a salary of $1,620; the
increase probably reflected postwar inflation.[5] In 1925 Miss
Isabella Ackerson signed on as an assistant librarian.

These two women, along with Violet G. Williams, managed
the organization's operations for the next forty-four years, but
between John Newton's death in 1897 and Dohrmann's arrival
in 1924, the Mercantile Library Association was directed by
six different head librarians. The longest tenure was the 6½
year period served by Taylor. At the same time, after Caroline
Gaither's retirement in 1912, assistant librarians showed a
steady turnover as well. This revolving door among the staff
certainly contributed to the Library's difficulties during the
first quarter of the new century.

Most members of the Association surely remained unaware
of either the Association's financial struggles or its internal

4   This reduction in salary, since McCurdy had started at $1,500, could have been due to the
    Association's financial difficulties or to less experience on the part of Miss Coy; on the
    other hand, women generally were paid less than men.
5   *Cincinnati Times-Star*, September 10, 1941, 2.

staffing problems. Checking out new books or reading news-papers and magazines remained largely unaffected by such matters, and so the Mercantile drifted into the 1920s. Even the First World War escaped comment in the board minutes with two very revealing exceptions, when emotions briefly trumped the Library board's usual common sense.

In May 1917, just one month after the United States declared war against Germany, the board canceled the subscription to *Der Volksblatt*, one of the city's most important German-language newspapers. The board stated that it no longer wished to give it "room in our files."

Then, three months later, the Enquirer ran an article under the headline "Attorneys Warm Up," which reported a disagreement between attorneys Frank H. Freericks and Charles B. Wilby. In "a circular letter of protest," Freericks had described the Library's cancellation of *Der Volksblatt* as "either an impotent hatred or an assumed right of censorship." Wilby, identified in the paper as secretary of the League Against the Teaching of Foreign Languages in Elementary Schools as well as a member of the Mercantile Library board of directors, retorted: "[T]he action of the board is approved by every loyal American." Wilby went on to point out that earlier in the year Freericks had publicly criticized a meeting held to protest German atrocities in Belgium. Also, at a recent concert at the Grand Opera House, he claimed Freericks had expressed annoyance at the playing of "The Star-Spangled Banner." Freericks responded that *Der Volksblatt* was "a truly loyal American paper and a credit to the city," and that he had never slighted "The Star-Spangled Banner."[6] Five months

---

6 *Cincinnati Enquirer*, August 3, 1917, 7. Frank Freericks had a law office on the 10th floor of the Mercantile Library Building.

after this flap, Thomas Powell moved, seconded by Johanna Hochstetter[7] and no doubt supported by Wilby, that the librarian place on the bulletin board a list of school board candidates who favored eliminating German in the elementary schools.

Other than these two outbursts of anti-German feeling, business as usual prevailed during the war years, although the Library donated unneeded books to the YMCA for use by soldiers stationed at Fort Thomas and permitted the Navy League to place its leaflets in books being checked out. And so the war passed.

The Twenties brought few changes. Board meetings mention the purchase of new equipment (a vacuum cleaner, a typewriter, cuspidors for the Chess Room), the selling of "the old books," periodic discussions about the Chess Club's use of Library space, management of the Association's investments, and the selling of various properties. Indeed, the sale of a piece of property at the corner of Fourth and Broadway to the Queen City Club netted the Mercantile some $16,000, a much-needed financial boost. In 1926 Charles Wilby, five-time president of the Association and a longtime director, worked out an arrangement with the Historical and Philosophical Society of Ohio (now the Cincinnati Historical Society Library) in which that organization would purchase the Mercantile's collection of old Cincinnati newspapers for $3,000. This sum was added to the slowly growing endowment fund.

The critical issues remained unchanged, however. By 1918 membership had fallen almost to five hundred, and it remained well below one thousand for the first part of the next decade.

---

7   Later in 1917 the Hochstetters changed the family name to Hilton.

Periodically the board discussed ways to attract new members. These efforts produced few results; as the secretary reported laconically in 1930, a "good deal of work [was] done" but "not much had been accomplished." In 1928 the board finally raised annual dues from $5 to $7.50 as a way to ease pressure on the budget, but it apparently showed no interest in pushing the Association into a more public role. The only hint of an event for members during the 1920s was a tea held in 1928, served by Mrs. Robert Bonner Bowler "for members, friends, and descendants of founders."[8] The board minutes failed to mention it.

The one constant during the decade was the continuing series of problems with the building's owners, Thomas Emery's Sons, mostly over the air and light easement on the south and east sides of the building. The Mercantile wanted to protect its view of the river, but the Emerys did not wish to jeopardize future development of its adjacent property on the northeast corner of Fourth and Walnut Streets. This tug-of-war lasted from 1925 to at least 1932; usually it was conducted between Robert Black Sr., representing the Library, and Charles J. Livingood, representing the Emerys. In April 1931 an exasperated Black wrote in a memorandum: "Saw Livingood. Urged him to consider lease. He said he would not do so; it had gone so long there was no hurry. He complained of the bitterness of the Library Board and especially [Charles] Wilby

---

8 *Cincinnati Enquirer*, February 26, 1928, n.p., clipping in "Mercantile Library" scrapbook, Cincinnati Historical Society Library, Cincinnati Museum Center. Also see an article titled "Mercantile Library Seeks Friends in Its Distress," *Cincinnati Times-Star*, February 23, 1928, 10; this account indicates that Mrs. Bowler, described as "a fairy godmother," hoped to raise funds to restore the Library's rooms to their former glory. A few years later she gave part of her tea service to the Library.

and [Frederick?] Hinkle.[9] At one point, in January 1932, a frustrated Mercantile board brought up the idea of taking legal action to secure its rights. Eventually lawyers Black and George Hoadley convinced fellow board members that the original lease protected their rights sufficiently and that court action would not help.

In his "President's Report" for 1929, Robert Black summarized the past several years for the Mercantile. He noted that from 1923 to 1927 expenditures had exceeded receipts and that membership had declined slightly. In 1929, however, his first year as president, profits had reached almost $1,700 and the board had been able to increase salaries. Yet he cautioned that salaries "must not be further increased," perhaps in recognition of the early signs of the Great Depression. Black also mentioned proudly that membership had risen to 1,229, and he singled out the special Christmas letter that had "brought in a substantial number of new members.... " Black's basic social conservatism emerged when he expressed the view that "the membership generally is and will, it is hoped, always be recruited from the well-bred and cultured."[10] One wonders what the early members would have thought of that.

In the next decade the ennui of the Twenties continued, aggravated by the Great Depression. Investments suffered, although previous emphasis on blue chip stocks protected the Library from the worst of the financial collapse.[11] Facing an

9   Robert Black, memorandum, April 16, 1931, in Mercantile Library Association archives, shelf box: "Emery Lease & Related Items," folder: "Copies of Correspondence Found in Library Files, 1901-1932."

10 "President's Report," February 20, 1930, in Mercantile Library Association archives, shelf box: "YMMLA (2)," folder: "1930 President's Report."

11 In November 1930 the Mercantile Library treasurer invested $20,000, half in common stocks, half in preferred, in businesses such as Procter & Gamble, The Norfolk and Western Railroad, General Electric, General Motors, American Telephone and Telegraph, United States Steel, and Cincinnati Gas & Electric.

operating deficit of $800 in 1932, the board authorized 10 percent pay cuts for the staff but managed to continue purchasing new books, without which the Library might as well have closed. By 1933, the worst year of the Depression, the economic malaise seems to have invaded board meetings. On three occasions during that year, the minutes simply state, "No quorum." From July through September no meetings were called, apparently because of summer recess. When the board did convene, comments such as "very little business" or "nothing of importance done" illustrate the prostrating effects of those years. A few events of note brightened the decade, however.

In March 1931 President Black announced that Mr. and Mrs. John Galsworthy would soon be in the city, and he proposed that Library members be invited "to meet them at tea."[12] On March 31 about five hundred people—"a brilliant and festive company," stated the *Enquirer's* society reporter—crowded the room. Galsworthy, who had just spoken on some of his favorite English novelists to an audience in the Sinton-St. Nicholas Hotel, joined the friendly gathering around Mrs. Bowler's tea table. Although he did not lecture, the Nobel Laureate talked informally and quite wittily about the differences between British and American humor.[13] To commemorate the occasion, W. H. Howe, vice-president of the American Book Company and the Galsworthys' host in the city, donated to the Association an etching of the distinguished English author.

The Galsworthy visit, so strongly reminiscent of the Mercantile's early lectures, stimulated an interest in promoting

---

12 Galsworthy, a prolific writer, is best known for the series of books titled collectively as *The Forsyte Saga*.

13 *Cincinnati Enquirer*, March 31, 1931, 7; April 1, 1931, 5.

literary events. Just weeks later, Mrs. Dohrmann established a "Poet's Corner" in the library. In December President Black suggested that the Association should invite "literary celebrities," naming author Allen Tate and his wife as possibilities. Three months later, director Shelley Rouse picked up the idea, and Johanna Hilton (formerly Hochstetter) agreed "to be on the alert" for literary men who might be visiting the city.

However, 2½ years passed before the Association sponsored another lecture. In October 1933 Van Wormer Welch of the University of Cincinnati spoke on "Russia."[14] Thirteen months later, Dixie Selden, a local artist and Mercantile Library member, presented her impressions of China and Japan based on a recent trip to Asia. Once again Mrs. Bowler presided over a tea, with the assistance of the "well born and highly educated" Mrs. Dohrmann.[15] Three weeks later Dorothy Thompson (wife of Sinclair Lewis), a prominent journalist and political commentator, chatted informally about the immortality of knowledge.[16]

In 1935 this mini-blossoming of the lecture tradition continued. In January Dr. Frank W. Chandler, former dean of the University of Cincinnati's College of Arts and Sciences, provided a personal look at "Some Novels I Like." He expressed admiration for Pearl Buck's *The Good Earth* and James Hilton's *Good-bye Mr. Chips*. Less to his liking were Stark Young's *So*

---

14 Dale Brown lists Welch in the appendix to *Brilliance and Balderdash*, but the board minutes of October 9, 1933, suggest that this lecture did not take place; see Brown, 158.

15 *Cincinnati Enquirer*, November 18, 1934, Section 5, p. 1. The reporter's comment about Mrs. Dohrmann seemed to express surprise that a librarian might be something other than a bookish spinster.

16 Brown, *Brilliance and Balderdash*, 158. Earlier in the day (December 15, 1934) Thompson had spoken at the Gibson Hotel to the Cincinnati Peace League, describing the Nazi regime in Germany as being supported by those who came of age during the Great War and the turbulent 1920s; see various newspaper clippings in "Scrapbook," compiled by Clara M. Stimson, Mercantile Library archives.

Red the Rose and Thomas Stribling's *Unfinished Cathedral,* both popular "Southern" novels of the era. Tea was not served. Chandler was soon followed by Cincinnatian Miss Helen Hinkle, who spoke on "The Story of the English Churchyard."

By the time Dr. Chandler spoke at the Library, plans were underway for the Association's centennial celebration. On April 2, 1935, the Mercantile president, the Reverend John Malik, presided at a dinner held at the Alms Hotel. Cincinnati Mayor Russell White, who earlier had declared that day Mercantile Library Day, gave the opening address, followed by former Mercantile president Thomas Powell, who delivered a "short and very interesting talk." Next came the four invited speakers: Pulitzer Prize-winning historian Herbert Agar; Seward Collins, editor of the American Review and an early admirer of Hitler; and two members of the Southern Agrarian literary movement, Allen Tate and Andrew Nelson Lytle. All espoused the "new conservatism" that was critical of the New Deal and what they considered the corruption of American values. Several in the audience felt that their general tone was inappropriate for the occasion.[17] Rabbi David Philipson of Hebrew Union College closed the evening.

The 256 members and guests who attended the celebration also enjoyed two surprises. Thomas Powell announced that he had purchased a life membership for his daughter, "commemorating the presentation of one to himself by his father" many years earlier; and Robert Black presented the Association with a miniature portrait of Moses Ranney, a gift from Mrs. John A. Cochran (née Catherine Ranney) of Oklahoma City.[18]

17 *Cincinnati Enquirer*, April 3, 1935, 8. In all likelihood Robert L. Black, who had pushed earlier for a lecture by Allen Tate, arranged for the four speakers.
18 The framed Ranney miniature portrait on ivory hangs in the library and is the only known image of the Association's first president.

Unfortunately, after the excitement faded, the board was left with a deficit of almost $270, which included the cost of Robert Black's short printed history of the Association, the several teas that led up to the dinner, and various expenses associated with the four speakers. This was unwelcome news in the midst of the Great Depression, and the board launched a subscription drive to cover the costs.

This concern over expenses is a reminder that the Mercantile Library continued to struggle with membership decline and budget problems. A year before the centennial celebration, Mrs. Charles Greve, a director, had called for a special meeting of the members to launch a recruiting drive tied to the upcoming event. When only seventeen members showed up, the drive was suspended. Later that year, the board, with an eye to attracting younger people into the Association, created a "junior membership" category available to all high school and college students.

In the summer of 1936, still worried about losing members, the board contacted city manager Clarence A. Dykstra about reserving parking spaces on Walnut Street for members who increasingly were driving into the city and found it difficult to access the Library. There is no record that the city obliged.

Finally, in October 1936, the board took the drastic step of reducing staff. Mrs. Clara Stimson, an assistant librarian for nine years, agreed to work half time for $40 a month. Somewhat later she wrote the board that she would need $50 per month for daytime work, as a lesser amount would not be worth her time and carfare. President Malik interpreted this request to be a demand for a salary increase and wrote Mrs. Stimson a letter that offended her greatly. In her response to the board, she concluded that "a serious fault" lay somewhere in the management of the Library's affairs. Either just before or just after writing this letter, she resigned.[19] The other librarians kept their jobs.

Just when it appeared that the hard times might only grow harder, two bequests eased the Mercantile's financial crisis. Late in 1936, Alice B. (Mrs. Robert) Bowler died and left the Association $1,000, which the board immediately designated for the installation of much-needed new lighting in the stacks. The primary relief, however, came from the Stephen H. Wilder estate.[20] In 1937 Wilder's will left the Library almost $30,000 in securities, with annual dividends of about $3,300, plus real estate for which the board eventually accepted $8,500. With this unexpected infusion of funds the directors restored staff salaries to their previous levels, but now they had to wrestle with an unfamiliar question: what to do with the $12,860 now on hand? Careful investment proved to be the answer; for the next several years the Mercantile Library budget showed sizable net gains.

Even so, stagnant membership levels continued to plague the organization. In 1936, knowing that one way to compete with the public library was by emphasizing personal service, Robert Black Sr. suggested mailing books to members who "were unable or unwilling" to call for them (possibly because of the parking problem). That summer the Library experimented with the idea by offering the service to members who were out of the city for the season. This initial step was such a success that the service soon was made available to everyone

19 CMS [Mrs. Stimson] to Board of Trustees, Young Men's Mercantile Library, December 23, 1936. A copy is held in the Mercantile Library Association archives, shelf box: "Library Histories, Letters, & Awards," folder: "Correspondence."
20 Stephen H. Wilder was a former general manager and part owner of the *Cincinnati Commercial Gazette*.

throughout the year. The Association also worked out a trial arrangement with the Welcome Wagon by which its representatives promoted the Mercantile Library to new residents of the area. The number of members showed little change, however.

In October 1940 an ominous statement appeared in the board minutes: Mrs. Dohrmann was sick again. The previous year the board had granted her a month's paid leave of absence due to illness, but in 1941 her health deteriorated rapidly. She died on September 10 of heart disease. The board quickly appointed first assistant Violet Williams as the Mercantile's next librarian. Williams had been with the Library since 1924 and filled the position very capably.

During these internal changes, war broke out in Europe. Although the United States officially remained neutral until December 8, 1941, there was little question as to where American sympathies lay, and the Mercantile Library reflected the general antifascist attitude. Just as in 1861 and 1917, however, the board minutes say little about the war, although on a few occasions the subject crept into discussions of Association matters. In May 1940 the Library received a pamphlet titled "Polish Acts of Atrocities Against the German Minority in Poland," sent by the German Library of Information in New York City. The directors unanimously refused to accept it, stating that they had "no desire to receive such propaganda." Then, just 10 days before the Japanese attack on Pearl Harbor, the Library shipped several boxes of surplus books to Camp Shelby in Mississippi. At the same time the board resolved to continue membership for members called into military service. In November 1942, one of the darkest periods of the war, the directors extended library privileges to all military personnel in uniform, including WAACs, WAVES, and public health officers.[21]

In his 1943 annual report, outgoing president Robert Black outlined the Association's situation: membership had dwindled to 663, approximately half of the 1929 number, and circulation of books had decreased in "an alarming way." He attributed this not only to the war but also to the poor quality of contemporary literature, to other diversions such as radio and movies, and particularly to the gasoline rationing that discouraged suburban members from driving downtown. Still, Black did not want to end his report on a discouraging tone. He noted that membership had increased slightly over the past year due to "the work of Miss Williams and her staff," and that the Wilder investments kept the annual budget above the red line. "The Library will fight a losing battle as long as the war goes on," he concluded, "but, surviving, it will flourish after its fashion in the years of peace."[22] Indeed, by 1944 the Association's financial picture had brightened enough to allow an increase in staff salaries, a response to wartime inflation, and to introduce much-appreciated Christmas bonuses, a tradition that continues today.

The Mercantile survived the war, although "flourish" would be too strong a word, and the postwar years proved

21 WAAC stood for the Women's Auxiliary Army Corps (later shortened to Women's Army Corps). WAVES, a unit within the United States Navy, stood for Women Accepted for Volunteer Emergency Service.
22 Robert L. Black Sr., "President's Report, 1943" (Cincinnati: Mercantile Library Association, 1944), 6-8.

somewhat dispiriting for the venerable institution.[23] The end of the war brought a new librarian, however. In September 1945, following the death of Violet Williams, long-time assistant Isabelle Ackerson[24] accepted the responsibility of running the organization. She held that position until 1969, having served on the staff for a total of forty-four years. The change in leadership brought little internal change. A succession of Library boards continued to wrestle with recruitment of new members, proper investment of the Library's funds, and the organization's relationship with the Chess Club.

During these years the Association struggled to find an identity. The emergence of television, accelerated suburbanization, and the slow decline of downtown as a retail and entertainment center added to the Library's reputation as a rather quaint institution that appealed to a small number of men and women who enjoyed archaic surroundings and a retiring, somewhat musty atmosphere. In other words, the Library seemed out of step with the times. Most Cincinnatians, in the prosperous decades following the war, embraced glass-and-steel office buildings, chrome-bedecked, high-powered automobiles, suburban split-level houses, and more active forms of entertainment. What was the Mercantile Library to do?

23 The Mercantile Library was not alone in its struggle to survive. In 1944 the Historical and Philosophical Society of Ohio (now part of the Cincinnati Museum Center) brought in Harvard University librarian Keys D. Metcalf to evaluate its operations. One of his suggestions was to merge with the Mercantile Library Association. Nothing came of this, although Robert Black Sr. and Herbert Koch were active in both organizations; see Metcalfe report in Mercantile Library Association archives, box: "Letters, 1940s & 1950s."

24 In a profile published in the *Cincinnati Times-Star*, Ackerson was described as an outstanding golfer, an avid reader, and a person who "has stayed up-to-the-minute in thought, dress, and manners." She lived in the suburb of Wyoming with her mother and a collection of more than two hundred pitchers. See *Cincinnati Times-Star*, October 27, 1945, 7.

Successive boards of directors had few ideas. Indeed, meetings again often failed to draw enough members to reach a quorum, a reflection of a failure of vision. The 1947 board revised the constitution by expanding the board to fifteen members and allowing the directors to select their own officers, but this change did nothing to address the problem of community presence. Most board meeting minutes reflect few ideas and little energy.

An example of this lethargy comes from the humorous pen of Herbert Koch, acting secretary on October 16, 1947, at a lunch meeting reportedly held at 12:15 at the University Club. "In order to preserve for posterity the reputation for promptness on the part of the existing Board of Directors the time of meeting has been set down as that announced in the notice of call," Koch wrote. "As a matter of fact, it was two minutes shy of one o'clock when the last of the necessary quorum had assembled.... The President, having followed the commendable precedent he had set of having libations prior to the luncheon, the problems to be presented were attacked with unusual vigor." Thereupon the board vigorously discussed Saturday evening hours, a change in book cover advertising (from the Central Trust Company to Cincinnati Gas & Electric), possible new board members, and the book-purchasing policy.

The topic of changing book covers ignited a long political discussion, according to Koch, "raising the question of whether, in view of the fact that both banks and public utilities are considered public enemies, this step was one of going from bad to worse or vice-versa. As is so often the case in directors' meetings, this question led to greater and greater digressions, finally involving public ownership, relative merits and demerits of various members of [City] Council, the qualifications of

Albert D. Cash,[25] etc., etc., etc." The president finally pointed out that the change had already been made, and "further discussion was fruitless."

As to potential board members, the discussion included "the personal opinion of the elevator operator concerning certain users of the library... and digressed to the point of elucidating the fact, hitherto unknown to many members of the board, that said elevator operator has a wooden leg, and a further discussion as to whether or not termites had attacked it."[26]

On changing the book-purchasing policy, Joseph Sagmaster remarked that "some of the modern literature was 'pure trash,' whereupon Edgar Pinger, ever the purist in English, raised the question of whether trash could be 'pure.'" The board did not arrive at a conclusion.

Despite Herbert Koch's witty account of the meeting (a welcome relief for any researcher), his minutes reveal both a lack of direction on the board's part and the ease with which minor matters, in a parallel to Gresham's Law, often drove out serious consideration of the Mercantile Library's real problems.[27]

Over the next twenty years, few changes were made in the Library's affairs. Under Ackerson's steady hand, the Library functioned quite well. In addition, the investments from the Wilder endowment and other funds maintained financial stability, but static or declining membership remained a problem.

The Chess Club was another nagging concern. For many

---

25 Albert D. Cash was a member of Cincinnati City Council at this time and became mayor the following year.

26 Since 1922 Bill Riley had operated the special elevator that served the eleventh and twelfth floors. He often returned books for Library members who lacked sufficient time to make the trip up, and occasionally he held packages for women members who were shopping in the area; see *Cincinnati Times-Star*, December 17, 1948, 24.

27 The official minute book includes a second, more sober account of the meeting.

years the club had rented space on the twelfth floor, where its members played chess and held their meetings.[28] A succession of boards complained about the club's failure to pay its rent, and on several occasions they passed motions asking the club to vacate.[29] Presumably, rent money was paid and the club retained use of the space. The association between the Chess Club and the Library did not end until 1967, when the Library decided to lease the twelfth floor space for $1,350 a year.

Board minutes still did not reflect many issues of note during these years. In 1949, however, Dr. David Philipson died. Philipson, the Reform Jewish rabbi of the K. K. Bene Israel congregation, had served on the Library board for 39 years. To replace him, President Webb Hill suggested "young Bob Black" (Robert L. Black Jr.), who Hill said might "come up with some new ideas as how to attract new young members to the library."[30] Black was duly elected, and on November 17, 1949, his father swore him in, a father-son first for the Library. In 1954 the board explored the idea of selling off valuable books. W. Russell Warner undertook the task of identifying salable volumes, but the minutes do not mention whether any books were sold.[31] The following year, an Employees Benefit

---

28 For example, see Robert L. Black Sr., "President's Report" for 1929, in which he stated that the Chess Club "remains more or less on sufferance."

29 In the 1950s alone, Mercantile Library boards discussed the problem of the Chess Club in 1951, 1952, 1956, 1957, and 1958. They rehashed the relationship in 1964 and 1965; the latter discussion led to the wry comment in the minutes that "The Chess Club status continues a mystery." Much of the correspondence between the Library and the Chess Club may be found in Mercantile Library Association archives, shelf box: "Miscellaneous" folder: "Chess Club."

30 Indeed, just three months after becoming a director, Robert Black Jr. proposed placing "placards in strategic locations throughout the City" in order to secure new members. This was done (Procter & Gamble and the Fifth Third Union Trust Co. were two of the locations). Although there is no record that this succeeded as a recruitment device, at least "young Bob," like his father, brought some energy to the board of directors.

31 The only financial record remaining from that period is a cash journal, and it shows no record of any sale; see Cash Journal #7 in Mercantile Library Association archives.

Subscription was established as a memorial to longtime board member Edgar E. Pinger. The fund got off to a slow start, so in 1956 the board committed itself to paying $50 a month into the fund from the operating budget.

At about the same time, the board held a lengthy discussion on the installation of alternating electrical current. The Library was the only floor in the building still using direct current, and the Emery Estates, the building's owner, wanted to know how much the Library would contribute to the estimated $2,200 cost of conversion. When Clark Wilby pointed out that the Emerys were not obligated to pay any of the cost, the board dropped the whole idea.

As usual, money remained the Association's most pressing concern. In 1955 the board sent the members a questionnaire to gather information about library services, as well as about raising annual dues. Most of the members expressed few complaints about Library services and even mildly supported an increase in annual dues to $10. The board also began advertising for new members in the *Cincinnati Enquirer's* Sunday book section and considered the possibility of advertising on "streetcars and buses."[32]

An unanticipated problem also emerged at this time. Isabelle Ackerson lost sight in one eye and suffered partial damage to the other. Although she returned from her leave of absence and remained at her post until 1969, it became clear that none of the present assistants, mostly part-time, were prepared to take on the librarian's responsibilities. The board then advertised for a full-time assistant who could be trained to replace Miss Ackerson when that became necessary. Only one person

---

32 By December 1955, when this was discussed, trolley cars and buses had largely replaced streetcars.

responded and she considered the salary of $2,700 too low. (That equals about $25,000 today.) There is no record that the position was filled.

At last, in March 1957, the board of directors held a long meeting to discuss the Library's future. The board secretary described it as "one of the most informative and beneficial meetings... in the past twenty years"; informative and beneficial it may have been, but unfortunately the minutes tell almost nothing about what was discussed. The only apparent immediate result was the establishment of a committee for the "Promotion and Development of the Library," chaired by Edward B. Evans. Most important, however, the meeting suggests a much-needed sense of urgency on the part of the board.

Whether or not as a direct result of this meeting, several initiatives for recruiting new members surfaced during the next few years. Early in 1958 the Library inaugurated a newsletter that included book reviews, to be sent three or four times a year to members, in the hope that this would "stimulate greater activity." A book prize to members (not to exceed $5) was re-introduced as an inducement to bring in new members. Despite these admittedly modest efforts, membership again slid towards the five hundred mark.

At this time the Emery Memorial Fund inquired about purchasing the Mercantile's ten thousand-year lease. The board decided to have the lease evaluated and also considered the possibility of transferring the lease to another conveniently located Emery property. In February 1959 the board met with several Emery Fund trustees. They took the opportunity to introduce the idea of the Library's giving up some of its space at the south end of the eleventh floor, a not-so-subtle attempt to gain control of the light and air rights on that side. Nothing resulted from this meeting.

In 1960 the Mercantile Library Association celebrated its 125th anniversary, a low-key affair highlighted by the establishment of a collection of pictures of past presidents. Clark Wilby had secured images for all but four of the presidents since 1900, and other board members promised to help locate images of the pre-1900 group. This collection, kept up to date, now watches over the spiral staircase, encouraging brave users to watch their step.

The Library's difficulties continued in the 1960s. Two serious problems emerged, both linked to finances. The first of these involved a major refurbishing of the rooms, including, finally, conversion of the electrical system from direct current to alternating current, refinishing the floors, and repairing and painting the plaster walls. Although most of the expense was met by a subscription drive among members, the annual budget was needed to cover almost $1,500 of the total.

When all the work was completed, the Library held an open house in May 1964 in hopes of remedying the second problem, a shortage of members. This effort failed. That year dues-paying membership declined to 362, the lowest level in well over a century. The following year, the board again explored possible ways to increase membership. Suggestions included establishing junior memberships, allowing installment payment for dues, emphasizing the Library's historical interest, following "Mr. Vitz's suggestion,"[33] and advertising in newspapers.

Other expenses threatened to drive the budget into the red. The board raised salaries in 1961 and made Blue Cross membership available to the staff. Also, the staff pension fund

---

33 Although the suggestion was not explained, the Vitz in question was probably Carl Vitz, former librarian of the Public Library of Cincinnati and Hamilton County.

remained so inadequate that the directors had to double the contribution to the fund from the annual budget, from $50 to $100 per month. An increase in annual dues from $10 to $15 helped somewhat, but the real problem was membership, which remained stagnant. In February 1962 William F. Dohrmann proposed to the board that they sell the lease to the Emery interests before the Mercantile was forced to negotiate at a disadvantage.[34] This idea failed to gain support. Three years later, however, John H. Clippinger, on behalf of the Emery Memorial Trust, queried Robert Black Jr. about purchasing the lease. The Mercantile responded that it had "no intention of surrendering the lease" nor of vacating the premises.[35]

Behind all of this maneuvering was a plan by the Federal Reserve Bank to build on the space immediately to the south of the Library and to obtain the Mercantile building site for future expansion. In a letter to Library president Walter H. Alexander, Black expressed some concern that the city might condemn the Mercantile Library Building, now almost sixty years old, in order to open the way for the Federal Reserve Bank.

Eventually the Federal Reserve chose to build a block away, but the pressure on the Library continued. The Emery trustees, who owned the Fourth and Walnut property, the area just south of the Library, proposed that the Mercantile Library Association move to Lytle Park and share a nineteenth-century house with the Emery Memorial Trust office and the

---

34 William F. Dohrmann to Board of Directors, February 15, 1962, in Mercantile Library Association board minutes, February 20, 1962.

35 Robert L. Black Jr. to John H. Clippinger, April 23, 1965, in Mercantile Library Association archives, shelf box: "Miscellaneous," folder: "Miscellaneous Correspondence."

recently established Miami Purchase Association.[36] Such a move would have reduced the Library's space and would have taken it to the outer edge of the downtown area; the proposal met with no enthusiasm from the Mercantile board. With the Federal Reserve out of the picture, however, the struggle now became a matter of the light and air rights, particularly on the south side of the Library building.

In December 1965 the city notified the Mercantile Library that it had condemned the property adjoining the library on the south, and talk soon surfaced that an eleven-story building was planned for the site. The board hired attorney Hawley Todd to defend the Association's light and air rights. It also arranged for an appraisal of the famous lease in order to set a value on those rights. In 1969, unable to block construction of the new building, after lengthy litigation, the Mercantile Library Association finally accepted $24,000 from the Emery Trust in exchange for giving up its light and air easement.[37] With that step, forty-plus years of quarreling came to an end. As a result, the Library lost its view of the Ohio River, and the windows on the south end of the Reading Room were closed off. The two stained-glass windows went into temporary storage, from which they were later sold at auction (but not by the Library; see Chapter 8). As for the air and light situation to the east of the Library, the directors received assurance that any new building erected there would not extend above the

---

36 The Emery people planned either to move a house from Mount Auburn, possibly the Gorham Worth house, or to reconstruct one that was "in Mr. Fleischmann's basement"; see Black to Alexander, April 30, 1965, in Mercantile Library Association archives, shelf box: "Miscellaneous," folder: "Miscellaneous Correspondence."

37 During the negotiations, the Emery Trust had offered the Library $20,000, but the Library wanted $25,000. Judge Gilbert Bettman pushed for a settlement of $24,000, and both sides eventually accepted that amount. Details may be found in Mercantile Library Association archives, shelf box: "Miscellaneous;" folder: "Miscellaneous Correspondence."

10th-floor ceiling of the Mercantile Library Building.

The 1960s ended on a sad note. In 1966 both Isabelle Ackerson and her primary assistant, Margaret Sebastiani, suffered bad falls, a foreshadowing of things to come. A year later Sebastiani, who had never fully recovered, retired after twenty-seven years with the Mercantile. She died in 1968. Then, in early 1969, two other assistants, Mrs. Culbertson and Mrs. Sagmaster, announced their resignations; both cited age and health issues.

By this time the board was already seeking a replacement for the aging Ackerson. In January 1969 they interviewed Jean Springer, then working at the Cincinnati Science Center. They offered her a position as assistant librarian at a salary of $8,000, with the idea that in three or four months she would be ready to replace Ackerson. Springer began work on April 1, 1969; two weeks later Ackerson informed President Alexander that her physician had "ordered" her to retire. A grateful board voted to provide her with a pension of one-half her salary for the rest of her life. They planned a testimonial luncheon as well, but she declined that honor. Ackerson also received a life membership to the Library and a "gold, double bar pin."

Springer suddenly found herself librarian and executive director of the Mercantile Library. Soon she would take the Association in new directions.

*"Old and distinguished we are, but backward
and dusty we're not."*
Jean Springer, 1975

---

*"It is my goal to carry on the remarkable tradition
of service Jean Springer has set."*
Albert Pyle, 1993

CHAPTER 7

Finding Its Voice: The Springer Years

J EAN SPRINGER brought much-needed energy and a welcome breath of fresh air into the Mercantile Library. A native of Long Island, she served as a WASP[1] during the Second World War, ferrying newly built aircraft from manufacturing plants to U.S. Army airfields. Shortly after the war's end she moved to Cincinnati with her first husband. Never one to sit still, she worked in public relations with the Cincinnati Symphony Orchestra for much of the 1960s, and then spent several years as assistant to the director of the Cincinnati Science Center.

When the Mercantile Library began searching in 1969 for someone to replace Isabelle Ackerson, board member Harry Whittaker recommended Jean Springer, a friend of his, who was not comfortable in the world of science. The result was one of those unforeseen but mutually beneficial relationships: Jean Springer managed the Mercantile for the next twenty-four years.[2]

When Springer accepted the position, President Walter

1 See *The Downtowner*, May 23, 1995, 5; WASP stood for Women Airforce Service Pilots.
2 Author's interview with Jean Springer, June 26, 2009.

Alexander made it clear that he wanted her to reinvigorate the Library.[3] That she did. Forty years later, with a mind still sharp for anecdotal detail, she recalled her first impressions of the board and the staff. She liked to say, with understandable exaggeration, that the Library had only ninety members and they were all over ninety, and that the board was a sort of "old men's club." Miss Ackerson appeared to her as "forbidding"; a person who often somewhat sternly asked members who approached her, "What do you want?" The two assistant librarians, a Miss Margaret Bolger and a Mrs. Veirs Scallan, seemed fussy and officiously protective. Bolger sometimes placed "salty books" under the counter, telling inquiring members that they were checked out. To Springer the Library seemed old-fashioned and unwelcoming; even the spiral staircase now led nowhere.[4] Springer began the process of recruiting younger replacements to the staff, beginning with Mary Jo Cannon. She also encouraged the directors to recruit younger, more civic-minded men and women to the board, and within a few years Peter Strauss, Hope Taft, Thomas Huenefeld, and others brought their own brand of enthusiasm to board meetings.[5] The Springer years were under way.

Although the board had instituted a membership drive in 1968, the year before Springer's arrival, like most of its pre-

---

3 Some sense of the Mercantile Library's drowsy atmosphere can be found in Jeanne Powell, "Mood of Mercantile Is Serene," *Cincinnati Enquirer for Women*, November 16, 1969, 1.
4 Springer interview.
5 Strauss and Taft went on to become board presidents; Huenefeld chaired several important committees during his long tenure on the board.

decessors, it had achieved very limited success.[6] According to board minutes, the number of active members in December 1969, when Springer became executive director, was just over four hundred.[7]

Among her first actions, Springer sought funding from the Ford Foundation to support a lecture series involving young authors. The Foundation rejected this request, but the new executive director was not discouraged. Drawing on her public relations skills, she entertained representatives of the news media at the Library, and followed that step with the first in a series of informal "Literary Lunch" programs at which current issues were discussed. With the help of Harry Whittaker she engaged William "Foss" Hopkins, a prominent local criminal attorney and author of *Murder Is My Business*, to speak on the benefits that would accrue from a city curfew.[8] More than two hundred members and guests attended "the hearty sandwich luncheon," and with that the Mercantile Library was back in the lecture game.

Springer also explored other ways to enliven the Library's activities. As a way of exposing potential new members to the Library, she suggested hosting chamber music recitals and encouraging other cultural organizations to use the facilities

---

6 The campaign included the distribution of a brochure in downtown office buildings, an extensive mailing by the women's committee, a flattering article in the *Cincinnati Enquirer*, and an open house for prospective members. A telling indicator of the Association's near-moribund state was the board's failure to secure quorums at its meetings in January, February, and March of 1968. This situation encouraged Whittaker, and no doubt several others on the board, to seek a different type of executive director/librarian.

7 Although Mercantile Library membership figures can be confusing, even contradictory, when possible I have relied on the numbers given in annual reports or board minutes.

8 *Cincinnati Enquirer*, April 8, 1970, 10. According to this account, Hopkins stated that a curfew would reduce crime in the city by fifty percent; three hundred new beat patrolmen by another twenty-five percent; and improved lighting by ten percent more. The remaining 15 percent, he argued, represented psychopaths.

for various functions. Also, very early in her tenure, she set out to change the atmosphere in the Reading Room. She wanted the Mercantile to be warm and inviting, not to be regarded as a musty private English club. Old World dignity was fine, but something more was needed. Springer encouraged members to bring their lunches into the Reading Room (although she reminded them to sweep up any crumbs), and encouraged the staff to learn and use members' first names. Remaking the Library's image included several cosmetic improvements, and by the end of Springer's first year floors had been waxed, new window shades installed, an IBM Selectric typewriter purchased (much to the delight of the staff), and a window air conditioner installed in the Ladies' Lounge. She mailed out quarterly a list of new acquisitions; in his annual report for 1970, president John A. Benjamin commented on the list's enthusiastic reception. These seemingly small changes helped push membership to 472 by the end of the year.

This flurry of activity, however, did not change the Library's underlying financial picture. The pressure of rising costs had left a deficit of about $10,000 in 1970, and the board searched for new sources of income. The directors created two new tax-deductible classes of contributors: the Lamplighters ($100-$249) and the Patrons ($250 and up), while a women's committee helped by raising over $3,500 through a subscription. In April 1971 Irving Stone, author of several popular biographies, spoke at a luncheon on "Passions of the Mind," his perspective of Sigmund Freud. Yet this addition to the expanding lecture programs netted only a modest $156 for the Mercantile.

In October 1971 the Mercantile ventured into unexplored waters: it held its first ever public book sale. Needing more room on the shelves as well as more revenue, Springer and the Young Men's Wing (soon to be known simply as the Young Wing) of the organization came up with the idea of a two-day sale on Fountain Square. First, however, members would have an opportunity to purchase books at a "Sherry Hour Preview" in the Library's Reading Room.

"Generations of Books," as the sale was titled, drew an excited crowd to the eleventh floor. In an atmosphere something like Filene's basement, hundreds of members and their guests milled around the makeshift bricks-and-boards shelving in search of bargains. Items were priced from 10¢ to $1. Eleanor Adams, in the *Enquirer's* "In Society" column, sprinkled her account with the names of many of the city's most prominent citizens.[9] The three-day event, squeezed in just before the one hundredth-anniversary rededication of the Tyler Davidson Fountain, removed more than five thousand books from the Library's cramped shelves and raised over $1,000 for the operating budget.[10]

Financial pressures continued, however. Almost from her first day at the Library, Jean Springer had urged the board to install central air conditioning but had met strong resistance. Eventually the board decided to explore alternatives such as installing several window units and adding floor fans, but at last the city's summer humidity and the increasing annoyance of pigeons roosting on the windowsills overcame the board's reluctance towards modernization.[11] To cover the projected

9 *Cincinnati Enquirer*, October 14, 1971, 19, 45. The idea of selling books on Fountain Square was then adopted by the Friends of the Public Library. Their sale is now an annual event held in the atrium of the Public Library's main location during the first week in June.

10 *Cincinnati Enquirer*, October 16, 1971, 1.

11 Springer interview.

$21,000 cost, the indefatigable Robert Hilton headed a campaign to raise $40,000, which would pay for installation, future maintenance, and some additional refurbishing of the rooms. The directors pledged the first $10,000.[12] On July 27, 1972 the Mercantile gave an "Air Conditioning Party" to celebrate the installation of the new system, and some eighty-two new members were feted as the guests of honor. Sangria mixed by Nick Niehoff and served in pitchers enhanced the celebration.[13]

In the meantime, Springer continued to expand the Library's activities. She arranged for a special private screening of the soon-to-be-released "Slaughterhouse-Five," which drew a full house to the Studio Cinema on East Seventh Street. Then she instituted a series of evening bridge parties, with local expert Manny Isralsky providing tips.

The author luncheons continued as well. In 1972 Garson Kanin, actor, director, playwright, and author of *Tracy and Hepburn*, entertained members and guests, followed in 1973 by David Halberstam, a Pulitzer Prize winner for his coverage of the Vietnam war and author of the 1972 bestseller *The Best and the Brightest*. Halberstam's talk drew 275 people; almost 150 others were turned away. Local authors Stephen Birmingham and Polk Laffoon IV followed.

Springer also decided to move beyond traditional writers. She invited choreographer Agnes de Mille for that May, but de Mille was "unavailable." Undiscouraged, Springer then

---

12 Hilton, a member of the Library's board of directors, was the nephew of former longtime director Johanna Hilton and always a good friend of the Mercantile. The campaign reached its goal in 1974, aided greatly by a $10,000 gift from Mr. and Mrs. Louis Nippert.

13 See Mercantile Library Association archives, box: "Miscellaneous," folder: "Air Conditioning Party." Nick Niehoff, then president of the Cincinnati Stock Exchange, was a brother of future Mercantile president, H. C. Buck Niehoff.

sought to bring Gina Lollobrigida to the Library for a program in connection with her recent book *Italia Mia*. Unfortunately, negotiations broke off when it was discovered that the sultry Italian actress "had either never heard, or didn't want to hear, of Cincinnati." As the board secretary noted wryly, "Regrets were expressed by male directors." The minutes do not mention how the female directors responded.

In 1975, in conjunction with the University of Cincinnati, Springer organized the "Lecture While You Lunch" series. Various University faculty members presented their favorite topics; in 1976 Warren Bennis, the University president, participated.[14]

About this same time, the Mercantile organized the first of a series of excursions to interesting cities. In October 1977, thirty members and friends, led by Springer, spent an "enormously successful" four days in Washington, D.C., attending a performance of "A Chorus Line" at the Kennedy Center, visiting the Library of Congress, and in general having a wonderful time. The trip also brought in $440 for the Library. The following year, a group traveled to Toronto, with side trips to Niagara Falls and to Stratford for some Shakespeare. In 1979 Springer planned a trip to Great Britain, but that proved overly ambitious and had to be canceled. Instead the group visited Montreal.

These fund-raising travel adventures went on for almost twenty years, almost always led by the affable Mrs. Springer. Boston, New York, Philadelphia, Chicago, and New Orleans

---

14 Among the first topics were "Why Do We Believe?," "What Mao Is Up To Now," "Anxiety Is Nothing New: From Epicurus to Rabbi Liebman," and "Play It As It Lies: A Trend in American Fiction."

all made her selection list.[15] In 1985, the Library's one hundred fiftieth anniversary year, England proved more attractive than in 1979, and four years later Library members went to Ireland. In subsequent years Mexico, France, Czechoslovakia, Italy, and Turkey all proved popular destinations, but then problems emerged. In 1994, the year after Springer's retirement, no trip was planned, and in the following year plans for Chicago had to be canceled because of low enrollment. Then, in 1996, a return trip to England failed to gain enough support. Perhaps the program had been tied too closely to Springer, or interest in travel among a core group may have run its course. Whatever the reason, the Mercantile turned to other ways to raise money.

Along with these annual trips, the Library continued to emphasize its lectures. In 1977 Springer scored a coup. Pushed by a "ruthless board member" to contact Julie Harris, she eventually reached the Broadway actress's New York agent. She made her pitch, but was somewhat discouraged by the agent's seemingly unenthusiastic response. Several weeks later, while Springer was eating a bologna sandwich in the Library, the phone rang. Julie Harris herself was on the line. "What do you mean by a 'reading'?" she asked.[16]

On March 11 Harris, in town for a professional engagement as Emily Dickinson in "The Belle of Amherst," mesmerized a capacity Mercantile lunch crowd of three hundred fifty with a presentation based on her Tony-winning role as Mary Todd Lincoln.[17] The Wheel Cafe, a longtime fixture on Vine Street,

---

15 Often these trips became regional visits. For example, the Philadelphia excursion included visits to the Winterthur Museum, Longwood Gardens, and the Brandywine Museum.

16 Springer interview.

17 Harris returned to the Mercantile in late October 1979 for another equally successful appearance. By that time, she and Jean Springer had developed a warm relationship.

handled the catering, and the Library netted $1,850.

By contacting publishers or agents directly, Springer often engaged lecturers who were already coming to Cincinnati on tour, thereby reducing the cost to the Mercantile. In 1979 she landed Sloan Wilson, author of *The Man in the Gray Flannel Suit*, in this way, but overtures to Joseph Heller (*Catch-22*) and to Supreme Court Justice Arthur Goldberg met with "regrets."

Springer also arranged more programs for the general public. In rapid succession the Library hosted a six-week writing workshop led by Stephen Birmingham, a short story contest with the winning entry to be published in *Cincinnati Magazine*,[18] and a series of courses on literature presented by Professor Thomas L. Siebert of The College of Mount Saint Joseph. In 1980 the board used the Library's one hundred forty-fifth birthday as an opportunity to showcase the institution. Calling the occasion the Mercantile's "very first Birthday Party, at least as far as our records show," the directors and staff mapped out an evening that included cocktails, a buffet dinner, an auction of library-oriented items, music by the Queen City Brass ("proficient in everything from classical to rag"), and a multitiered cake, with dancing at the end.[19] Although attendance proved rather disappointing, the cel-

---

18 The first short story contest, which drew more than 125 entries, also included a $350 prize for the winning story and was underwritten by Robert H. Allen, a director and future president of the Mercantile. Local author Stephen Birmingham; Patrick O'Connor, editor of *Cincinnati Magazine;* John Brady, editor of *Writer's Digest;* and Professor James K. Robinson of the University of Cincinnati's Department of English served as judges. In 1980 or 1981 the contest was dropped but was revived in 1989. Over time, two winners of the contest, John Wessel in 1994 and Jack Kerley in 2003, signed handsome book contracts with publishing houses.

19 *Cincinnati Enquirer*, March 31, 1980, C: 3; also see Mercantile Library Association archives, box: "Founders Day & Annual Meeting," folder: "Mercantile Birthday – 145 Years."

ebration netted more than $7,000.

The 1970s were not all lectures, parties, and travel, however. The Library continued to face problems, many very familiar. In 1974, just as the financial picture began to brighten, Fleischmann Enterprises, the building's new owner, notified the board that the Library was liable for about $13,000 of the projected cost to bring the main staircase within the fire code. Peter J. Strauss, one of the newer, younger members of the board, challenged the assessment in a letter to John J. Kelley Jr. of Fleischmann Enterprises. As in previous conflicts, Strauss cited the 1849 lease and the 1902 agreement with the Emery brothers. That June, the Fleischmann organization threatened legal action and the Mercantile board prepared for lengthy litigation.

Then, in August, the landlord unveiled plans to wall off the service elevator from eleventh-floor access. The board instructed Strauss again to call Fleischmann Enterprises' attention to the 1902 agreement, and in October the Fleischmanns abandoned the plan to block the elevator. They still wanted the $13,000, however, but that suit was eventually dropped.[20] Another lawsuit involving the air and light easement on the east side of the building was decided in a way "almost wholly favorable to the Library," resulting in a settlement of $1,500 for the Mercantile.

While Strauss and other attorneys on the board steered the Mercantile through dangerous legal waters, other directors, with the Library's annual expenses still greater than income, searched for new sources of revenue. Salary increases, maintenance costs, utility rates, book purchases, legal fees, and

20 I have presented the conflict from the Mercantile Library's point of view; probably the records of Fleischmann Enterprises would provide a different perspective.

needs for new equipment all increased during that inflation-ary decade, and the Library was hard-pressed to gain control of its budget.

Navigating between rising costs and the need for additional programs, Springer and the board explored numerous possi-bilities. The Library continued to promote its trips to cities around the world, adding a built-in $100 contribution to the overall cost. In 1983, in cooperation with the Taft Museum and the Contemporary Arts Center, the Mercantile cosponsored the "Cultural Chow Line," a progressive evening of food and art that concluded with dessert and dancing at the Library. This proved a "roaring success," especially for younger members and their guests, and was repeated for a number of years.[21] The Young Wing chipped in with monthly dinners, often accompanied by a film and discussion. Then, in 1985, the engaging courses started by Professor Siebert were resumed by Jonathan Kamholtz of the University of Cincinnati. His popular exploration of literary themes remains a staple of the Mercantile's annual programs.

In the midst of all this new activity, the Mercantile suffered a blow to its institutional pride. Throughout the nineteenth century, boards had confronted numerous cases of theft and vandalism (rarely with much success), but by the early twenti-eth century those acts had all but ceased. Then, in 1973, after some suspicious behavior on the part of a teenager who fre-

---

21 Hope Taft and the Young Wing of the Library had pushed for this event. A typical Cultural Chow Line included hors d'oeuvres at the Taft Museum, a first course in the lobby of the Atrium II building, and the main course at the Contemporary Arts Center (then on Fifth Street), with the evening ending at the Mercantile. A local band, fre-quently "The Four Hubcaps," provided the dance music. At each stop attendees could enjoy some type of art exhibit. Among the younger members who enjoyed the Cultural Chow Line was H. C. Buck Niehoff, who later served as president of the organization and established the Niehoff Lecture Series; author's interview with Buck Niehoff, October 27, 2009.

quented the Reading Room, Jean Springer discovered that the Library was missing almost two hundred volumes, all pertaining to Cincinnati or Ohio history. Once the staff was alerted, the culprit was soon caught and turned over to the police. Embarrassingly, he was a Timothy Crane Day scholar, who had impressed the Library staff with the amount of time he spent in the Reading Room. Although authorities recovered most of books, the permanent volumes missing included Daniel Drake's *Natural and Statistical View, or, Picture of Cincinnati and the Miami Country* (Cincinnati: Looker and Wallace, 1815), B. Drake and E. D. Mansfield's *Cincinnati in 1826* (Cincinnati: Morgan, Lodge, and Fisher, 1827), and about a dozen early Cincinnati city directories. The missing books were appraised at just over $2,500. The teenager was convicted in juvenile court, fined $10 and court costs, ordered to attend school, and banned from the Mercantile for one year.[22] Given the genteel nature of the Mercantile and the Association's pride in its Day Scholars program, the theft weighed heavily on their spirits.

Book thievery aside, the increase in programs brought in new members. By late 1981 active memberships had climbed to about 650; two years later the number approached 700. Revenue increased as well. In 1980 and 1982 the treasurer proudly reported that the Mercantile had achieved annual net gains of several thousand dollars, and in 1983 a proposal to the Gannett Foundation resulted in a $3,000 grant to help pay for a word processor. The Mercantile had entered the computer age! The next year, another grant proposal, this time to the Reakirt Foundation, brought in $5,000.

Unfortunately the operating budget still showed a deficit

22 Mercantile Library Association archives, box: "YMMLA (2)," file: "Rogers, Marshall–Book Theft."

of almost $10,000 at the end of 1984. This cast a shadow over plans to celebrate the Library's 150th anniversary, scheduled for 1985. All through 1984 the board and staff had been discussing ideas for the Library's sesquicentennial. Eventually the plans called for a Mercantile Library Day to be held on Fountain Square, with Mayor Charlie Luken proclaiming the week of April 15 as Mercantile Library Week. Other plans called for downtown banners advertising the celebration, a cocktail party sponsored by the Young Wing, and a dinner at $150 per couple. The capstone would be a lecture by a major literary figure.

Robert Hilton recommended that the dinner be a black tie affair, arguing mischievously that it would give more meaning to the event, that it would be more compatible with the Library's storied past, and that the participants would become the decorations, thus saving on expenses. The board agreed. Hilton also headed a fund drive to be tied to the milestone date, this time with a goal of $150,000. He had hoped to find a symbolic 150-year-old to serve as honorary chairperson, he informed the board, but had "to settle" for Mary Louise Burton, "a mere 100 year old."[23]

The 150th anniversary celebration proved very successful. As Molly Whittaker, wife of Harry Whittaker and a fourth-generation member, said to a reporter, she hoped the week of activities would "forever shed (the Library's) 'stuffy and elitist' image."[24] On Monday the mayor issued his proclamation, while banners hanging from the downtown streetlights informed the public of the milestone event. On Tuesday, 280

---

23 Unfortunately Mary Louise Burton died the next year, but she left a $5,000 bequest to the Mercantile.
24 Alice Hornbaker, "A Booklover's Hideaway," *Cincinnati Enquirer*, April 14, 1985, F:1.

people turned out for the cocktail party at the Library; the special guest was Jonathan Valin, a local writer of detective stories. The festive week culminated with the dinner, where Nobel Laureate Saul Bellow provided the literary punch. As a result of the festivities, the Mercantile gained enormous public exposure, leading to more than 200 new members, and Bellow's appearance enhanced its reputation as a literary center. The "stuffy and elitist" image was gone forever.[25]

More importantly, the sesquicentennial led to two important results. First, the anniversary fund eventually reached its goal, for which the board at the annual meeting in 1988 presented Bob Hilton with a leather wing chair and ottoman. Hilton responded (rather typically) "It was the first modern thing [I have] seen in the Library in 35 years."

Second, while the anniversary fund drive helped compensate for the sudden drop in the stock market in October 1987, the inauguration of the Niehoff Lecture Series provided the Library with its signature event. Buck Niehoff, whose mother was a member, had been searching for an organization that would provide literary stimulation, both for himself and for the city as a whole. (He briefly describes his and his wife Patricia's somewhat unusual path to literary patronage in his charming book *Something Funny at the Library*, published by the Mercantile in 2004.)

Although Niehoff had found Saul Bellow's talk almost incomprehensible, he said he was "enthralled by the literary

---

25 Except in the local press: two years later, when comedian Jonathan Winters spoke at the first Niehoff lecture, *Enquirer* reporter Jim DeBrosse described the Reading Room as a place of "over-stuffed leather chairs, musty books, and fine old wood." See *Cincinnati Enquirer*, April 30, 1987, E:1. Even as late as 1993, the headline on David Wecker's column about Springer's retirement read: "Retiree will miss musty library." See *Cincinnati Post*, November 25, 1993, clipping in Mercantile Library archives, box: "Newspaper Clippings," folder: "Newspaper Clippings, 1990-1996."

wind that blew through [his] convoluted sentences, and the accompanying dinner with friends in the library was my idea of a special occasion."[26] He and Patricia mulled over how they might respond to this, and some months later Buck met with Mercantile president Douglas Cole, director Robert Allen, and Jean Springer at the Maisonette, the city's five-star restaurant. Niehoff proposed to annually underwrite a major speaker to be part of a black tie dinner, open to the public, with the idea that this would become the Library's major fund-raising event.[27] Springer was enthusiastic; Cole and Allen "were intrigued but seemed dubious," especially when Niehoff said he wanted comedian Jonathan Winters, a genius of improvisation, to be the first speaker. Although some people wanted to restrict attendance to Mercantile Library members, Niehoff insisted that the lecture be open as a way of increasing the Library's public exposure and attracting new members.[28]

Buck, though a lawyer by training, and Patricia had a long-standing personal interest in literature. In the early 1980s they had attended the annual Santa Barbara Writers Conference. There they became friends with Barnaby Conrad, the founder of the conference. Jonathan Winters, a native of Dayton, Ohio, now lived in Santa Barbara and was also a friend of Conrad, so, when Niehoff needed to contact the comedian, he turned to Conrad as a go-between.

With the help of a lunch, a letter, the gift of a Cincinnati Reds baseball cap, a follow-up telephone call (complete with typical Winters impersonations), and further prod-

26 Buck Niehoff, *Something Funny at the Library* (Cincinnati: Mercantile Library, 2004), 5-8. Unless otherwise indicated, information on the various Niehoff lectures comes from this warm and "funny" account.
27 Buck Niehoff underwrote some early Kamholtz courses.
28 Author's interview with Buck Niehoff, October 27, 2009.

ding by Conrad, Jonathan Winters finally agreed to come to Cincinnati in late April 1987. Perhaps the clincher was the invitation to throw out the ceremonial first pitch at a Reds-Braves baseball game.[29]

That first Niehoff lecture proved more than successful. Winters, reading from the Library's list of recent acquisitions, used the titles and authors' names for his improvisations; the capacity audience of 280 people never stopped laughing. By bringing in the popular comedian, the Mercantile had caught the city's attention and secured an enviable reputation for the event.

While Winters' appearance established the Niehoff Lecture as the Library's primary fund-raising event, the Mercantile board still had to wrestle with the usual affairs and problems. Even so, the comedian's visit apparently injected humor into the usually lackluster monthly board meetings.[30] In November 1985, in discussing destination possibilities for a future trip, Chadwick Christine suggested going by train to Banff, Canada, and then on to Alaska by boat. One director retorted that he found it too difficult to play bridge on a train because chairs did not face each other; another director countered with the suggestion that upturned garbage cans (presumably empty) made fine tables. Then, while the board mulled over the merits of garbage-can tables, Mrs. Charlee Blaine recommended a summer trip to Santa Fe for opera. At this, according to the secretary, Edward Terrill blanched noticeably. For several months, opera became a *leitmotif* in the minutes: the following April, when an unnamed director, probably presi-

29 Patricia Niehoff's mother was a first cousin of Marge Schott, the Reds' principal owner.
30 Humor may always have been present at board meetings, but secretary Ernest Eynon had a flair for capturing board proceedings, and he deserves much of the credit for this and the following paragraph.

dent George Palmer, suggested an opera or a ballet as part of the planned New York trip, another director commented that he didn't need to go to New York City "to fall asleep." In June 1986, when Palmer again urged the addition of a good opera to the New York agenda, his motion died for lack of a second. Palmer then ended the meeting "lickety-split."

Secretary Ernest Eynon's deft pen captured another jocular boardroom conversation, this time on the annual budget. When treasurer Thomas Huenefeld presented the budget on May 20, 1986, the board routinely approved it "with appropriate guarantees and warrantees from Mr. Huenefeld" (as Eynon described it). The following month, when the previous minutes were handed out, the treasurer good-naturedly objected to the phrase "guarantees and warrantees," pointing out that bankers[31] "obtain guarantees and warrantees, and never give them." He was certain that "he had never done such a thing and it was unfair to so charge him." The board, expressing great sympathy for the aggrieved treasurer, then "instructed" the secretary "not to be unfair to Mr. Huenefeld ever again." Of course the secretary had the last word, writing in the minutes that "Mr. Huenefeld's budget is not to be relied upon as Mr. Huenefeld neither warrants nor guarantees any single number contained therein even though the year is half over and some people have been known under similar circumstances to be able to demonstrate a very high degree of accuracy in the budgeting process, especially for the first six months, but such standard shall not be observed for Mr. Huenefeld."

Three years later, when the board discussed whether to give

---

31 At the time, Huenefeld was a senior vice-president at First National Bank, now a part of U.S. Bancorp.

the executive director greater discretion in routine tasks such as window and drapery cleaning, Eynon recorded: "Some of us felt the Board should concentrate on more important matters while others thought a discussion of dirty floors helped enliven the luncheons." The minutes do not mention whether the board increased the executive director's authority.

Friendly ribbing aside, the 1980s brought a number of significant changes to the now not-so-staid Mercantile Library. In 1983 the board elected Carol Allgood president, another first in the Association's gender equity development. Two years later the board discussed a retirement pension for its executive director, although it was unable to carry through on this. Then in 1986 it elected Buck Niehoff to the board. In 1987 the board changed the Timothy Crane Day awards ceremony, replacing the grade criterion with an essay contest for eligible high school juniors. The directors also invited Barnaby Conrad to speak at a special awards luncheon that year; in 1988 they followed that with a writing contest in recognition of the two hundredth anniversary of Cincinnati's founding. The topic selected was "If experience is the best teacher, what experience of Cincinnati's first 200 years has best equipped it to face the future?" The following year, 1989, the board renewed the short story contest for the region's aspiring authors. First prize was $300, publication in *Cincinnati Magazine,* and a scholarship to the Santa Barbara Writers Conference, funded by the Niehoffs. The Provident Travel Company and American Airlines generously paid travel expenses.[32]

Also in 1988, the board decided to inventory the collection

---

32 See information in Mercantile Library archives, box: "Short Story Contest, 1978-1996."

to determine the value of rare books. Previous boards had sold or donated books, mostly volumes of little value, although in 1970 a "book buff" by the name of Weidel had offered to evaluate the entire collection "in exchange for some volumes that he desired." The board apparently hired him, but there is no record of his evaluation nor of any books he may have selected for himself.

In April 1988 the board brought in an English book dealer–a Mr. John Hodgkins–to handle the appraisal. This turned out to be less an appraisal than a shopping expedition. Hodgkins found thirty items to his liking, mostly European volumes and books with botanical prints, and offered $28,000 for the lot. Concerned about the ethical question of allowing the appraiser to be the buyer as well, the board hastily sought local assistance. Yeatman Anderson, head of the Rare Book Room at the Public Library of Cincinnati and Hamilton County, examined the thirty volumes and concluded that because of their condition the offer was fair. He also noted that in several cases, the prints would most likely be removed and sold separately. By June the books had been sold and the endowment fund was richer by $28,500.[33]

Always in search of revenue, the Mercantile board pursued additional book sales. In January 1989 Hodgkins and another English book dealer arrived at the Library. Following a "full English Tea" provided courtesy of the Cincinnatian Hotel, they offered appraisals of members' personal books before looking over the Library holdings. When they had finished, some two hundred to three hundred more books were headed

---

33 This amount is recorded in the board minutes for June 21, 1988. Yet in the financial statement appended to the minutes of the annual meeting in January 1989, the sum listed is $23,662, which may reflect some additional costs or the cost of the appraisal.

across the Atlantic, for which the Library received $13,500.

Here again, without a list of titles, it is difficult to know whether these two boards made the right decisions. Inevitably, however, directors' concerns about financial stability almost always overcame any objections to deaccessioning. As one director commented about the latter batch of books to be sold, "none... had been checked out since 1924," as though circulation were the only criterion for determining value to the Library.[34] On the other hand, annual deficits had recurred, and interest from the growing endowment fund was the only way to keep the Mercantile going.

Various boards tried other methods. They periodically raised dues and sold Mercantile ties, note cards, and a specially designed Robert Flischel photographic poster depicting Library books. They continued with the popular tours and brought in some revenue from the Kamholtz courses, but they had to relinquish the Cultural Chow Line in 1989, when both the Taft Museum and the Contemporary Arts Center pulled out. When Fifth Third Bank donated a Cincinnati Bicentennial print by noted historical artist Frank McIlwain, the directors chose to sell it rather than pay $100 for framing.[35] Yet even collectively these efforts could not balance the annual budgets, and this situation made the Niehoff Lectures almost indispensable. Indeed, in retrospect one wonders how the Mercantile could have survived without them.

By 1989, after just three years, the Niehoff Lectures had generated more than $36,000 for the Library; much of that

---

34 If that were the case, given recent circulation numbers, the Library should sell most of its collection. It is not uncommon to find books in the stacks that have not been checked out for thirty to forty years. Many of the books purchased in the nineteenth-century have not been checked out in well over one hundred years.

35 Besides, there was no wall space for such a large print.

went into the endowment fund. Every year the event was a virtual sellout, attesting to the impressive list of speakers. Jonathan Winters was followed in 1988 by William F. Buckley, prominent author, conservative newspaper columnist, and editor of *The National Review*. As Niehoff described Buckley, he appeared to wrap himself in the mantle of a distracted intellectual: he deliberately rumpled his just-pressed, borrowed tuxedo before his appearance at the Library. In his speech Buckley covered the Western intellectual tradition from Plato to Jesse Jackson, but according to the *Enquirer's* reporter, more than a few in the sold-out audience nodded off "during his rambling treatise...."[36] Niehoff seemed to agree: "[F]ew, if any, of us actually understood what he said." Nevertheless, Buckley spoke for a substantially reduced fee, and the Library's coffer was the beneficiary. George Plimpton, who made a career of writing about his amateur experiences among professional athletes, spoke in 1989. He gave a polished, witty talk; to better accommodate the large crowd, the board moved the function across the street to the Westin Hotel, with cocktails in the Library preceding the dinner and speech.

In selecting the speaker for 1990, the board considered Carl Sagan, Gore Vidal, John Updike, and Julia Child. For a short time the directors believed they had secured the famous chef and cookbook author, but she canceled. After that they arranged to bring in Tom Wolfe, author of *The Right Stuff*, *The Bonfire of the Vanities*, and other books exploring the American condition.

Anticipating another very large turnout, the board planned

---

36 *Cincinnati Enquirer*, quoted in Niehoff, *Something Funny at the Library*, 29.

the dinner for the Hall of Mirrors in the Art Deco-style Omni Netherland Plaza Hotel. But when they considered moving the pre-dinner cocktails to the hotel as well, Jean Springer objected strongly, emphasizing that the physical association with the Mercantile Library far outweighed any inconveniences. Cocktails thus remained at the Library. Almost four hundred people enjoyed the "very festive and elegant" evening; few, if any, expressed displeasure at walking the two blocks from the Mercantile to the hotel.

So the Niehoff lectures continued: John Updike, creator of the *Rabbit* quartet, spoke in 1991, followed by a rather "difficult" Margaret Truman Daniel, who tried both her host's and her audience's patience.[37] Originally the scheduled lecturer for 1993 was John Grisham, whose third novel, *The Client*, had just arrived at bookstores, but he took advantage of a 30-day cancellation clause because he needed to focus on his next book, *The Pelican Brief*. A disappointed Jean Springer described the late cancellation to an *Enquirer* reporter as "a low blow."[38] On short notice, however, journalist David Halberstam agreed to pinch-hit. He probed the 1950s, the subject and title of his most recent book, and to a full house at the Library he elaborated on the importance of that decade to an understanding of the present.

John Grisham's withdrawal underscores the difficulties in obtaining top-flight speakers. In 1988, before inviting William Buckley, the Mercantile had approached Hal Holbrook, the popular actor and Mark Twain impersonator. He declined because his "Mark Twain Tonight" required a full stage, pro-

---

37 In the minutes for November 19, 1991, the Updike talk was described as "first class and stylish," whereas Margaret Truman Daniel's presentation in 1992 was considered "substandard." In his book, Niehoff agreed with this assessment.

38 *Cincinnati Enquirer*, August 31, 1993, C2.

fessional lighting, and at least four hours just for his makeup. Gore Vidal explained that he preferred not to give lectures, while John McPhee wrote that he was "just not a maker of pre- pared speeches." For others, such as Scott Turow and the Irish Nobel laureate Seamus Heaney, scheduling simply proved too difficult.

In addition to the Niehoff Lectures, the Mercantile hosted an impressive number of other writers, national figures, and locally prominent citizens. Tracy Kidder, winner of both a Pulitzer Prize and the National Book Award in the nonfic- tion category, addressed a luncheon audience at the Library in 1993. Indeed, that year proved particularly fruitful for Library supporters. Kentuckian Wendell Berry, whose novels and poems often reflect his environmental concerns, spoke in December. Northern Kentucky University professor Robert Wallace discussed the connections between Herman Melville's writings and J. M. W. Turner's art, the subject of his recent book, *Melville and Turner: Spheres of Love and Fright*. Under John Ryan's vigorous leadership, the Young Wing brought in speakers from the local political community: state senator William Bowen, congressman Charles Luken, councilwoman Roxanne Qualls, and Robert J. Portman, deputy assistant to President George H. W. Bush.

The Young Wing also started its "Lunchtime Thing," at which often-controversial topics were discussed. John Frohnmayer, chairman of the National Endowment for the Arts during the Robert Mapplethorpe controversy, drew a large audience in April 1993.[39] He discussed the problems of

39 *Cincinnati Enquirer*, April 25, 1993, 1J. The Mapplethorpe exhibit of homoerotic pho- tographs (funded by the National Endowment for the Arts) at the Contemporary Arts Center earlier that year had created an uproar in Cincinnati, and it added to the political pressure that convinced the Bush administration to ask for Frohnmayer's resignation.

censorship and public funding for the arts, and made a few comments about his recent departure from Washington. A month later, a "diverse crowd" gathered to hear John Dolibois, former United States ambassador to Luxembourg and a resident of Oxford, Ohio, speak on current problems in Yugoslavia. Also in 1993 Charles Vere, Earl of Burford, made a case for his ancestor Edward de Vere, Earl of Oxford, as the actual author of the works attributed to William Shakespeare, a view dear to several Cincinnatians.[40] The Library also brought in a former CIA agent to present his views on the John F. Kennedy assassination.

Other lunchtime forums during the early 1990s included a presentation concerning the planned new arts center for Cincinnati,[41] a panel discussion titled "Is Cincinnati in Decline?", and a four-person debate over the location of the new ballpark for the Cincinnati Reds. Suddenly the Mercantile Library had become the place to hear the latest news and views on hot topics.

Under Jean Springer's firm hand, public programs had become the new face of the Library. In 1993 the board recognized this by producing a new mission statement that reflected the change: "The Mercantile Library provides a contemplative environment for the enjoyment of books and ideas through reading, lectures, discussions of current issues and literary events." But the board did not neglect one of its principal responsibilities—namely finances. Two years earlier the directors had explored the qualifications they desired in new board

---

40 Mercantile member Morse Johnson was particularly strong in advocating the Earl of Oxford as the actual author of "Shakespeare." After his death, his widow gave his collection of "Shakespeare" authorship to the Library, where it is now housed in a fine bookcase designed by Bruce Petrie and constructed by Jim Wellinghoff.

41 This became the Stanley J. Aronoff Center.

members, and chief among these were skills in fund-raising, grant writing, and marketing. Money was still the necessary ingredient for making the Library successful. With that point in mind, in 1992 the board increased annual dues to $45 and established the Thackerary Society for members who annually contributed $500 or more.[42]

In 1991 Jean Springer jumped at the opportunity to include the Mercantile Library in an informal network of the country's membership libraries. In 1993 the Mercantile hosted the network's annual meeting, which included an opportunity to attend the Niehoff Lecture that year.[43] Springer also pushed for general cleaning of the Reading Room. (Some years earlier she had replaced the drab institutional green paint with a cheerful yellow.)

At the same time, the board began to take the art collection more seriously. Tom Huenefeld stepped in to chair the committee charged with restoring several paintings, repairing frames, preserving several documents,[44] repairing the grandfather clock, and cleaning the numerous busts. The cleaned-up busts, which usually were kept on top of the bookcases, were taken down from their lofty perches in May 1994 for a special exhibit in their honor. By then, however, Jean Springer had left the Mercantile.

In mid-1993 Springer informed the board that she would be retiring at the end of the year, after twenty-four years of devoted service. When asked why by a local writer, she

---

42 Benefits at this level originally included one ticket to the annual Niehoff lecture, one free gift membership, free admission to all Mercantile Library programs, and a Mercantile Library poster.

43 See the assortment of material on membership libraries in Mercantile Library archives, box: "YMMLA (3) & Misc.," folder: "Membership Libraries."

44 Among the documents preserved was the original charter granted by the State of Ohio.

responded, "It's just time to retire. There are a million things I want to do; I'll enjoy being a little footloose."[45] First, however, the board faced the problem of replacing her.

At a board meeting held on July 20, 1993, Springer and the directors engaged in a long discussion about her replacement's qualifications. President Buck Niehoff pointed out that librarian skills were no longer a high priority, a reflection of the recently crafted mission statement. Carol Allgood suggested that solid computer skills should be a requirement. Springer, after emphasizing the importance of public relations experience and an ability to cultivate local media, suggested that this would be an opportunity to hire a separate director of development. Treasurer Vere Gaynor responded bluntly that the budget would not permit the creation of a new position.

When discussion returned to the position of executive director, Charles Powers argued for a person "who is comfortable dealing with sophisticated people." This director, he continued, should also possess "good motivational skills and have previous experience serving on various non-profit boards." Everyone seemed to agree that a local person would be best and would require a less expensive search; nobody mentioned a superhero. By September the search committee had narrowed the list of candidates to three, and in October the board voted unanimously to offer the position to local writer Albert Pyle.

In her almost quarter-century as the Mercantile Library's executive director, Jean Springer played the key role in remaking the institution. Through aggressive programming she transformed the Library into the city's premier center for

---

45 *The Downtowner*, November 16, 1993, clipping in Mercantile Library archives, box: "Newspaper Articles," folder: "Newspaper Articles, 1990-1995."

literary activities and civic forums. She also took the lead in improving the Reading Room's physical and psychological image; certainly the Library shed most of its "musty" atmosphere.[46] A younger, friendlier staff (notably Mary Gruber, hired in 1986)[47] did much to air out the mustiness. As Springer liked to say, it's a place where "your face is your library card."[48] Because of all these changes during her tenure, the membership more than doubled: it stood at about nine hundred by the time Springer left office. Equally important, the members' average age had decreased significantly.

President Niehoff, in an interview for *The Downtowner*, praised Springer's services. "Aside from upholding the library's standard of intellect, wit and grace," he commented, "[she] allowed this institution to flourish during a time when it surely would have withered."[49] High praise indeed. The board acknowledged "her remarkable career" with a special Jean Springer Day, as proclaimed by mayor Mayor Roxanne Qualls, and established a special Springer Fund for the purchase of travel books.

---

46 As an example of this change in atmosphere, when Thomas Huenefeld joined the Library in the early 1970s, he found it a "fun, exciting place" where one could learn about issues facing the community; author's interview with Thomas E. Huenefeld, July 1, 2009.

47 In 1986 the board minutes make no mention of Gruber's appointment as second assistant librarian, but in December 1991, in approving an eleven percent raise for her, the directors referred to Gruber as "the invaluable assistant librarian." Before she was hired, Gruber, a Xavier University student who was dissatisfied with college and looking for a temporary job, recalls that she had a five-minute interview with Jean Springer and submitted a handwriting sample. Among her first duties were addressing envelopes, learning members' names and reading interests, keeping the catalog up to date, and reading new books. She became first assistant librarian in 1987; in 2004 she became literary programs manager, taking the position vacated by Judy Sharp. Cedric Rose then became collector, a title revived a few years earlier by Albert Pyle.

48 *Cincinnati Post*, January 25, 1994, 3B; May 3, 1994, 3B.

49 *The Downtowner*, November 16, 1993; in Mercantile Library archives, box: "Newspaper Clippings," folder: "Newspaper Clippings, 1990-1996."

"Somebody has to hang onto the books."

ALBERT PYLE, 1999

*"The Mercantile Library [is] a center
of civilized mirth and merriment combining
Shakespearean revels with discussions about civic
challenges and Cincinnati architecture.
A mighty roar for the Merc!"*

MARY PAT AND DALE MULLANEY, 2007

CHAPTER 8

To the New Millennium and Beyond

FOR MOST MEMBERS of the Mercantile Library, the change from Jean Springer to Albert Pyle appeared seamless, and in many ways that was true. Daily operations continued as before, and most of the programs for 1994 were already in place. Yet Pyle brought a different style and a new perspective. In the Mercantile he saw an institution that could become an even more important center for public discussion of municipal issues. The author of three Cesar Franck detective novels and a freelance writer for some years, the forty-eight-year-old year old Pyle also introduced both a more businesslike approach and an expanded vision of the Library's role as a literary center for the city.[1] As Jean Springer said, "Albert will bring imagination, spirit, humor, warmth—not to mention brains—to our library. He'll do a wonderful job."[2]

Pyle was no stranger to the Mercantile Library. His wife had been a member for a number of years, and he had served

---

[1] *The Downtowner*, November 23, 1993, 9; author's interview with Pyle, August 5, 2009.
[2] See news release in Mercantile Library archives, box: "Library Programs, 1970-1996"; folder: "Jean Springer Farewell Party."

as a judge for the 1991 short story contest. In accepting the position he was aware of the Mercantile's declining role as a traditional library, and he felt that members deserved more for their annual dues. Although he inherited a wealth of programs, he believed there was room for more. He also understood that the Library was one of Cincinnati's essential institutions.[3]

Just a month after Pyle's arrival, the Library hosted a discussion about Broadway Commons, a space on the northeast edge of downtown, as a possible future site for the Cincinnati Reds. The Reds had expressed a need for a baseball-only facility that would replace Riverfront Stadium, which they shared with the Cincinnati Bengals.

Jim Tarbell, founder of the Over-the-Rhine Chamber of Commerce and at that time owner of Arnold's Restaurant on East Eighth Street, spearheaded the noon program on a December day in 1993. Complete with models, computer simulations, sketches, and various parking and traffic charts, his argument for Broadway Commons impressed many in the audience. Tarbell hoped for construction of a "retro" stadium that would also provide an economic stimulus to the Over-the-Rhine area, and the Mercantile Library discussion helped launch an extensive community debate over the future site of the ballpark.[4]

Although the event had been arranged during Springer's final months, Pyle embraced the idea of using the Mercantile as a center for any number of community discussions. In subsequent years he arranged public forums on regional coop-

3 *Cincinnati Post*, December 20, 1993, 1C, 4C.
4 See *Cincinnati Enquirer*, December 7, 1993, D1-5; *Cincinnati Post*, December 6, 1993, clipping in Mercantile Library archives, box: "Newspaper Articles," folder: "Newspaper Articles, 1990-1995." Eventually the Cincinnati Reds constructed Great American Ball Park on the riverfront, just east of the old stadium.

eration for future development; on whether Cincinnati would benefit from a "strong mayor" system of government; on levying a county sales tax to pay for two new professional sports stadiums; and on the general future of the city's downtown.[5]

This expanded focus on community issues, particularly downtown problems, did not keep the Mercantile from continuing the programs established during Jean Springer's tenure. In Pyle's first year the Library sponsored thirty-three separate events, if one counts all of Jonathan Kamholtz's lectures. The Library's close relationship with Drew's Bookstore, owned by Drew Gores, brought in several speakers of distinction including Tim O'Brien, whose *Lake of the Woods* received *Time* magazine's nod as best novel for 1994; Gloria Steinem, a leading feminist author and activist, who spoke to a packed room; and popular English suspense writer Ken Follett,[6] who drew a large audience as well. Proceeds from the Follett lecture were earmarked for restoration and conservation of historic books in the Library. Pulitzer Prize-winning cartoonist Jim Borgman of the *Cincinnati Enquirer* chose the Mercantile that year for his return to the lecture circuit, and Kentuckian Bobbie Ann Mason appeared at a Literary Lunch to talk about her recent novel, *Feather Crowns*.

Two distinguished poets also spoke at the Library in 1994. Nikki Giovanni, who grew up in Lincoln Heights, a suburb of Cincinnati, and Andrew Hudgins, a University of Cincinnati professor, helped restore poetry to the Mercantile's "curriculum." (The 1999 Niehoff Lecture strengthened that relationship by bringing in Robert Pinsky, United States

---

5   *The Downtowner*, February 27, 1996; clipping in Mercantile Library archives, box: "Newspaper Articles," folder: "Newspaper Articles, 1996-1999."
6   Follett's best-known works are *Eye of the Needle* and *The Key to Rebecca*.

poet laureate, whose "celebration of language" impressed the large gathering.) In June 1994 Pyle organized a session with three "Cincinnaturalists," the artist John Ruthven and Dr. Robert Kennedy and Dr. Betsy Dresser from the Cincinnati Zoo and Botanical Gardens. Later that year, in recognition of the Cincinnati Symphony Orchestra's upcoming 100th anniversary, the Library hosted British author Carole Rosen. She discussed the career of Eugene Goossens, orchestra director from 1931 to 1947. To cap that year's literary activities, science fiction writer Ray Bradbury, author of *Farenheit 451*, delivered the Niehoff Lecture.

All in all, 1994 proved to be a stellar year with a wide array of speakers and events, but the Mercantile Library still could not shake off its traditional problems. Membership increased, inching towards the one thousand mark, but the endowment fund declined 10 percent, a reflection of a bear market. Worse, Drew's Bookstore closed, a victim of chain store competition and the recent opening of Joseph-Beth Booksellers, a larger bookstore just a mile away. Pyle quickly worked out an arrangement with the new bookstore to provide speakers, but that arrangement did not last long.[7] Where Drew's had no space for public events and used the Mercantile's facilities as its site for author lectures and book signings, Joseph-Beth invited prominent authors to speak in its own store, leaving the Mercantile with lesser names. The following year, the Mercantile ended its association with Joseph-Beth.

The Niehoff Lectures alone could not compensate for the loss of the bookstore partnership. Space limitations in the Library kept audiences well below two hundred for Ray

---

7   Among the lecturers brought in through Joseph-Beth was Gregory Howard Williams, who became president of the University of Cincinnati in 2009.

Bradbury in 1994 and Elmore Leonard in 1995. Once again, board meetings were filled with discussions about improving the organization's financial foundation. Several members even suggested drastically changing the format of the Niehoff Lectures in order to draw more guests.

Unexpected expenses compounded the situation. Early in his first year Pyle requested two new computers costing $1,800; then the restoration of the bust collection ran over budget.[8] For most of 1995 and 1996, membership sagged again. Fortunately the situation soon improved. By early 1997 the endowment had risen above $2 million, and the Niehoff Lectures brought in greater returns. The dinner was moved to the Contemporary Arts Center, so almost three hundred people now could attend Pat Conroy's lecture in the Library in October 1996. This event was described in the annual report as an "extraordinary evening," and president William Chatfield called it "one of the finest talks in the history of the Lecture."[9] The next year, William Styron's presentation brought a handsome profit of about $10,000, and there was no further talk about making changes to the Niehoff Lecture Series. By early 1998 membership had turned upward as well, and in December of that year Pyle informed the board that the number had finally passed one thousand.

Excitement at the Mercantile took other forms as well. In 1995 Navy veteran Pyle decided he needed a ship's bell to control possibly boisterous audiences at the Library. Eventually Robert Economou, president of the Cincinnati Council of

8 Both of these expenses were handled through the Goode bequests. In 1990 Dr. Ralph Goode and his sister Alice, both frequent travelers on Mercantile trips, left sizable bequests to the Library.
9 In *Something Funny at the Library*, Buck Niehoff describes how Conroy visited each table during the dinner to personally thank the guests for coming to his presentation.

the Navy League, arranged for the Mercantile to receive on permanent loan the ship's bell from the *U.S.S. Cincinnati*, a decommissioned nuclear submarine. Pyle took great pleasure in this acquisition, and promised to use it to convene meetings and "cut off droning speakers."[10] Much to the Library members' delight, and sometimes to the startled surprise of guests, the bell still announces the opening of every program in the Reading Room.

Perhaps less well known to members is the historical marker commemorating the Young Men's Mercantile Library Association that stands outside the Walnut Street entrance to the building. In 1996 the board had agreed to provide such a marker, supported by a generous contribution from president William Chatfield and his wife, Anne. Unfortunately the city's engineering department objected, apparently on the grounds that the building lacked a sufficient historical pedigree. It made little difference to City Hall that the marker would commemorate the Association, not the building. After two years of negotiation, however, the plaque was installed as the first in the city's "Historic Cincinnati" program to mark local sites.[11]

Pyle's interest in local history also surfaced in two other, if less significant, ways. In 1999 he dusted off the old staff title "collector"[12] and assigned it to first assistant librarian Mary Gruber. A few years later he pushed to have the organization's logo changed from the modernistic block lettering to the cur-

10 *Cincinnati Post*, January 15, 1996, 8A. The *U.S.S. Cincinnati* was the fourth naval vessel to carry the city's name; the first had been a Civil War gunboat, followed by a cruiser constructed in 1894 and a light cruiser that saw service in both world wars. Board member and future president Jim Wellinghoff constructed and contributed the lovely mahogany mounting for the bell.
11 *Cincinnati Enquirer*, August 31, 1999, 1B.
12 This title had been used for a few years in the mid-nineteenth century.

rent initials taken from the Mercantile Library Building's original doorknobs.[13]

The most extensive change to the facilities since the 19th century generated even more excitement. In 1997 word circulated about plans for a complete makeover of the space on the twelfth floor, previously rented to an insurance company. Plans included making the spiral staircase a usable connection between the two floors;[14] the stairs to nowhere would finally go somewhere. Architect Frank Russell, a Mercantile board member, offered to design the area pro bono. To cover the anticipated cost of construction and to pay for some other, much-needed physical improvements on the eleventh floor, James Schiff and Susan Rowe Gaynor, assisted again by Robert Hilton, led a capital campaign called the Spiral Staircase Fund, with a goal of $250,000. At the end of 1998 Hilton informed the board that over $200,000 had already been pledged, led by another generous donation from the Niehoffs. Renovation began early the next year. On April 6, 2000, Hope Taft, former Mercantile president and wife of Ohio governor Robert Taft, cut the ribbon at the base of the spiral stairs that led up to the sparkling Arts & Crafts-style lecture room and foyer. Russell, who designed the space, and Thomas Huenefeld, who chaired the board committee that oversaw the project, were both rewarded with life memberships.[15]

During all of this activity, the board sought the return of the two stained-glass windows that had been removed from

---

13 The design firm of Sanger and Eby donated its services in designing the new logo.

14 While cleaning out a filthy stairway storage closet, staff members found a nineteenth-century portrait of an unidentified man. After extensive restoration, the gentleman now hangs in the twelfth-floor meeting room, still unidentified.

15 Russell, in a labor of love, handcrafted the tile floor from pieces of the original floor; he also designed the light fixtures and ventilation covers to repeat ornamental detail on the building façade.

the south wall of the building some thirty years before. The Ogden memorial window, titled "Woman with a Book," had been installed by Augustine ("Gussie") Ogden in 1904 as a memorial to her late husband, Frank McGee Ogden.[16] The other window, "The Three Arts," came to the Mercantile in 1884, a gift from George A. Bowen. When construction of the Mercantile Center, the structure immediately to the south of the Mercantile Library Building, blocked the light, and with little available storage space, the board had to decide what to do with the two large windows. In June 1970 the directors voted that the House Committee was to dispose of them "at the best possible terms."

After that point, the trail fades. In January 1971 the directors agreed that the windows should go to the Cincinnati Art Museum, where they would be "recognized as our windows." A month later, after building owner Charles Fleischmann offered to pay for the removal, the board secretary recorded that the windows were to be "given to the Art Museum in the name of the Mercantile Library."

Twenty-one years later, the more recent search for the windows began. In November 1992 the "missing" windows came up for discussion, and board member Carol Allgood agreed to search out their location and condition. Several months later she reported that, according to the Cincinnati Art Museum, Fleischmann had "loaned the windows" to the Museum, and that in 1982 the Museum had returned the windows to him. Allgood learned that Fleischmann had paid the Mercantile

---

16 Frank McGee Ogden (1850-1901) and his wife, Augustine, had both been members of the Mercantile Library. The window was meant to memorialize Ogden for his "generous and kindly labors among those less fortunate than himself"; see Lewis Alexander Leonard, *Greater Cincinnati and Its People: A History* (New York and Chicago: Lewis Historical Publishing Co., 1927), III: 100.

$200 for the windows with the understanding that they would then be donated to the Art Museum.

That was not the end of the matter, however. In May 1995 board member Ernest Eynon decided to pursue the matter further. The following spring, April 1996, Eynon reported no progress in "the mystery of the vanishing windows," but five months later, he announced that he–a "private eye par excellence"–had a lead that "Skip" Fleischmann had given the windows to a church in Vevay, Indiana. A month later he announced that a "Mercantile SWAT team was being readied for retrieval of the windows."

Unfortunately, Eynon's lead proved unreliable, and the SWAT team never materialized. The church windows in question proved not to be the right ones, and in April 1999 Eynon wrapped up his two-year "investigation." It turned out that the Cincinnati Art Museum, at Fleischmann's request, in fact had turned over the windows to him in 1982. They were then delivered to the Main Auction Gallery and were sold on August 30, 1982. No one at the auction house could recall the buyer, and they kept sales records for only seven years.[17]

High-profile programs and sleuthing for missing windows aside, the regular operation of the Library called for constant attention. After decades of neglect, the card catalog required updating. In 1999 assistant librarians Mary Gruber and Mark Pierce, with the help of a Northern Kentucky University student, began the tedious and time-consuming task of reconciling the catalog with the books on the shelf. They found

---

17 Anita Ellis to Thomas E. Huenefeld, February 9, 1999, in Mercantile Library archives, box: "Miscellaneous," folder: "Stained Glass." Although the windows cannot be located, there is nothing to suggest that anyone involved acted with less than good faith.

many discrepancies but eventually completed the project.[18]

This exercise in traditional librarianship did not preclude the need to stay current with new technology. In 1999 the board authorized the installation of a new telephone system. They followed that with plans for a Library website, which was completed in 2002. So much modernization encouraged a name change as well: in 2003 the Young Men's Mercantile Library Association shed its antiquated name and officially became the Mercantile Library Association.

Less expensive changes came through the work of the "Busted Thumbnail Society." Led by Edward Marks, who coined the name, and Jim Wellinghoff, these energetic and talented workers in wood repaired and restored various pieces of 19th-century furniture including the circulation desk, several newspaper and magazine stands, and a number of bookcases. This work was not without physical dangers, however: in taking apart and rebuilding the George McLaughlin bookcase, the "esteemed librarian" suffered "a minor head wound." That this information found its way into the board minutes suggests that the "Busted Thumbnail" gang enjoyed the weekend fellowship as much as the sprucing-up of the Reading Room.

A more ambitious project was launched in 2003, when plans surfaced for restoring the elevator lobby and adjacent stairway. Supported by a $25,000 grant from the Greater Cincinnati Foundation and by contributions from many members, the project moved forward quickly. Designed to highlight the original beauty of the building, the work opened up the space to light from the large arched windows on the

18 In 2009-2010 the card catalog was digitized; thus, one of the last vestiges of a nineteenth-century library has disappeared from the Reading Room. Digitization, however, will facilitate research, allow more efficient updating of the collection, and permit members to access the holdings from their homes.

east wall. At the same time, the women's restroom received some much-needed redecoration, and the Ladies Lounge was re-named the Members' Lounge, bringing an end to a tradition of gender separation more than century old.[19]

The physical improvements did not end there. In 2008 the board authorized a major restoration of the Reading Room, which included new shelving against the south wall, a platform for speakers, the relocation of the circulation counter, an enlarged, handicap-accessible restroom, the elimination of the Members' Lounge, the placement of *Silence* in the entrance lobby, and the construction of a special display area for the Elizabeth Nourse Collection–all to be completed in time for the Mercantile's 175th anniversary celebration in 2010.[20]

Remodeling, refurbishing, and installation of new equipment were all necessary and good, but programs remained the heart of the Mercantile Library. In 1999 Pyle hired Judith Sharp as a part-time events coordinator, and the program schedule soon became even busier.[21] The Mercantile board of directors remained very active as well, especially the Events Committee, chaired first by James Schiff and then by Dale P. Brown. Both shared Pyle's passion for literature and local history, and their committee produced several additional signature events to complement the annual Niehoff Lecture. In 2000 the Library started its Winter Author Series, sponsored initially by the Lois and Richard Rosenthal Foundation. Each year three distinguished writers entertained and enlightened audiences. In the program's first season, Edward Ball, Bobbie Ann Mason, and Ernest Gaines set the bar high. Since

---

19 Board member William Friedlander suggested this change of name and function.
20 This work was underway when this chapter was written.
21 This step also freed librarian Pyle for other responsibilities such as ringing the ship's bell.

then the series has brought in such prominent writers as E. L. Doctorow, John Updike, Mary Gaitskill, Paul Theroux, Dorothy Allison, Michael Cunningham, Jane Smiley, and David Quammen.[22]

The Literary Lunch Series also continued. Before it ended in 2007, the program featured almost every local writer of note, including Sharon Draper, Stephen Birmingham, University of Cincinnati professor Austin M. Wright, photographer Robert Flischel, mystery writer Jonathan Valin, and Kentuckians Wendell Berry, Ed McClanahan, and Nick Clooney. The Cincinnati Art Museum's Anita Ellis and Julie Aronson spoke about the Museum's new Cincinnati Wing; Miami University historians Andrew Cayton and John H. White tied their talks to the Ohio bicentennial celebration; *CityBeat's* sassy columnist Kathy Y. Wilson entertained and educated her audience with a talk titled "Your Negro Tour Guide." Fittingly, board member Ann Hagedorn, discussing her latest book, *Savage Peace: Hope and Fear in America, 1919,* closed the series on June 28, 2007.[23]

In connection with the 150th anniversary of the publication of Uncle Tom's Cabin, the Mercantile commissioned a bust of Harriet Beecher Stowe. The Events Committee then decided to organize a Harriet Beecher Stowe Festival in recognition of the most famous author associated with Cincinnati. In February 2003, after two years of planning, the festival opened with the unveiling of a limestone bust of Stowe,

---

22 After the first two years, funding came first from the Robert and Adele Schiff Foundation and then from the Duke Energy Foundation.

23 The Books by the Banks program, for which the Mercantile is one of the sponsors, currently provides recognition for local authors.

sculpted by local artist Walter Driesbach.[24] Over the next three weeks, subsequent events included an evening of musical excerpts from the play *Harriet*, a timely discussion of the sentimental novel led by University of Cincinnati professor Martin Wechselblatt, a bus trip to underground railroad sites in the area, and a capstone lecture by Joan Hedrick, Pulitzer Prize-winning author of *Harriet Beecher Stowe: A Life*.[25]

Even before plans for the festival had been completed, the board decided to make the Harriet Beecher Stowe Lecture a major event, each year bringing in a speaker whose writing has helped "change the world." Gail Collins, *New York Times* editorial page editor and Cincinnati native, spoke in 2004, followed by Linda Lear, biographer of Rachel Carson; Dorothy Rabinowitz of the *Wall Street Journal;* Samantha Power, an Irish-born journalist; and prominent syndicated columnist Cynthia Tucker. Both Power and Tucker were Pulitzer recipients. In 2009 the speaker was George Packer, author of The *Assassin's Gate: America in Iraq*. An impressive list, indeed.

Success always increases aspirations. In 2003 Dale Brown's and Albert Pyle's shared enthusiasm for local history resulted in two more significant annual events. The annual meetings, held in January, had become nothing more than a pro forma election of new board members and an occasional vote to change the constitution. Since 2004, however, this meeting has included a talk on some aspect of the Library's history,

24 The bust depicts Mrs. Stowe in 1852, at age forty-two. Because the five hundred-pound block was too heavy for the artist's studio, it had to be carved outside; see *CityBeat*, January 29-February 4, 2003, 45-46.

25 *Cincinnati Magazine*, January 2003, 16. Outside funding for the festival came from the Luther Charitable Foundation, and an anonymous Northside resident who contributed $2,000 in memory of her mother, "who loved to read." Other event sponsors included the National Underground Railroad Freedom Center, the University of Cincinnati Center for Women's Studies, and the Greater Cincinnati Consortium of Colleges and Universities.

accompanied by a traditional afternoon tea. Professor Andrew Cayton opened the new format with a lively talk on James E. Murdoch, nineteenth-century local actor and frequent presenter at the Mercantile.

After revamping the annual meeting, the board turned to the Association's anniversary, which fell in April. During the mid-nineteenth century the April meeting had been used to celebrate the Association's founding, complete with a dinner, a main speaker, and an anniversary poem, but this tradition faded away. By the end of the century, only major anniversary years were recognized. Now, on Founders Day, a speaker is brought in to discuss some aspect of the region's literary history. Over the past few years, thanks to the Founders Day programs, Mercantile audiences have enjoyed learning about James Thurber, Fannie Hurst, William Dean Howells, Paul Lawrence Dunbar, and Lafcadio Hearn.[26] These programming changes did not take place in a vacuum, however. In 2002 the board developed a strategic plan. This has been critical in achieving most of the recent changes, not only in programs but also in physical alterations.

Life at the Mercantile was not all authors and lectures, important as these might be. The first ten years of the new millennium have seen a variety of new programs that appeal to a range of people: many of the ideas emerged from the fertile minds on the events committee. In 2004 both the Walnut Street Poetry Society and the Canon Club were founded, and these year-round discussion groups now have well-established, devoted followings. The Walnut Street Poetry Society reflects the members' growing interest in poetry as a means

26 See Mercantile Library archives, box: "Founders Day & Annual Meeting."

of expression. The Canon Club, co-founded by the Cincinnati Shakespeare Festival (now the Cincinnati Shakespeare Company), gathers with Northern Kentucky University professor emeritus William McKim and the CSC's managing director, Rebecca Bromels, to discuss the bard's works. In many ways, Albert Pyle's most important contribution has been his receptiveness to new ideas. In his first year he helped launch Sunday musical concerts, beginning with soprano Blythe Walker's delightful presentation of songs and poems.[27] When Sundays proved unappealing to many people, the concerts became the autumn "Noon Music" series, which remains popular.[28]

In 1997 the Mercantile Library began hosting monthly book discussion groups, followed three years later by the "Great Debate," the brainchild of a group of members. In typical Pyle fashion, the press release described this event as "a cross between the bare-knuckled, ear-biting competition of nineteenth-century America and the flamboyant fencing seen in Britain's House of Commons." In June 2000, over the course of three evenings, a wide range of city leaders and personalities had at it, sometimes having to argue positions repugnant to their own beliefs. Participants included mayor Charlie Luken, *Cincinnati Enquirer* editorial page editor Peter Bronson, and two students from Covington's Holmes High School. On the final evening "The God Squad" (Reverend Harold Porter and Xavier University professor Arthur Dewey) entered combat with "The Forked Tongues" (attorney Eric H. Kearney and radio personality and advertising executive Jerry M. Galvin).

27 *Cincinnati Enquirer*, December 15, 1994, 31.
28 Robert Allen funded this series in memory of his first wife, Elise Eaton Allen, through the Elise Eaton Allen Performing Arts Fund of the Greater Cincinnati Foundation.

Judge Thomas Crush, who once threatened to break out into a Gilbert and Sullivan aria, moderated the contest. After a thorough debate on the question of the government's right to impede the sale of liquor on the Internet, the evening's judges declared Kearney and Galvin the winners.[29]

All of this was quite tongue-in-cheek, but librarian Pyle hoped to restore formal debate to its rightful place of honor, especially debates on community issues. Later in 2000 he arranged for Charterites Edward Burdell and William K. Woods to argue the question of campaign finance reform with Republican supporters Aaron Herzog and Fred Nelson. This was soon followed by a second debate between Robert Bedinghaus and Todd Portune, candidates for Hamilton County commissioner. In 2002, in the same vein, the Mercantile joined with the Architectural Foundation of Cincinnati to promote discussion of downtown development. Topics included the future of downtown, the rebuilding of the Over-the-Rhine neighborhood, and a joint presentation by architect David Niland and architectural historian Walter Langsam Jr. In 2003, John Alschuler, a New York-based consultant on public space usage, led a lively and timely discussion on downtown Cincinnati projects. Alschuler challenged his audience to rethink how Fountain Square might be used, as well as how "The Banks" riverfront project and the area around Washington Park might be developed.[30]

In 2004 the Mercantile hosted its first Holiday Book

---

29 *Cincinnati Herald,* June 30, 2000, clipping in Mercantile Library archives: gray three-ring binder.

30 *Cincinnati Post,* June 5, 2003, 1A, 8A. Since Alschuler's visit to the city, Fountain Square has been refashioned into a major downtown entertainment center, construction on The Banks has been started, and the Washington Park area has seen the arrival of the School for the Creative and Performing Arts and, just three blocks away, a new home for the Art Academy of Cincinnati.

Bazaar, in cooperation with the Bookshelf of Madeira. More than 20 local writers attended, giving readings and talks.[31] This event later was replaced by the much larger Books by the Banks Cincinnati USA Book Festival, for which the Mercantile served as one of the organizing partners.[32]

Also in 2004, when a British production company contacted the Mercantile about using its facilities as a site for filming part of a planned documentary on Charles Dickens' 1842 American tour, Albert Pyle jumped at the opportunity. Although there is no evidence that Dickens actually visited the Mercantile while in the city that year, the Reading Room proved to be a most suitable setting for an informal chat on the British author's interest in America.[33]

Two years later, despite considerable trepidation among the staff, the Library launched its first annual Grandparents Day. Some twenty children, described as "angels" in the board minutes, invaded the Library's usually quiet chambers for several Saturday-morning hours of entertainment, education, and eating. Both the Library and the staff survived.

In 2003 Buck Niehoff, Ann Hagedorn, and Dale Brown organized the Writers Workshop for aspiring writers. The instructors were local authors Brock Clarke and Michael Griffin of the University of Cincinnati, as well as Stephen Birmingham. In 2007 this event morphed into the

31 *The Downtowner*, November 2, 2004, 6.
32 Other original organizing partners of Books by the Banks were The Public Library of Cincinnati and Hamilton County, *Cincinnati Magazine*, the University of Cincinnati Libraries, the Kenton County Public Library, Borders Books, and Cincinnati Educational Television.
33 See email, Suzie Samant to Albert Pyle, September 22, 2004, in Mercantile Library archives, box: "Membership," folder: "BBC." A welcome by-product of the BBC film crew's visit was the identification of a previously unidentified bust as representing a young Charles Dickens, by American sculptor Henry Dexter; see *Cincinnati Post*, November 13, 2004, 10A.

LateBloomers Nonfiction Writers Conference, which continues to support beginning writers. The Mercantile also has entered the book business, overseeing the publishing of Buck Niehoff's *Something Funny at the Library* (2004), his *Breathing in Africa* (2006), and Dale Patrick Brown's *Brilliance and Balderdash: Early Lecturers at Cincinnati's Mercantile Library* (2007).[34]

The Mercantile Library has reached its 175th anniversary in a strong position. Membership hovers around the 1,500 mark; the endowment is healthy despite the recent economic downturn; and while the Library board still worries about balancing the annual budget, the Association has achieved a measure of financial stability. The facilities have never been so well maintained. The organization is ably led; the staff is first-rate, and the board continues to find energetic, visionary members.

Still, programming remains the Library's vital force. What Jean Springer started in 1969, Albert Pyle has continued and expanded. The Niehoff Lecture Series annually brings in a high-quality writer[35] and remains the Library's highest-profile function, but the Harriet Beecher Stowe Lecture, the Founders Day festivities, the annual meeting, the Winter Author Series, and the more recent Modern Novel event maintain the Mercantile Library's reputation throughout the year. Debates, discussion groups, community forums, and even some of the musical performances have enhanced the

34 Brown's book was supported by a $6,500 grant from the Ohio Humanities Council.
35 More recent authors who have given the annual lecture include Joyce Carol Oates, Jonathan Winters again, Arthur M. Schlesinger Jr., Christopher Buckley, Salman Rushdie, Annie Proulx, Calvin Trillin, David Baldacci, and, in 2009, Booker Prize winner A. S. Byatt. Bill Bryson is scheduled to appear in 2010.

Mercantile's position as the city's literary center.[36]

What has allowed the Mercantile Library not only to survive but also to become such an essential part of Cincinnati's intellectual life? From its inception it has benefited from outstanding leadership. Boards of directors have taken their roles seriously; their members almost always have been hard-working, and sometimes visionary. Presidents have stepped forward to steer the Association through fires and wars, through internal disputes and economic crises. Librarians have played critical roles in keeping the Library on an even keel, from Charles Cist in the mid-nineteenth century to Jean Springer in the late 20th century. Albert Pyle continues this role today. Staff members often have provided the glue that has held the Library together: Alice McLean, Caroline Gaither, Violet Williams, Mark Pierce, and, today, Mary Gruber, Cedric Rose, Sandra Geiser, and Chris Messick.

All of these people have been important in maintaining the Mercantile's equilibrium, but another group deserves recognition as well—the membership. Few institutions in the city can boast such a devoted following. Members rescued books from the early fires; they defended the Association's lease when a shortsighted board decided to give it up; and on countless occasions they have generously contributed funds to keep the facilities up to the highest standards. Whether they have enjoyed the Mercantile for its access to information, for its literary programs, or simply as a quiet place of refuge, the members have always been the Library's foundation. All of them, past and present, can be proud of this history.

36 Buck Niehoff and Dale Brown, in working on a mission statement, came up with the tag line "The Literary Center of Cincinnati" while on a return flight from the annual outing of the Commercial and Commonwealth Club. Brown recalls that "it was written out on the back of a barf bag." Dale Brown to Robert Vitz, email, September 21, 2009.

Eventually Albert Pyle will retire, but a future board of directors certainly will find a capable replacement. Staff members will come and go, and at some point a new building will replace the current structure. But there is no reason to think that the Mercantile Library isn't looking forward to the next 175 years at the same address... or even another 9,825 years, when the current lease expires.

Board Presidents

1835	Moses Ranney	1858	Samuel M. Murphy
1836	Moses Ranney	1859	Charles W. Rowland
1837	Rowland G. Mitchell	1860	Theodore Cook
1838	William Watts	1861	Caleb B. Marsh
1839	Isaac D. Wheeler/	1862	Augustus S. Winslow
	Charles S. Sackett	1863	C. Taylor Jones
1840	Moses Ranney	1864	C. Taylor Jones
1841	Charles Duffield	1865	Adolph Wood
1842	William Watts	1866	S. C. Newton
1843	John W. Ellis	1867	S. C. Newton
1844	R. M. W. Taylor	1868	F. H. Baldwin
1845	R. M. W. Taylor	1869	F. H. Baldwin
1846	R. M. W. Taylor	1870	George W. Jones
1847	John W. Hartwell	1871	Hugh Colville
1848	John W. Hartwell	1872	Wiliam P. Anderson
1849	George T. Stedman	1873	Samuel B. Warren
1850	Joseph C. Butler	1874	William B. Munson
1851	Joseph C. Butler	1875	William J. Armel
1852	James Lupton	1876	Herman Goepper
1853	James Lupton	1877	Earl W. Stimson
1854	Henry D. Huntington	1878	Charles A. Wilson
1855	Charles R. Fosdick	1879	Henry J. Page
1856	Andrew B. Merriam	1880	Robert F. Leaman
1857	W. I. Whiteman	1881	W. S. Mitchell

1882	William Wirt Peabody	1914	Thomas Carr Powell
1883	Henry B. Morehead	1915	Luke W. Smith
1884	Henry DeBus	1916	Luke W. Smith
1885	James L. Foley	1917	Luke W. Smith
1886	John A. Townley	1918	Ferdinand Jelke Jr.
1887	Chapman Johnson	1919	Charles H. Stephens
1888	William B. Carpenter	1920	Charles H. Stephens
1889	Reverend Dudley W. Rhodes	1921	Thomas B. Paxton Jr.
		1922	Thomas B. Paxton Jr.
1890	Joseph C. Carew	1923	Thomas B. Paxton Jr.
1891	Joseph Cox Jr.	1924	George Hoadley
1892	Frederick H. Alms	1925	George Hoadley
1893	Frederick H. Alms	1926	Charles B. Wilby
1894	Frederick H. Alms	1927	Charles B. Wilby
1895	E. O. McCormick	1928	Charles B. Wilby
1896	E. O. McCormick	1929	Robert L. Black
1897	E. O. McCormick	1930	Robert L. Black
1898	Rudolph Kleybolte	1931	Robert L. Black
1899	Guy W. Mallon	1932	George Hoadley
1900	Guy W. Mallon	1933	George Hoadley
1901	John E. Bruce	1934	Shelley Rouse
1902	John E. Bruce	1935	John Malick
1903	John E. Bruce	1936	John Malick
1904	John E. Bruce	1937	Clinton Galway
1905	John E. Bruce	1938	Charles H. Stephens
1906	William B. Melish	1939	Charles H. Stephens
1907	William B. Melish	1940	Stephen W. Jones
1908	Frederick Hinkle	1941	Stephen W. Jones
1909	Charles B. Wilby	1942	Robert L. Black
1910	Charles B. Wilby	1943	Robert L. Black
1911	Charles B. Wilby	1944	Joseph W. Sagmaster
1912	Charles B. Wilby	1945	Joseph W. Sagmaster
1913	Thomas Carr Powell	1946	W. Webb Hill

236

1947	W. Webb Hill	1980	Robert H. Allen
1948	W. Webb Hill	1981	Robert Westheimer
1949	W. Webb Hill	1982	Robert Westheimer
1950	W. Webb Hill	1983	Carol H. Allgood
1951	W. Webb Hill	1984	Carol H. Allgood
1952	W. Webb Hill	1985	George H. Palmer
1953	W. Webb Hill	1986	George H. Palmer
1954	W. Webb Hill	1987	Hope Taft
1955	W. Webb Hill	1988	Hope Taft
1956	W. Webb Hill	1989	Chad W. Christine
1957	W. Webb Hill	1990	Chad W. Christine
1958	W. Webb Hill	1991	Ernest A. Eynon II
1959	W. Webb Hill	1992	Ernest A. Eynon II
1960	W. Webb Hill	1993	H. C. Buck Niehoff
1961	Hal D. Balyeat	1994	H. C. Buck Niehoff
1962	Spencer F. Kuhn	1995	H. C. Buck Niehoff
1963	Spencer F. Kuhn	1996	William H. Chatfield
1964	Spencer F. Kuhn	1997	William H. Chatfield
1965	Walter H. Alexander	1998	John Ryan
1966	Walter H. Alexander	1999	John Ryan
1967	Walter H. Alexander	2000	Vere Gaynor
1968	Walter H. Alexander	2001	Vere Gaynor
1969	Walter H. Alexander	2002	James Wellinghoff
1970	John A. Benjamin	2003	James Wellinghoff
1971	John A. Benjamin	2004	Edward Marks
1972	Douglas G. Cole	2005	Edward Marks
1973	Douglas G. Cole	2006	Joseph Tomain
1974	Harry W. Whittaker	2007	Joseph Tomain
1975	Harry W. Whittaker	2008	Dale Patrick Brown
1976	Peter J. Strauss	2009	Dale Patrick Brown
1977	Peter J. Strauss	2010	Dale Patrick Brown
1978	Peter J. Strauss		
1979	Robert H. Allen		

Librarians

1836-1837	Benjamin F. Doolittle
1837-1839	Nathaniel Holley
1839-1844	James Wildy
1844-1847	Charles E. Cist
1848	Thomas Gales Foster
1849-1853	Charles E. Cist
1853-1859	Reuben H. Stevenson
1860-1861	George A. Morris
1862-1863	Sylvester Taylor
1864-1865	James G. Barnwell
1866-1878	M. Hazen White
1879-1897	John M. Newton
1898-1900	William Holden
1904-1911	William B. A. Taylor
1911-1915	Robert M. McCurdy
1915-1918	Alice Coy
1919-1922	Caroline Blanton
1922-1924	Anna E. Sechrest
1924-1941	Natalie B. Dohrmann
1941-1945	Violet G. Williams
1945-1969	Isabelle K. Ackerson
1969-1993	Jean Springer
1994-	Albert Pyle

Art Objects and Collectibles

CURRENTLY OR PREVIOUSLY IN THE LIBRARY

❦ **1841**
Andrew Jackson - Oil portrait
Source: R. H. Parry
Location: Unknown

❦ **1842**
Minerals and Fossils - McGrew ?
Location: Unknown

❦ **1842**
"Handsome clock" - "An excellent timepiece"
Source: Green and Beggs
Location: Unknown

❦ **1842**
Hamlet and Ophelia - Painting by Lily Martin
Source: Acquisition
Location: Unknown

❦ **c. 1843**
William H. Harrison - Oil portrait by J. Beard
Source: Subscription
Loaned to Cincinnati Art Museum/c. 1906; returned to family in 1919

❦ **c. 1843**
Charles Hammond - Oil portrait by J. Beard
Source: S. S. L'Hommedieu
Loaned to Cincinnati Art Museum/c. 1906

❦ **1844**
Henry Clay - Plaster bust by Joel T. Hart
Source: Purchase
Location: Library

❦ **1844**
Mr. Guthrie (?) - Plaster bust
Source: Purchase
Location: Unknown

❦ **1845**
William H. Harrison -
Marble bust by S. Clevenger
Source: Purchase
Location: Library

❦ **1845**
"Jolly Flatboat Men" -
G. Bingham (engraving?)
Source: American Art
Union
Location: Unknown

❦ **1845**
 Landscape painting? -
by Thomas Cole
Source: American Art
Union
Location: Unknown

❦ **1846**
Ornithology - Book by
J. Bonaparte
Source: John B. Coram
Location: Unknown

❦ **1846**
*Nicollet's Topographical Map
of the... Mississippi*
Source: James T. Morehead
Location: Unknown

❦ **1846**
"Hiram Powers" - Engraving
Source: N. Longworth
Location: Unknown

❦ **1846**
Truman Safford - Engraving
Source: N. Longworth
Location: Unknown

❦ **1846**
Mineral specimens - From
Lake Superior
Source: Crafts J. Wright
Location: Unknown

❦ **1846**
Declaration of Independence
(facsimile)
Source: Albert G. Day
Location: Unknown

❦ **1846**
Andrew Jackson - Portrait by
Miner Kellogg
Source: Unknown
Location: Unknown

❦ 1846
Geo. Washington -
Autograph
John Kennett
Location: Library archives

❦ 1846
Maps and Engravings - No
further information
J. H. Perkins
Location: Unknown

❦ 1847
Benj. Franklin - Autograph
Lewis J. Cist
Location: Unknown

❦ 1847
Execution warrant for
Charles I (facsimile)
Albert G. Day
Location: Unknown

❦ 1848
John Quincy Adams - Bust by
John C. King
Source: Purchase
Location: Unknown

❦ 1849
Mr. Abbey (?) - Portrait by
Brannon [sic]
Source: Purchase
Location: Unknown

❦ 1849
"Youth" - Engraving of
Thomas Cole's Painting
American Art Union
Location: Unknown

❦ 1851
Views from Pompeii - Book
Source: Dudley Hall
Location: Unknown

❦ 1851
History of... Indian Tribes
- Book by H. Schoolcraft/
Seth Eastman
Source: U.S. Commissioner
of Indian Affairs
Location: Unknown

❦ 1851
G. Washington - Signed
letter
Source: S. S. L'Hommedieu
Location: Unknown

❦ 1851
John Adams - Signed letter
Source: John B. Russell
Location: Unknown

❦ 1851

Louis Agassiz - Signed
letter to Jas. Lupton
Source: Helen Crane
Location: Library archives

❦ 1852

John Adams - Signed letter
Source: Andrew J. Reynolds
Location: Unknown

❦ 1852

London, Paris, etc. -
Embossed maps
Source: Henry D.
Huntington
Location: Unknown

❦ 1852

French Dictionary, 16th
century
Source: C. Augustus Smith
Location: Unknown

❦ 1852

Latin pamphlets - Bound in
sharkskin
Source: C. Augustus Smith
Location: Unknown

❦ 1852

Gospel of Matthew - Printed
in Persian
Source: C. Augustus Smith
Location: Unknown

❦ 1852

Louis Kossuth - Signed
letter to J. Lupton
Source: W. T. H. Howe
Location: Library archives

❦ 1852

Geneva Regulator - Clock
Source: Charles Stetson
Location: Library

❦ 1852

Bible - Printed in Germany
c. 1500
Source: C. Augustus Smith
Location: Unknown

❦ 1852

Thomas Jefferson - Signed
letter
Source: Charles D. Drake
Location: Unknown

❦ c 1855

Hezekiah Flint - Portrait by
Miner Kellogg
Source: John Baker
Location: Library, 12th
floor

❦ 1856
Daniel Webster - Bust by
John C. King
Source: Purchase
Location: Library

❦ 1856
Louis Agassiz - Bust by John
C. King
Source: Purchase
Location: Library

❦ 1856
Daniel Drake - Plaster bust
by Chas. Bullett
Source: Samuel M. Murphy
Location: Library

❦ 1856
Silence - Statue by Joseph
Mozier
Source: Davis Lawler
Location: Library

❦ 1857
Sabrina - Statue, sculptor
unknown
Source: Unknown
Location: Unknown

❦ 1857
John C. Breckinridge - Plaster
bust
Source: C. W. Rowland
Location: Unknown

❦ 1857
Edward Everett - Oil
painting by J. O. Eaton
Source: A. B. Merriam
Location: Library

❦ 1858
Jonathan McLean - Plaster
bust by J. Frankenstein
Source: Thomas Gallagher
Location: Library

❦ 1858
Christy Cabinet - Shells,
fossils, and minerals
Source: Purchase
Sold in Europe

❦ 1858
Stephen Douglas - Plaster
bust
Source: Charles Rule
Location: Unknown

❦ 1859
Salmon P. Chase - Plaster
bust by T. D. Jones
Source: S. C. Newton
Location: Library

❦ 1859
John P. Foote - Plaster Bust
by C. Bullett
Source: Davis B. Lawler
Location: Library

🐦 **1859**

Map of Cincinnati, printed in 1819
Source: W. S. Johnson
Location: Library

🐦 1859

Ethan and Ira Allen - Autographs
Source: George B. Read
Location: Unknown

🐦 **1859**

Planetarium
Source: a Mr. Barlow
Location: Unknown

🐦 1860

Thomas Ewing - Plaster bust by T.D. Jones
Source: John Caldwell
Location: Unknown

🐦 1860

Mineral specimens
Source: "Donated by Eggers & Wilde"
Given to Society of Natural Science in 1870

🐦 1861

George Washington -
Marble bust by Powers
Source: L. B. Harrison et al.
Location: Library

🐦 1862

Abraham Lincoln - Plaster bust by T. D. Jones
Source: a Dr. Hamlin
Location: Library

🐦 1862

Andrew Jackson - Signed letter
Source: J. S. Pugh
Location: Unknown

🐦 **1864**

Napoleon Bonaparte - Marble bust by A. Canova
Source: Lewis C. Hopkins
Location: Library, 12th floor

🐦 1867

Geanette Cummins
- Oil portrait
Source: John W. Owens
Returned to a Miss J. Cummins

🐦 1867

Susan Ludlow - Oil portrait
Source: John W. Owens
Location: Unknown

❦ **1867**
Washington Irving - Marble medallion
Source: William Powell Jr.
Location: Library

❦ **1868**
Declaration of Independence (in Chinese)
Source: Isaac J. Allen
Location: Unknown

❦ **1872**
Gli Edifizi Antichi dei Contorni di Roma (6 vols.) - Book by Luigi Canina, with engravings
Source: David Sinton
Location: Library

❦ **1873**
Shakespeare - Variorum edition
Source: Purchase
Location: Unknown

❦ **1873**
Shakespeare - 1623 edition (facsimile)
Source: Robert Clarke
Location: Unknown

❦ **c. 1875**
Abraham Lincoln - Henry Gugler engraving of portrait by John Littlefield
Source: M. Hazen White et al.
Location: Library

❦ **1876**
Explorations in the West, by Lt. George Wheeler
Source: Alphonso Taft
Location: Unknown

❦ **1876**
Photographs of Wheeler expedition, by T. Sullivan
Source: Alphonso Taft
Sold to Walter Burton in 1983

❦ **1877**
Bible, folio-size, printed in Nuremburg, 1479 (in Latin)
Source: Robert Clarke
Location: Unknown

❦ **1877**
Joel Barlow - Plaster bust by Jean Houdon
Source: Daniel Bolles
Location: Library

❦ 1877
E. S. Thomas - Full-
length portrait by John
Frankenstein
Source: Calvin W. Thomas
Location: Unknown

❦ 1879
Illuminated design - Henry
F. Farney
Source: Robert F. Leaman
Location: Unknown

❦ 1880
"Beautiful vase" (no other
identification)
Source: T. J. Wheatley
Location: Unknown

❦ 1880
Le Costume Histoire - Book
by Auguste Racinet
Source: C. H. Justis
Location: Library

❦ 1884
"The Three Arts" -
Stained-glass Window:
Source: George A. Bowen
Location: Unknown

❦ 1888
Symmes land grant
- Document

Source: Lawrence
Mendenhall
Location: Unknown

❦ 1892
"The Ruins of Rome" - Five
Photographs by Carlo Ponti
Source: Herman M. Moos
Location: Library

❦ 1892
Panoramic view of Rome
(engraving?)
Source: Herman M. Moos
Location: Library, 12th
floor

❦ 1904
"Woman with a Book" -
Stained-glass Window
Source: Augustine Ogden
Location: Unknown

❦ 1907
Oil portraits (unidentified)*
Source: Emery H. Barton
Location: Unknown

❦ 1910
Signed letters from
William Howard Taft
Source: Thornton W. Hinkle
Location: Library archives

❦ **1911**
"Four Pictures": Charles
Dickens, Robert Burns,
Oliver Wendell Holmes,
and Whistler's portrait
by Nicholson (probably
reproductions)
Source: Emery H. Barton
Location: Unknown

❦ **1915**
Isaac M. Wise - Oil portrait
Source: Max B. May
Location: Unknown

❦ **1930**
Thomas J. Gallagher - Oil
portrait by T.B. Read
Source: The Misses
Gallagher
Location: Unknown

❦ **1931**
John Galsworthy - Etching
by R. H. Sauter
Source: W. T. H. Howe
Location: Library

❦ **1935**
Moses Ranney - Watercolor
on ivory
Source: Ranney's
granddaughter
Location: Library

❦ **1940**
Grandfather clock - Duhme
Jewelry Co.
Source: Mrs. David May
Location: Library

❦ **1983**
Morgan Ewing
- Daguerreotype
Source: E. Remelin (?)
Location: Library archives

❦ **1987**
Grand piano - Steinway
Source: Melba Schott
Location: Library

❦ **1995**
Buck Niehoff - Oil by Stacey
Davidson
Source: Patricia Niehoff
Location: Library

❦ **1997**
Robert Frost - Bust by G.W.
Lundeen
Source: Buck and Patricia
Niehoff
Location: Library

❦ **1998**
H. W. Longfellow - Bust by
Thomas Brock (?)
Source: Virginius Hall
Location: Library

❦ **1998**
Charles Dickens - Wax
bas-relief portrait
Source: Chas. Fleischmann
Stolen

❦ **1998**
Works by Octavio Paz
- Illustrations by Robert
Motherwell
Source: Buck and Patricia
Niehoff
Location: Library

❦ **2003**
Dombey and Sons (First ed.)
- by Charles Dickens
Source: Mr. and Mrs. Joseph
Andrews
Location: Library

❦ **2003**
*Harriet Beecher Stowe
Limestone* - bust by Walter
Driesbach
Source: Purchase
Location: Library

❦ **2003**
Our Mutual Friend (First ed.)
- by Charles Dickens
Source: Brad Wigor
Location: Library

❦ **2004**
Portrait of a Married Woman
- Watercolor by E. Nourse
Source: Patricia Niehoff
Location: Library

❦ **2004**
"Seven Owls" - Oil,
charcoal, mixed media on
burlap by E. Nourse
Source: Patricia Niehoff
Location: Library

❦ **2008**
"Washington," "Franklin,"
and *"Grant"* - Engravings by
George Meinschausen
Source: R. Vitz
Location: Library

❦ **2010**
Two Rooks - Ceramic
sculptures by Brenda Tarbell
Source: Deborah and Louis
Ginocchio Jr. and Marilyn
and James Wellinghoff
Location: Library

❦ Miscellaneous
No Known Date of Acquisition

Mr. Ernst - Probably oil portrait
Location: Unknown;
Loaned to Cincinnati Art Museum in 1906

Portrait of Mr. Hunt - (Oil?) by a "colored artist"
Location: Unknown
Donated to a "colored institution" in 1919

Thomas Buchanan Read - Self-portrait (?)**
Source: Unknown
Location: Library

Benjamin Franklin - Engraving
Source: Unknown
Location: Library

Abraham Lincoln - Picture
Location: Unknown
Given to Berea College, 1931

Nicholas Longworth - Plaster bust (attr. to H. Powers)
Source: Unknown
Location: Library

Charles Dickens - Plaster bust by Henry Dexter
Source: Unknown
Location: Library

Shakespeare - Plaster bust
Source: Unknown
Location: Library

White walnut case - Carved by Henry Fry
Source: Unknown
Location: Unknown

Rookwood vase (1897) - K. Shirayamadani
Source: Unknown
Location: Library, 12th floor

Rookwood vase (1896) - K. Shirayamadani
Source: Unknown
Location: Library, 12th floor

Photograph of William Howard Taft
Source: Unknown
Location: Library, 12th floor

Rookwood pot (1895) - K. Shirayamadani
Source: Unknown
Location: Library, 12th floor

Rookwood vase - MJD (Matthew Daly?)
Source: Unknown
Location: Library, 12th floor

Sèvres urn - L. Malpass
Source: Unknown
Location: Library

Etching - Edmund T.
Hurley
Source: Randy Sandler
Location: Library, 12th
Floor

Watercolor - Drisler
Source: Unknown
Location: Library

Hand-colored lithograph -
Cecil Aldin
Source: Unknown
Location: Library

Andersonville Prison -
Lithograph by Henry Blatz
Source: Unknown
Location: Librarian's Office

---

* One of these may be the
unknown portrait found in a
Location: Library storage closet
in 1999, which was cleaned and
restored, and now hangs in the
12th-floor lecture hall.

** This may be the portrait of
Thomas Gallagher given in 1930.

Primary Sources

❧ Newspapers

Chic, 2 (January 10, 1891), 16.

Cincinnati Advertiser and Ohio Phoenix, 1835.

Cincinnati Commercial, 1853-69.

(Cincinnati) Daily Evening Post, 1835.

Cincinnati Daily Gazette, 1835-78.

Cincinnati Daily Times, 1846-57.

Cincinnati Enquirer, 1870-2009.

Cincinnati Graphic, 3 (April 11, 1885), 239.

Cincinnati Herald, 2000.

Cincinnati Post, 1993-2003.

Cincinnati Times-Star, 1928-48.

Cincinnati Whig and Commercial Intelligencer, 1835.

CityBeat, 2003.

Downtowner, 1993-2004.

❧ Books

Cincinnati City Directories, 1834-1900.

Cist, Charles. Cincinnati in 1841: Its Early Annals and Future Prospects. Cincinnati, 1841.

_____. The Cincinnati Miscellany, or, Antiquities of the West and Pioneer History and General and Local Statistics. Cincinnati, 1846. Vol. 1.

_____. Sketches and Statistics of Cincinnati in 1851. Cincinnati, 1851.

Conway, Moncure Daniel. Autobiography, Memories and Experiences of Moncure Daniel Conway. Boston, 1904.

Drake, Benjamin and Edward D. Mansfield. Cincinnati in 1826. Cincinnati, 1826.

"Glimpses into Cincinnati's Past: The Gest Letters, 1834-1842." Edited by Charles Schultz. Ohio History, 73 (Summer, 1964), 151-57.

Niehoff, H. C. Buck. Something Funny at the Library. Cincinnati: Mercantile Library, 2004.

Trollope, Frances. *Domestic Manners of the Americans.* New York: Oxford University Press, 1984. Reprint of 1832 edition.

Weld, Charles Richard. *A Vacation Tour of the United States and Canada.* London, 1855.

Young Men's Mercantile Library Association. Minutes of the Board of Directors. Mercantile Library Association archives.

_____. *Quarterly and Annual Reports.* Mercantile Library Association archives.

❦ Interviews by Author

Mary Gruber, July 16, 2009

Thomas E. Huenefeld, July 1, 2009

H.C. Buck Niehoff, October 27, 2009

Albert Pyle, August 5, 2009

Jean Springer, June 26, 2009

❦ Secondary Sources

Aaron, Daniel. *Cincinnati, Queen City of the West, 1819-1838.* Columbus: Ohio State University Press, 1992.

Bahra, Peter J. "Everything, However Trifling." *Queen City Heritage,* 55 (Winter, 1997), 38-41.

Barringer, Sallie H. and Bradford W. Scharlott. "The Cincinnati Mercantile Library As a Business-Communications Center, 1835-1846." *Libraries and Culture,* 26 (Spring, 1991), 388-401.

[Black, Robert L. Sr.]. *The Young Men's Mercantile Library Association of Cincinnati.* Cincinnati, 1935.

Brown, Dale Patrick. *Brilliance and Balderdash: Early Lectures at Cincinnati's Mercantile Library.* Cincinnati: Mercantile Library, 2007.

Clubbe, John. *Cincinnati Observed: Architecture and History.* Columbus: Ohio State University Press, 1992.

Cowan, C. Wesley. "A Historical Overview of the Mercantile Library's Furnishings." Talk delivered at the Mercantile Library on January 15, 2006. Copy in Mercantile Library archives.

Fleischman, John. "The Ironclad Lease." *Ohio Magazine* (July, 1992), 26-29.

_____. *Free & Public: One Hundred Years at the Public Library of Cincinnati and Hamilton County.* Wilmington, OH: Orange Frazer Press, 2002.

Ford, Henry A. and Kate B. Ford. *History of Cincinnati, Ohio.* Cincinnati, 1881.

Glazer, Walter Stix. *Cincinnati in 1840: The Social and Functional Organization of an Urban Community during the Pre-Civil War Period.* Columbus: Ohio State University Press, 1999.

Greve, Charles T. *Centennial History of Cincinnati.* Chicago: Biographical Publishing Company, 1904.

Hanlon, David R. "Arts and Letters: The Baker Family Papers." *Ohio Valley History*, 9 (Summer 2009), 89-93.

Herz, Walter P. "Influence Transcending Mere Numbers: The Unitarians in Nineteenth-Century Cincinnati." *Queen City Heritage*, 51 (Winter, 1991), 2-22.

Hurley, Daniel H. "Mercantile Library Annual Meeting Presentation." Talk delivered at the Mercantile Library, January 16, 2007. Copy in author's possession.

Komlos, John H. *Louis Kossuth in America, 1851-1852.* Buffalo: East European Institute, 1973.

Leonard, Lewis Alexander, editor-in-chief. *Greater Cincinnati and Its People.* Chicago and New York: Lewis Historical Publishing Co., 1927.

Meade, David. "Brownson and Kossuth in Cincinnati." *Bulletin of the Historical and Philosophical Society of Cincinnati*, 7 (April, 1949), 89-97.

Merrihew, Murray E. "Young Men's Mercantile Library Association, 1835-1905." Cincinnati, 1905.

Miller, Ernest I. "Libraries in Cincinnati." *Bulletin of the Historical and Philosophical Society of Cincinnati*, 16 (July, 1958), 240-244.

Miller, Orloff G. "Man of Letters, Man of Service: Alphonso Taft & The Mercantile Library." Paper delivered at Mercantile Library, January 20, 2009. Copy in Mercantile Library archives.

Pierson, George Wilson. *Tocqueville and Beaumont in America*. New York: Oxford University Press, 1938.

Shapiro, Henry D. and Jonathan D. Sarna, editors. *Ethnic Diversity and Civic Identity: Patterns of Conflict and Cohesion in Cincinnati*. Urbana: University of Illinois Press, 1992.

Venable, William H. *Beginnings of Literary Culture in the Ohio Valley*. Cincinnati: Robert Clarke & Co., 1891.

Vitz, Robert C. *The Queen and the Arts: Cultural Life in Nineteenth-Century Cincinnati*. Kent, OH: Kent State University Press, 1989.

Wendorf, Richard, editor. *America's Membership Libraries*. New Castle, DE: Oak Knoll Press, 2007.

Wunder, Richard P. *Hiram Powers, Vermont Sculptor, 1805-1873, Vol. 1: Life*. Newark, DE: University of Delaware Press, 1989.

Index

A. B. Closson Jr. Company, 116
Ackerson, Isabella, 161
Adair, John F., 83
Adams, Eleanor, 189
Adams Express Company, 72
Adams, John, 99, 243, 244
Adams, John Quincy, 23, 30, 51, 98, 243
Addy, Caroline, 78
Agar, Herbert, 168
Agassiz, Louis, 59, 82, 102, 244, 245
Air Conditioning Party, 190
Alexander, Walter H., 180, 237
Alger Jr., Horatio, 131
Allen, James Lane, 129
Allen, Robert H., 138, 193, 199, 227, 237
Allgood, Carol, 202, 210, 220
Allison, Dorothy, 224
Alms & Doepke, 127
Alms Hotel, 168
Alschuler, John, 228
American Airlines, 202
American Art Union, 96, 98, 242, 243
American Express Company, 88
American Israelite, 125
American Ornithology, 42, 98
Ames, Daniel, 7
Anderson, Charles, 43
Anderson, William P., 85, 86, 120
Anderson, Yeatman, 203
Andrews, Joseph, 117, 250
Annan, James T., 39, 44
Anthony, J. G., 94
Apprentices' Library, 3
Arnold's Restaurant, 214
Aronson, Julie, 224
Assassin's Gate: America in Iraq, The, 225
Association for the Advancement of
    Science, 52
Audubon, John J., 100
Autobiography of an Actress, 47

Axtell Circulating Library, 135, 136
Bailey Jr., Gamaliel, 43
Baker, John, 103, 244
Baker, Nathan Flint, 101, 103
Baldwin, Almon, 103
Ball, Edward, 223
Bank of the United States, 1
Barnhorn, Clement, 152
Barton, Emery H., 248, 249
Baum, Martin, 3
Beard, James H., 95, 96
Bebb, William, 50
Bedinghaus, Robert, 228
Beecher, Henry Ward, 59, 68, 82, 122
Beecher, Lyman, 22, 59, 123
Beggs, J. P., 94
"Belle of Amherst," 192
Bellow, Saul, 198, f
Bellows, Henry W., 69
Benham, Joseph S., 10
Benjamin, John A., 188, 237
Benjamin, Park, 54, 57
Bennis, Warren, 191
Benton, Thomas Hart, 50, 55, 67
Berea College, 135, 136, 251
Berry, Wendell, 207, 224
Best and the Brightest, The, 190
Bettman, Gilbert, 181
Biggs, Thomas, 104
Bingham, George Caleb, 96
Birds of America, 100
Birmingham, Stephen, 190, 193, 224, 229
Black Jr., Robert L., 176, 180
Black Sr., Robert L., 5, 154, 157, 164-165,
    168-169, 170, 172, 176
Blaine, Charlee, 200
Blair Jr., Francis P., 69
Blanton, Caroline, 161, 239
Boccacio, 11
Bolger, Margaret, 186

Bolles, David, 100, 114
Bonaparte, Charles Lucien, 98
Bonfire of the Vanities, The, 205
Books by the Banks, 224, 229
Bookshelf, 229
Borders Books, 229
Borgman, Jim, 215, e, f
Boston Quarterly, 52
Bouldin, George W. R., 18
Bowen, George A., 114, 220, 248
Bowen, William, 207
Bowler, Mrs. Robert Bonner, 164
Bradbury, Ray, 216
Bradlaugh, Charles, 125
Brannan, William P., 103
Breathing in Africa, 230
Breckinridge, John C., 103, 245
Breckinridge, Robert J., 50
Brilliance and Balderdash, vi, 21, 39, 51, 54,
  60, 124, 126, 128, 152, 167, 230, 256, 266
Brown, Charles F., 72
Brown, Dale Patrick, iii, vi, vii, 21, 128, 124
  223, 230, 237
Brown, Henry Kirke, 101
Brown, H. W., 81, 83
Brown, John, 69
Brown, Robert, 5
Brown, S. G., 19
Brownson, Orestes, 52
Brown, W. W., 142
Bruce, John E., 149, 236
Bryant, William Cullen, 51
Buchanan, James, 63
Buchanan, John, 18
Buckley, Christopher, 230
Buckley, William F., 205
Buckner, William, 148
Bullett, Charles, 103
Burdell, Edward, 228
Burnet House, 52
Burnet, Jacob, 3, 41
Burnham, Daniel, 151
Burns, Jonathan G., 132
Burns, Robert, 115, 249
Burt & Greene's, 95
Burton, Mary Louise, 197
Burton, Walter, 113, 247
Bush, George H. W., 207
Butler, Benjamin F., 79
Butler, Joseph C., 17, 46, 75, 235
Byatt, A. S., 230
Caldwell, John D., 110

Calhoun, John C., 51
Cannon, Mary Jo, 186
Canon Club, 226, 227
Canova, Antonio, 110
Carew, Joseph T., 133
Carlisle, Florence, 78
Carnegie, Andrew, 143
Carnegie Foundation, 143
Cary, Alice, 78
Cash, Albert D., 175
Cass, Lewis, 50
Catch-22, 193
Cayton, Andrew, 224, 226
Century Magazine, The, 70
Chamber of Commerce, 214
Chandler, Frank W., 167
Chase, Salmon P., 13, 43, 57, 105, 245
Chatfield and Woods Building, 101
Chatfield, William, 217, 218
Chess Club, 75
Child, Julia, 205
Christine, Chadwick, 200
Christy Cabinet, 76, 77
Christy, David, 106
Cincinnatian Hotel, 203
Cincinnati Art Museum, 95, 96, 112, 115
Cincinnati Bengals, 214
Cincinnati Choral Society, 128
Cincinnati Circulating Library, 3
Cincinnati College, 15, 20, 31
Cincinnati College Building, 19, 20, 31,
  35, 37, 40, 89, 90, 95, 115, 121, 137-138,
  144-148
Cincinnati Commercial, 49, 55, 105, 114
Cincinnati Commercial and Advertiser, 114
Cincinnati Daily Commercial, 66, 68
Cincinnati Daily Times, 51, 56-57
Cincinnati Educational Television, 229
Cincinnati Enquirer, 214-215, 218, 227
Cincinnati Evening Post, 114
Cincinnati Female Seminary, 80
Cincinnati Gas, Light & Coke Company,
  136
Cincinnati Graphic, 127, 132
Cincinnati, Hamilton & Dayton Railroad,
  52, 53
Cincinnati Historical Society, 133
Cincinnati in 1826, 3, 196
Cincinnati Insurance Company, 74
Cincinnati Law College, 20, 21
Cincinnati Literary Society, 2, 13
Cincinnati Lyceum, 2, 19, 23

Cincinnati Magazine, 193, 202
Cincinnati Observatory, 30
Cincinnati Peace League, 167
Cincinnati Philanthropist, 43
Cincinnati Public Library, 49
Cincinnati Reading Room, 3
Cincinnati Reds, 199, 208
Cincinnati Science Center, 185
Cincinnati Shakespeare Festival, 227
Cincinnati Symphony Orchestra, 216
Cincinnati Times-Star, 129
Cincinnatus, 101
Cist, Charles E., 27, 30
Cist, Lewis J., 30, 98
Clarke, Brock, 229
Clarke, Robert, 3
Clark, Peter H., 84, 85
Clay, Cassius, 65
Clay, Henry, 65, 67
Clayton, Richard, 5
Clevenger, Shobal V., 95
Clippinger, John H., 180
Clooney, Nick, 224
Closson. *See* A. B. Closson Jr. Company
Cochran, Mrs. John A., 168
Cole, Douglas, 199
Cole, Thomas, 97, 98
Colfax, Schuyler, 82
College Building Board of Trustees, 144
College of Mount Saint Joseph, 193
College of Music, 122
Collins, Gail, 225
Collins, Seward, 168
"Columbiad, The," 114
Colville, Hugh, 85
Compromise of 1850, 65
Conrad, Barnaby, 199, 202
Contemporary Arts Center, 195, 204, 207
Conway, Moncure D., 56
Cook, Theodore, 75
Coram, John B., 42, 97
Corwin, Thomas, 57
Cowan, C. Wesley, 104
Cox, Joseph, 133
Coy, Alice, 160
Crush, Thomas, 228
Cummins, David, 111
Cummins, Geanette, 110
Cunningham, Michael, 224
Cushing, Caleb, 59
Daily Evening Post, 20
Dair, John F., 134

Daly, Matt, 119
Daniel, Margaret Truman, 206
Dartmouth College, 138
Davidson, Stacey, 117
Davidson, W. L., 129
Day, Albert G., 98
Day, Timothy Crane, 133
DeBrosse, Jim, 198
de Mille, Agnes, 190
Der Volksblatt, 162
Dewey, Arthur, 227
Dexter, Julius, 74, 85
Dickens, Charles, 115, 117
Doctorow, E. L., 224
Dodd & Company, 53
Dohrmann, Natalie B., 161
Dolibois, John, 208
Dombey and Son, 117
Domestic Manners of the Americans, 2, 4, 256
Dom Pedro II, 131
Doolittle, Benjamin F., 11, 239
Douglas, Stephen A., 104
Downtowner, 185, 210, 211
Drake, Benjamin, 3
Drake, Charles D., 99
Drake, Daniel, 3, 10, 99, 103, 111, 196, 245
Draper, Sharon, 224
Dresser, Betsy, 216
Drew's Bookstore, 215, 216
Driesbach, Walter, 225
Duke Energy Foundation, 224
Dumahut, R. C. H., 131
Dunbar, Paul Lawrence, 226
Dykstra, Clarence A., 169
Eastman, Seth, 99
Eaton, Joseph Oriel, 56
Ebert, Edward S., 143
Eckstein, Frederick, 104
Economou, Robert, 217
Edison, Thomas, 136
Egeria at the Fountain, 101
Ellis, Anita, 221, 224
Ellis, John W., i
Ellis, Samuel, 15
Emerson, Ralph Waldo, 54
Emery Estates, 177
Emery Hotel Annex, 150
Emery Memorial Fund, 178
Emery, Thomas J., 149
Encyclopedia Britannica (*Ninth Edition*), 135
Ernst, Sarah, 77

"Essays of Elia," 40
Evans, Edward B., 178
Everett, Edward, 56, 58
Ewing, Morgan, 116
Ewing, Thomas, 110
Ex Army and Navy Officers' Society, 135
Exposition of Textile Fabrics, 121
Eynon, Ernest, 200, 201
Farny, Henry F., 114
Federal Reserve Bank, 180
Fee, John G., 136
Field, Fanny, 159
Field, Kate, 129
Fifth Third Bank, 204
First National Bank, 201
First National Bank Building, 150, 151
First Unitarian Church (Cincinnati), 139
Fisher, Elwood, 64
Flagg, Mrs. W. D., 78
Fleischmann, Charles, 220
Fleischmann Enterprises, 194
Flint, Hezekiah, 101, 103
Flint, Timothy, 4, 103
Flischel, Robert, 204
Foley, James E., 127, 139
Follett, Ken, 215
Foote, A. R., 40
Foote, Henry S., 69
Ford Foundation, 187
Forster, Thomas G., 44
Fort Sumter, 70, 71, 73
Fort Thomas, 136
Fosdick, William, 59
Four Hubcaps, The, 195
Fourth National Bank Building, 150, 151
Frankenstein, John, 104, 114
Franklin, Benjamin, 98
Franklin Society, 2
Frazer, George, 47
Freericks, Frank H., 162
Friedlander, William, 223
Friends of the Public Library, 189
Frohnmayer, John, 207
Frost, Robert, 117
Fur Traders Descending the Missouri, 96
Gaines, Ernest, 224
Gaither, Caroline, 231
Gaitskill, Mary, 224
Gallagher, Thomas, 103, 116, 119
Gallagher, William, 14
Galsworthy, John, 116
Galvin, Jerry M., 227

Gannett Foundation, 196
Gano, Daniel, 111
Gaynor, Susan Rowe, 219
Gaynor, Vere, 210
Geiser, Sandra, 231
German Library of Information, 171
German National Bank Building, 150
Gibson & Company, 102
Gibson House, 87
Giovanni, Nikki, 215
Gli Edifizi Antichi dei Contorni di Roma, 112
Godkin, Edward L., 130
Goldberg, Arthur, 193
Good-bye Mr. Chips, 167
Good Earth, The, 167
Goode, Ralph, 217
Goodloe, Daniel Reeves, 65
Goossens, Eugene, 216
Gores, Drew, 215
Goshorn, Alfred T., 81
Grand Opera House, 162
Great American Ball Park, 214
Greater Cincinnati Consortium of Colleges
    and Universities, 225
Greater Cincinnati Foundation, 222, 227
Great Western Sanitary Fair, 110
Greek Slave, The, 104
Greeley, Horace, 51, 59
Greene, William, 41, 43
Greene, William N., 5
Green, James A., 129
Greenough, B. F., 29
Greve, Charles T., 103
Greve, Mrs. Charles T., 169
Griffin, Michael, 229
Grisham, John, 206
Groesbeck, William S., 58
Gruber, Mary, 211
Guthrie Grays, 73
Hagedorn, Ann, 224
Halberstam, David, 190, 206
Hale, John, 52
Hall, Dudley, 98
Halley's Comet, iii, 10
Hall, J. M., 51
Hall, Virginius, 117
Hamlet and Ophelia, 95
Hammond, Charles H., 96
Harbeson, Sarah, 78
Harriet Beecher Stowe Festival, 224
Harriet Beecher Stowe Lecture, 124, 225, 230
Harris, Julie, 192

Harrison, George T., 133
Harrison, Learner B., 104
Harrison, William Henry, 6, 21, 30, 35, 94, 95, 96, 115
Harte, Bret, 125
Hayes, Rutherford B., 122
Headley, J. B., 38
Heaney, Seamus, 207
Hearn, Lafcadio, 226
Hebrew Union College, 168
Hedrick, Joan, 124
Heller, Joseph, 193
Herron, Nellie, 152
Herzog, Aaron, 228
Heth, Henry, 130
Hilton, Johanna, 167, 190. *See also* Hochstetter, Johanna
Hilton, Robert, 219
Hinkle, Helen, 168
History, Condition, and Prospect of the Indian Tribes of the United States, 99
Hoadley, George, 165
Hochstetter, Johanna, 159, 163. *See also* Hilton, Johanna
Hodgkins, John, 203
Holbrook, Hal, 206
Holden, William J., 140
Holland, J. G., 70
Holley, Nathaniel, 12, 19, 25, 239
Holmes Sr., Oliver Wendell, 82
Hooker, James J., 85
Hooper, William, 59
Hopkins, Lewis C., 110
Hopkins. William "Foss", 187
Horton, S. Dana, 122
Houdon, Jean-Antoine, 104
Houston, Sam, 77
Howells, William Dean, 226
Howe, W. T. H., 116
Huddlesey, John, 38
Hudgins, Andrew, 215
Huenefeld, Thomas E., 186, 201, 209, 211, 219, 221
Huntington, Henry D., 99
Hunt, Samuel, 127
Hurst, Fannie, 226
Ingalls Building, 150
Irving, Washington, 112
Isralsky, Manny, 190
Italia Mia, 191
Jackson, Andrew, 1, 97, 110
Jackson, Jesse, 205

James M. Clark Company, 88
Jefferson, Thomas, 99
John P. Foote, 105
Johnson, Morse, 208
Jones, C. Taylor, 73, 75
Jones, Thomas D., 105
Joseph-Beth, 216
Justis, Charles H., 113
Kamholtz, Jonathan, 215
Kanin, Garson, 190
Kearney, Eric H., 227
Kelley Jr., John J., 194
Kellogg, Miner K., 97, 103
Kemble, Fanny, 77
Kemper, A. C., 127
Kennedy, Robert, 216
Kennett, John, 97
Kenton County Public Library, 229
Kerley, Jack, 193
Kesterman, Rick, 102
Kidder, Tracy, 207
Kilgour, Charles, 144
King, John C., 102
Kirby, Timothy, 134
Koch, Herbert F., 138
Kossuth, Louis, 52, 53
Kravchinsky, Sergius Mikhailovich, 129
Ladies' Academy of Fine Arts, 105, 106
"Lady of Lyon, The," 77
Laffoon I V, Polk, 190
Lane Seminary, 123
Langsam Jr., Walter, 228
Last of the Barons, The, 34
Lawler, Davis B., 101
Lawrence, Elbridge, 5
League Against the Teaching of Foreign Languages in Elementary Schools, 162
Leaman, Robert F., 114
Lear, Linda, 225
Le Costume Historique, 113
Lewis, Edmonia, 131
Lewis, Ella C., 128
L'Hommedieu, Stephen S., 96, 99
Lincoln, Abraham, 110
Lincoln, Fred T., 133
Literary Club, 138
Livingood, Charles J., 164
Lloyd, Henry Demarest, 130
Lloyd, John Uri, 135
Lloyd Library and Museum, 135
Logan, Eliza, 77

Lois and Richard Rosenthal Foundation, 223
Longfellow, Henry Wadsworth, 117
Longworth, Nicholas, 97, 104
Lotus Glee Club, 129
Ludlow, Susan, 110
Luken, Charlie, 227
Lupton, James, 6, 46, 53, 100, 120, 235
Luther Charitable Foundation, 225
Lyceum. *See* Cincinnati Lyceum
Lytle, Andrew Nelson, 168
Magoon, E. L., 59
Malik, John, 168
Manetti, Miss Fannie, 128
Man in the Gray Flannel Suit, The, 193
Mann, Horace, 54
Mansfield, Edward D., 3, 15, 22, 41, 255
Mapplethorpe, Robert, 207
Marks, Edward, 222
Marks, Edward G., 3
Marshall, Thomas F., 67
Martin, Lily, 95
Mason, Bobbie Ann, 215, 224
Massey, Gerald, 125
May Festival, 128, 130, 151, 152
May, Max B., 116
May, Mrs. David, 116
McArthur, Andrew, 80
McClanahan, Ed, 224
McCosh, James, 131
McCurdy, Robert M., 157
McGrew and Beggs, 94
McGuffey, Alexander H., 144
McGuffey, William Holmes, 89
McIlvaine, Charles P., 43
McIlwain, Frank, 204
McKim, William, 227
McLaughlin, George, 222
McLaughlin, James, 102
McLean, Alice, 231
McMicken, Charles, 105
McPhee, John, 207
Melodeon Hall, 127, 128
Melville, Herman, 55
Mendelssohn Club, 127
Mendenhall, Lawrence, 116
Menter's Band, 56
Merchants' Exchange, 42, 46
Merriam, Andrew B., 56
Messick, Chris, vii
Metcalf, Keys D., 173
Miami Purchase Association, 181

Miller, Isaac J., 113
Minister's Wooing, The, 124
Mitchell, Rowland G., 5
Mitchel, Ormsby M., 41
Moby Dick, 55
Moody, William, 111
Moore, Miss C. W., 50
Moos, Herman M., 116
Morehead, James T., 97
Motherwell, Robert, 117
Moulton, Richard G., 129
Mount Auburn Inclined Plane, 122
Mowatt, Anna, 48
Mozier, Joseph, 102
Mt. Vernon Ladies' Association, 56
Murdoch, James E., 226
Murphy, Samuel M., 102
Music Hall, 122
National Book Award, 207
National Underground Railroad Freedom Center, 225
Natural and Statistical View, or Picture of Cincinnati and the Miami Country, 196
Natural History of Birds in the United States, The, 98
Navy League, 218
Nelson, Fred, 228
Netherland Plaza Hotel, 206
Newport Barracks, 136
Newton, Clara C., 78
Newton, John Marshall, 138-140, 159
Newton, S. C., 105
New York Mercantile Library, 125
Nicollet, Joseph, 97
Nicollet's Topographical Map of the Basin of the Mississippi, 97
Niehoff, H. C. Buck, 117, 118
Niehoff, Nick, 190
Niehoff, Patricia, 117, 118
Niland, David, 228
Nippert, Mr. and Mrs. Louis, 190
Northern Kentucky University, 207
Nourse, Clara, 78
Nourse, Elizabeth, 78
Oates, Joyce Carol, 230
O'Brien, Tim, 215
O'Connor, Patrick, 193
Odeon Theatre, 126
Ogden, Augustine ("Gussie"), 115
Ogden, Frank McGee, 115
Ohio Life Insurance and Trust Company, 99
Ohio Mechanics Institute, 2, 106

Omoo, 55
On the Origin of Species, 48
Ostend Manifesto, 66
Ostrom, Lemuel A., 46
Our Mutual Friend, 117
Owen, Robert Dale, 50
Owens, John W., 110
Palmer, George, 201
Parry, R. H., 93
Parsons, Charles B., 66
"Patience," 54
Pattison, John, 148
Paz, Octavio, 117
Peabody, George, 112
Pelican Brief, The, 206
Peter, Sarah Worthington King, 105
Petrie, Bruce, 208
Philharmonic String Quartette, 129
Philipson, David, 168, 176
Phillips, Wendell, 67
Pierce, Mark, 221, 231
Pike, Samuel M., 59
Pike's Opera House, 59
Pinger, Edgar E., 177
Pinsky, Robert, 215
Pitman, Agnes, 78
Plimpton, George, 205
Plum Street Temple, 125
Plymouth Congregational Church, 123
Porter, Harold, 227
Portman, Robert J., 207
Portrait of a Married Woman, 117
Portune, Todd, 228
Powell Jr., William, 112
Powell, Thomas C., 157
Power, Samantha, 225
Powers, Charles, 210
Powers, Hiram, 131
Powers, Preston, 131
Probasco, Henry, 81
Proctor, R. A., 125
Proulx, Annie, 230
Provident Travel Company, 202
Public Library of New York, 160
Pugh, J. S., 110
Pullan, Richard B., 33
Punch, 71
Pyle, Albert, vii, 212-218, 223, 225-232
Qualls, Roxanne, 207, 211
Quammen, David, 224
Queen City Brass, 193
Queen City Club, 163

Queen & Crescent Railroad, 157
Rabinowitz, Dorothy, 225
Racinet, Auguste, 113
Ranney, Moses, 4, 11, 19, 116, 168, 235, 249
Read, Thomas Buchanan, 103, 116, 119
Reakirt Foundation, 196
Republican Party, 121, 122
Riley, Bill, 175
Rive-King, Julie, 128
Robert and Adele Schiff Foundation, 224
Robinson, James K., 193
Robinson's Opera House, 128
Root, Frederick W., 130
Rose, Cedric, vii
Rosen, Carole, 216
Ross, Ishbel, 152
Rouse, Shelley, 167
Rowland, C. W., 103
Rule, Charles, 104
Russell, William H., 73
Ruthven, John, 216
Ryan, John, 207
Sabrina, 103, 105
Saengerfest Hall, 122
Safford, Truman H., 97
Sagan, Carl, 205
Sagmaster, Joseph, 175
Sagmaster (Mrs.), 182
Sanger and Eby, 219
Santa Barbara Writers Conference, 199, 202
Sauter, Rudolf Helmut, 116
Scallan, Veirs, 186
Scarborough, William W., 98
"Scene on Lake George," 97, 98
Schiff, James, 219, 223
Schlesinger Jr., Arthur M., 230
Schneider, George, 128
Schott, Marge, 200
Schwab, Louis, 152
Schwab, Mathias, 88
Seasongood, Lewis, 86
Sebastiani, Margaret, 182
Sechrest, Anna E., 161
Selden, Dixie, 167
"Seven Owls," 117
Shakespearean Club of Cincinnati, 127
Sharp, Judy, 211
Shearer, J. L., 129
Shirayamadani, Kataro, 119
Shockley, H. S, 139
Sibley, J.W., 17

Siebert, Thomas L., 193
Silence, 102, 105
Silliman, Benjamin, 54
Simpson, Matthew, 51
Sinton, David, 112
Sinton Hotel, 150
Slaughterhouse-Five, 190
Smiley, Jane, 224
Smith Book Company, 156
Smith & Nixon's Hall, 65, 67, 73, 77
Smith, Richard, 122
Smith, William R., 5, 11
Snodgrass, James H., 85
Something Funny at the Library, 217, 230
So Red the Rose, 167
Spencer, Benjamin, 95
Spencer, Mary, 78
Spencer, Samuel S., 5
Springer, Jean, vi, vii, 185-193, 195-199, 206, 208-211, 213, 231
Springer, Reuben, 81
Stallo, Johann B., 53
Stanley J. Aronoff Center, 208
St. Clair, Arthur, 3
Steinem, Gloria, 215
Stephens, Alexander H., 82
Stephenson, Reuben H., 47
Stepniak, Sergius. *See* Kravchinsky, Sergius Mikhailovich
Stetson, Charles, 99
Stimson, Clara, 169
Stimson, Fred M., 133
St. Louis Public Library, 160
Stone, Irving, 188
Storer, Bellamy, 81
Stowe, Calvin, 123, 124
Stowe, Harriet Beecher, 59, 117, 123, 124, 224, 225, 230, 250
Strauss, Peter, 186, 194
Studio Cinema, 190
Styron, William, 217
Sullivan, Arthur M., 131
Sumner, Charles, 82
Sumner, William Graham, 131
Swedenborg, Emanuel, 114
Symmes, John Cleves, 116
Taft, Alphonso, 122, 138, 150
Taft, Charles P., 152
Taft, Hope, 219
Taft Museum of Art, 152
Taft, Robert A., 219
Taft, William Howard, 127, 151

Tarbell, Jim, 214
Tate, Allen, 167, 168
Taylor, Bayard, 54, 59
Taylor, R. M. W., 33, 39
Taylor, Sylvester, 76
Taylor, William B. A., 160
Terrill, Edward, 200
Textile Building, 150, 151
Thackeray Society, 209
Thackeray, William Makepeace, 56
Theroux, Paul, 224
Thomas, Calvin W., 114
Thomas Emery's Sons Company, 148
Thomas, E. S., 114
Thomas, George H., 131, 136
Thomas, Theodore, 122, 152
Thompson, Dorothy, 167
Thurber, James, 226
Times (London), 73
Todd, Hawley, 181
Todd, M. A. (Miss), 78
Tosso, Joseph, 6
Traction Building, 150, 151
Tracy and Hepburn, 190
Trillin, Calvin, 230
Trollope, Frances, 2, 3
Trubner & Company, 109, 110
Turner, Fanny E., 159
Turow, Scott, 207
Tyler Davidson Fountain, 189
Typee, 55
Uncle Tom's Cabin, 224
Unfinished Cathedral, 168
Union Central Life Insurance Company, 148
Union Trust Building, 150, 151
United States Geographical Surveys West of the One Hundredth Meridian, 113
United States Sanitary Commission, 69
Universalist Church, 39
University of Cincinnati, 215, 216, 224, 225, 229
University of Cincinnati Center for Women's Studies, 225
Updike, John, 224
U.S.S. Cincinnati, 218
Valin, Jonathan, 224
Vaughn, Daniel, 81
Vere, Charles, 208
Vickers, Thomas, 126
Vidal, Gore, 205, 207
Vitz, Carl, 179

INDEX

Voyage of Life, 98
Waldie's Select Circulating Library, 3
Walker, Blythe, 227
Wallace, Robert, 207
Walnut Street Poetry Society, 226
Walter, Henry, 37
Ward, Artemus. *See* Brown, Charles F.
Warner, W. Russell, 176
Watson, Luman, 104
Wealth Against Commonwealth, 130
Webster, Daniel, 102
Wechselblatt, Martin, 225
Welch, Van Wormer, 167
Wellinghoff, James, 117, 118, 208, 218, 222
Wertheimer, Emma, 78
Wessel, John, 193
West, Charles W., 81
Western Art Union, 98
Westin Hotel, 205
Westover, Kate, 78
Wheatley, Thomas J., 114
Wheel Cafe, 192
Wheeler, George M., 112, 113
Wheeler, Isaac D., 5, 18, 24, 235
White, John H., 224
White, M. Hazen, 159
Whittaker, Harry, 185, 187, 197
Whittaker, Molly, 197
Whittredge, Thomas Worthington, 103
Wigor, Brad, 117
Wilby, Charles B., 156, 162
Wilby, Clark, 177, 179
Wilde, Oscar, 131
Wilder, Stephen H., 138
Williams, Gregory Howard, 216
Williams, Violet, 231
Wilmot Proviso, 65
Wilson, John M., 72
Wilson, Kathy Y., 224
Wilson, Moses F., 81
Wilson, Sloan, 193
Wing-and-Wing, The, 34
Winslow, A. S., 75
Winters, Jonathan, 230
Wise, Isaac M., 125
Wolfe, Tom, 205
Woodburn, D. T., 75
Wood's Theater, 77
Woods, William K., 228
World's Fair, 122, 131
Worthington and Ranney, 4
Wright, Austin M., 224

Wright, Crafts J., 97
Wright, John C., 34
Writer's Digest, 193
Yancey, William L., 59
Yeatman's Tavern, 3
Yergason, Henry C., 138

About the Author

ROBERT C. VITZ joined the Northern Kentucky University faculty in 1972, following short teaching stints at the University of North Carolina at Greensboro and Purdue University at West Lafayette, Indiana. A native of Minnesota, he grew up in Cincinnati, received a B.A. degree from DePauw University (1960), an M.A. in history from Miami University (1967), and a Ph.D. in history from the University of North Carolina at Chapel Hill (1971).

His research interests include 19th century American artistic development, particularly art and music, and he has focused on the role of Cincinnati in this development. He has published numerous articles in professional journals; written one book, *The Queen and the Arts: Cultural Life in Nineteenth-Century Cincinnati* (1989); and served as a consultant for the recently opened Cincinnati Wing of the Cincinnati Art Museum. He is currently a member of the History Advisory Board of the Cincinnati Museum Center, the board of Directors of the Friends of the Public Library of Cincinnati and Hamilton County, and the board of Directors of the Friends of the William Howard Taft National Historic Site.

This book was designed by
TRIAD Communications, Cincinnati.
All text is set in a font called Balderdash,
a type family designed by Keith Bollmer
for the book *Brilliance and Balderdash*,
published by the Mercantile Library in 2007.
The initial caps are set in Catich Titling,
a design based on the lettering of
Father Edward Catich, the noted
calligrapher and typographic scholar.
The type ornaments are from
Hoefler Ornaments and ITC Bodoni.
The paper is Accent Opaque
by International Paper.
The printing and binding
was performed by CJK, Cincinnati.

Young Men's Men
INTE

Name	Resider
Henry D Lloyd	New Yo
A W Edward	Carlinvil
I. M. Palmer	de
J C Wells	Peoria
R A Anderson	Lene Ha
Wm E. Mc Lean	de
Thos A Stilwell	Anderson
Carl Schurz	Washi
Thos C Anderson	Ar
Edwin Bennett	Ar
H L Fletcher	Little Rock
Wm B Fleming	Crt